The Origins &
Evolution of the Field of

INDUSTRIAL
RELATIONS

in the United States

The Origins &
Evolution of the Field of

INDUSTRIAL
RELATIONS

in the United States

CORNELL STUDIES

IN INDUSTRIAL AND

LABOR RELATIONS

NUMBER 25

BRUCE E. KAUFMAN

ILR PRESS

Ithaca, New York

Cover and interior design by Ann Lowe

Library of Congress Cataloging-in-Publication Data

Kaufman, Bruce E.
The origins & evolution of the field of industrial relations in the United States.
p. cm.—(Cornell studies in industrial and labor relations; no.25)
Includes bibliographical references and index.
ISBN 0-87546-191-3 (alk. paper).—ISBN 0-87546-192-1 (pbk. : alk. paper)
1. Industrial relations—United States—History. I. Title.
II. Title: Origins and evolution of the field of industrial
relations in the United States. III. Series.
HD8066.K38 1993
331'.0973—dc20 92-19055

Copies may be ordered through bookstores or directly from

ILR PRESS
School of Industrial and Labor Relations
Cornell University
Ithaca, NY 14853-3901

Printed on acid-free paper in the United States of America

5 4 3 2 1

To Lauren and Andrew

CONTENTS

PREFACE

W HEN I STARTED this project three years ago I had no idea that it would grow to be a book or that the conclusions would take the shape they have. The book had its genesis in two developments. The first was that I was assigned to teach a new graduate course we had just introduced into the curriculum at Georgia State University, the purpose of which was to survey the evolution of thought and practice in the field of "employment relations"—a term the faculty adopted as a way to provide an intellectual umbrella for consideration of both industrial relations and personnel management in one course. The second development was that in 1989 I was appointed director of the newly created Beebe Institute of Personnel and Employment Relations at Georgia State. The institute had been the Institute of Industrial Relations, but in 1988, in response to declining student and faculty interest in industrial relations, a decision had been made to refocus the institute's activities on personnel and human resource management.

These events stimulated my interest in learning more about the histories of the fields of industrial relations and personnel management and their underlying theoretical paradigms, both because I had to discuss these matters in class and knew precious little about them (having been trained as a labor economist) and because I soon discovered in my new role as institute director that faculty from the industrial relations and personnel wings of the field have quite different conceptual and methodological approaches to research on the employment relationship. To learn more, I set off for the library, where I soon discovered that relatively little had been written on the histories of either industrial relations or personnel management but particularly the former. I also discovered that what had been written was almost completely silent with regard to the relationship of one field to the other, especially the differences and commonalities in intellectual origins, theoretical paradigms, and underlying philosophies and ideologies.

This book is the result of my investigations. The book has three objectives. The first is to provide a detailed account of the intellectual history of the field of industrial relations, its relationship to personnel management (and related fields such as organizational behavior), and the historical development of the major institutions of industrial relations in American academe, including university degree programs and professional associations. The second objective is to assess the reasons for the marked decline in the field's intellectual and organizational fortunes over the last two decades, a decline that has proceeded to the point that the continued existence of industrial relations programs at a number of universities is threatened. Finally, the third objective is to develop a strategy for change that will preserve and strengthen industrial relations as a field of study, if not in name then in intellectual spirit.

My findings and conclusions are both revisionist and critical; revisionist with respect to the conventional wisdom regarding the intellectual roots of industrial relations as a field of study and its early (pre-1950s) relationship to the study and practice of personnel management, and critical of the direction the field has taken since the late 1950s and of the role played therein by the field's major professional group, the Industrial Relations Research Association. When I started this project, I had neither revisionism nor criticism in my heart since both strike at the institutional tradition in industrial relations, which, given my University of Wisconsin background in labor economics, holds a strong appeal for me. Nevertheless, as I dug deeper into the history of the field I came to realize that institutionalism was but one of two major streams of thought in industrial relations (rather than the predominant stream, as often alleged) and that some of its major assumptions, and the policy conclusions that flow from them, are in serious need of critical evaluation and revision. These conclusions, and my perception that the majority of academics active in industrial relations in the post-1960 period have held opposite views, inevitably led me to take a revisionist and critical stance. While I have not shrunk from identifying shortcomings where

I see them, I have also labored to be fair and accurate to all parties and points of view. My intent is to stimulate constructive dialogue, not to cause heartburn.

A central theme of this book is that research in industrial relations has been animated by two very different impulses: science-building (the advancement of knowledge for its own sake) and problem-solving (the application of knowledge to solve practical problems). These impulses have given the field a split personality—researchers interested in science-building seek to turn the field into a distinct discipline with its own overarching theoretical framework, while the problem-solvers find its multidisciplinary nature a rich source from which to mix and match specific theories and concepts to issues of practice and policy.

This book exhibits much the same split personality. In part, it is a science-building exercise in historical analysis (albeit of an interpretive nature) in which I attempt to trace the origins and evolution of institutions and ideas in industrial relations. But the book also has a problem-solving dimension to it, for I am interested not only in chronicling the development of the field but also in offering a vision for change that will reverse the decline in the field's intellectual vital signs. The danger in mixing these two motives, as in the broader world of IR research, is that it blurs the purpose of the book and the nature of the intended audience. Readers who want a straightforward history of thought text, for example, will find the amount of space given to curricular and programmatic developments and the development and organizational details of the Industrial Relations Research Association to be excessive. From my point of view, however, a consideration of these institutional details is crucial if we are to chart a new path for the field. Such are the tensions between science-building and problem-solving!

This book has benefited from the contributions of many people, foremost among them Clark Kerr, Richard Lester, and George Strauss. Each of these men spent considerable time with me during the research phase of the project discussing the key events, people, and ideas in the field from the time of their first involvement with it in the 1940s to the present time. After I had completed a first draft of the manuscript, they also gave me detailed comments and suggestions. The manuscript has benefited greatly from their efforts.

During the research phase of the project I also benefited from written and telephone communications with numerous other scholars in the

Preface

field. A partial list includes Chris Argyris, Jack Barbash, Don Cullen, Milton Derber, William Form, John Fossum, Dallas Jones, Robert Lampman, David Lewin, H. Gregg Lewis, Charles Myers, Maurice Neufeld, Lloyd Reynolds, Richard Rowan, Tony Sinicropi, Philip Way, Hoyt Wheeler and William Foote Whyte. I also received valued assistance from the staff of the Industrial Relations Research Association. After completing a first draft, I sent the manuscript to numerous people for review. I received written or telephone comments from Jack Barbash, Don Cullen, John Delaney, John Dunlop, John Fossum, Sanford Jacoby, Thomas Kochan, Morris Kleiner, Michael Lee, Robert McKersie, Peter Sherer, James Stern, Hoyt Wheeler, William Foote Whyte, and Daniel Wren. I wish to express my sincere appreciation to each of these people for their help and assistance. All contributors and reviewers are, of course, absolved from responsibility for errors of fact or interpretation.

Finally, I wish to acknowledge a number of other people who also made valuable contributions to this book: Fran Benson, Erica Fox, Andrea Fleck Clardy, and Patricia Peltekos, all of ILR Press, and Donna Smith, who assisted me in preparing the manuscript for submission to the publisher. Completion of this project was also aided by financial assistance from the College of Business Administration of Georgia State University. Last, but not least, I owe a debt of thanks to my wife, Deborah, who somehow managed her own full-time career and two young children while her husband worked nights and weekends to complete this manuscript.

Introduction

I NDUSTRIAL RELATIONS (IR) developed as a distinct academic subject and field of study nearly three-quarters of a century ago. In this book I provide a historical survey of the origins and development of the field in the United States and an analysis of the factors that contributed both to the field's ascendancy in the decade after World War II and to its sharp decline in the 1980s.[1]

The book is motivated by three considerations. The first is that no comprehensive account of the intellectual history of industrial relations in the United States has heretofore been written. This omission is in sharp contrast to the detailed histories available for the closely allied fields of labor economics (McNulty 1980) and personnel management (Ling 1965; Wren 1987). The only studies that provide even a modest historical treatment of the development of the field are Milton Derber's (1967) book on pre-1960s research on labor problems, the chapter in Thomas Kochan's (1980) collective bargaining textbook on the historical evolution of the American industrial relations system, the survey article by George Strauss and Peter Feuille (1981) on trends in post–World War II IR research, and a soon-to-be-published article by Roy Adams (1992). Other useful but more topical accounts of the field's development are provided by James Cochrane (1979), George Strauss (1989, 1990), Jack Barbash (1991a), and Ronald Schatz (1993). All of these studies deal with the evolution of thought in industrial relations. No study I am aware of has attempted to chart the institutional and organizational development of industrial relations, including when and where the first IR academic programs were established and the structure and historical evolution of IR curricula.

The second consideration is that substantial controversy exists in the field concerning its intellectual boundaries and core subject area (Begin 1987; Boivin 1989; Strauss 1989, 1990). Several IR scholars, for example, define the field broadly to include the study of all aspects of the employment relationship (Heneman 1969; Fossum 1987). From this point of view, IR subsumes all subfields relevant to the employment relationship, such as human resources management, collective bargaining, industrial psychology, and labor law, and covers in its coursework and research all dimensions of work, including the practice of employment relations in both union and nonunion situations.

Other people adopt a narrower interpretation that defines industrial relations as the study of organized employment relationships, with a particular focus on unions and collective bargaining (see Behrend 1963; Strauss 1990). Juxtaposed to the field of IR, in this view, is the separate field of human resources (HR), which has become associated with a largely behavioral science approach to the study of nonunion work situations, with particular emphasis on the practice and organization of management. This bifurcation in the study of the employment relationship is attested to, for example, in the title of the University Council of Industrial Relations and Human Resource Programs and the title of a textbook by Thomas Kochan and Thomas Barocci (1985), *Human Resources Management and Industrial Relations.*

These starkly different visions of industrial relations have created a significant identity problem for the field, a situation exacerbated by the attempt of IR scholars to have it both ways—to stake out a broad, all-inclusive jurisdiction for industrial relations when discussing the nature of the field but to focus primarily on collective bargaining when conducting research. I hope this book helps to resolve this intellectual paradox or, if not to resolve it, at least to identify its origins and underlying causes.

The third consideration motivating this book concerns the recent decline in the vitality and academic stature of industrial relations as a field of study and its prospects for survival and growth in the future. A variety of signs indicate that the field of industrial relations experienced a significant decline in the 1980s as a focal point for teaching and research in employment relations (W. Franke 1987; Begin 1987;

Strauss 1990). Examples include the elimination, consolidation, or significant downsizing of a number of academic IR programs; the elimination of the term *industrial relations* from academic units; the substantial shift in students from IR courses to HR courses; and the decline in the number of academics in the field's major professional organization, the Industrial Relations Research Association. The hard times that have befallen industrial relations have led some scholars to question the field's long-term prospects for survival. Indicative of this sentiment is the question posed by Arnold Weber (1987b:9)—"Will industrial relations institutes and the study of industrial relations go the way of home economics?"—and the statement by George Strauss (1989:257): "Short of an unexpected resurgence of union victories academic IR will have to make major adjustments. Otherwise it may follow the example of the Cigarmakers and the Sleeping Car Porters, both leaders in their times."

Why has academic IR fallen on hard times? Will IR institutes and IR programs stage a comeback, or will they ultimately fade from the academic scene? What can be done to improve the prospects for the field? Successfully answering these questions requires, I believe, a thorough understanding of the field's history and, in particular, the events and decisions that brought industrial relations to its current state. The remainder of the book attempts to provide this context.

The Origins &
Evolution of the Field of

INDUSTRIAL
RELATIONS

in the United States

1

THE ORIGINS OF
INDUSTRIAL RELATIONS

T HE TERM *industrial relations* entered the American lexicon in 1912 when President William Howard Taft proposed and Congress approved the creation of a nine-person investigative committee called the Commission on Industrial Relations.[1] The commission was formed as the result of the public outcry over the death of twenty persons in the dynamite bombing of the *L.A. Times* building in 1910 by two leaders of the Structural Ironworkers Union (Harter 1962:131–59). The charge given to the commission was to determine the conditions responsible for conflict between employers and employees and possible remedies for such conflict. The commission held 154 days of hearings and published its findings and conclusions in 1916 in eleven volumes.[2] The importance of this new subject of industrial relations was attested to in the opening sentence of the commission's report (U.S. Congress 1916:1): "The question of industrial relations assigned by Congress to the commission for investigation is more fundamental and of greater importance to the welfare of the Nation than any other question except the form of our government."

In its initial usage, the term *industrial relations* was little more than a shorthand for "the relations between labor and capital in industry," a phrase encountered frequently before 1912. The meaning of the term soon expanded greatly, however, and by 1920 it had come to represent an academic field of study, a reform movement in industry, and a professional vocation.

The birth of the term *industrial relations* and its metamorphosis into a subject of academic inquiry was critically influenced by several events and ideas in the preceding half-century. An appreciation of the origins and development of the field requires brief mention of these events and ideas.

LABOR PROBLEMS

The intellectual precursor of industrial relations was the concept of "the labor problem." The term *labor problem* came into vogue in the latter part of the nineteenth century and was used to connote the general struggle between labor and capital over the control of production and the distribution of income and the conflict engendered by this struggle (see Barnes 1886; Olson 1894). The concept then evolved in two steps.

The first step, which occurred shortly after the turn of the century, was a movement away from the unitary conception of *the* labor problem to a pluralistic conception of labor *problems* (Adams and Sumner 1905; Watkins 1922).[3] The pluralistic version represented an intellectual advance in that it recognized that labor problems take many different forms besides labor-management conflict, that labor problems afflict both employers and workers, and that labor problems exist in both socialist and capitalist economies. Commonly cited examples of labor problems facing employers were high employee turnover, worker "soldiering" (loafing), and excessive waste and inefficiency in production, while labor problems affecting workers included insecurity of employment, low pay, child labor, and unsafe working conditions.

The second step, which occurred gradually after World War I, was the replacement of *labor problems* with a terminology that was more field-specific. Thus, the term *labor problems* continued to be used in labor economics but was gradually replaced by *personnel problems* in personnel management, *social problems* in sociology, and so on.[4] It was not until the late 1940s–early 1950s that the "problems" perspective began to fall out of favor in the social sciences, for reasons discussed in chapter 6.

The concept of labor problems was crucial to the development of industrial relations because it provided both an intellectual justification for the field and a focal point for research and teaching (Derber 1967). When the labor problems perspective first emerged it was as a reaction against the policy conclusions derived from the intellectual doctrines of classical economics and social Darwinism. As discussed in more detail in chapter 2, classical economics purported to show that competition in free, unregulated labor markets promotes efficiency in production and a harmony of interests between labor and capital. Social Darwinism held that economic and social progress is best promoted by unrestrained competition since the competitive struggle weeds out the weaker members of society and allows the strongest members to rise to the top to take their place as the nation's business and political leaders. Both doctrines were used by conservatives to justify the prevailing system of laissez-faire capitalism, the dominance of the existing business and political elites, and the hostile attitude of legislatures and courts toward labor union activity and protective labor legislation (Bendix 1956; Dorfman 1959).[5]

The concept of labor problems was thus developed by both social reformers and socialist revolutionaries as a means to attack the status quo in industry since, if it could be shown that the employment relationship contained serious maladjustments and defects, then the case for laissez-faire was weakened and the case for reform (or revolution) was strengthened. The reformers and revolutionaries diverged, however, as to the best approach to resolve these problems.

The reformers accepted the capitalist system but sought to improve the efficiency and equity with which it operated through more scientific and humane management methods, an equalization of bargaining power between workers and employers, and the introduction of democracy and due process into the workplace. This approach was to become the intellectual and policy core of the new field of industrial relations. From the point of view of the reformers, labor problems and industrial relations were opposite sides of the same coin—labor problems were the undesired behavioral outcomes generated by the defects and maladjustments in the employment relationship, while industrial relations was the body of theory and methods that would resolve or ameliorate the problems (Watkins 1922).

Marxists and socialists were antagonistic to the new field of industrial relations since it sought to save through reform what they hoped to replace through revolution.[6] These groups largely shunned industrial relations and instead subscribed to Marxist economics, political action through the Socialist party, and direct job action through unions such as the Industrial Workers of the World (IWW).

CAUSES OF LABOR PROBLEMS

Just as the concept of labor problems provided the intellectual justification for the field of industrial relations, the perceived causes of

5

labor problems heavily influenced its theory, practice, and philosophy. Labor problems, such as conflict between employers and workers, insecurity of employment, and worker soldiering on the job, did not suddenly appear in the late nineteenth century. To one degree or another, these problems had been evident since the emergence of free labor markets and a wage labor force several hundred years earlier. What was new was the scope and intensity of many of these problems, a development most graphically illustrated by the unparalleled violence and radicalization of emotions associated with such labor-management disputes as the Homestead, Pullman, and anthracite coal strikes of the late 1800s.

Early writers on the subject of labor problems identified three reasons in particular for this trend (Adams and Sumner 1905; Commons 1911; Watkins 1922; Furniss 1925). The first was the rise of large-scale, capital-intensive, bureaucratic forms of business organization. Before the late nineteenth century, most of the country's employment was in agriculture. Nonagricultural forms of business, such as in manufacturing, mining, and construction, were typically small-scale operations that employed skilled craftsmen using hand tools and were managed by the owner-entrepreneur. After 1870, however, the industrial sector experienced a fundamental transformation (Nelson 1975). From 1870 to 1920, average employment in manufacturing plants in most industries doubled and tripled. Likewise, the production process was transformed as machines replaced hand tools, skilled craftsmen were replaced by semiskilled or unskilled operators and assemblers, and standardized, interchangeable parts replaced customized parts. Finally, the corporate form of business organization gained popularity, with a consequent separation of ownership and control, as a salaried cadre of management officials took over responsibility for day-to-day operation of the firm. These events increased the potential for conflict and other forms of labor problems in the workplace by increasing the physical and social distance between workers and employers, "proletarianizing" the work force into a large, relatively undifferentiated group of manual workers, and removing the status, bargaining power, and high earnings that went with being a skilled craft worker (see Peterson 1987:9–70).

The second reason was the downward pressure on money wages and working conditions during the last thirty years of the nineteenth century exerted by the chronic unemployment in the labor market. The large number of jobless workers during this period was caused by both demand and supply factors. On the demand side, the economy was in recession or depression roughly half the years between 1870 and 1900. The scarcity of jobs because of the insufficient demand was exacerbated on the supply side by the influx of millions of immigrants into the country. The result in many urban areas was a persistent pool of unemployed workers and cut-throat competition for jobs. Faced with numerous job seekers, many of whom were foreign-born and unskilled, and continual downward pressure on prices in the product market (prices fell by one-third between 1870 and 1900), the competitive struggle to stay in business forced employers to reduce labor costs wherever possible, be it by lowering wages, speeding up the pace of work, or skimping on even elementary safety precautions. The working life of most manual workers during the period, therefore, was marked by considerable insecurity and hardship (Lescohier 1935). The resulting social tensions were further exacerbated by the growing affluence of the upper classes and the notable trend toward a greater inequality in income and wealth (Williamson and Lindert 1980).

The third reason for the increase in labor-management conflict was the arbitrary, unsystematic, and authoritarian methods of personnel management used in industry (Jacoby 1985). Employers generally regarded workers as a commodity from which maximum production should be extracted for the least cost and then discarded when no longer needed. Personnel departments and written policies were nonexistent before World War I. In most plants, top management delegated all personnel matters such as hiring, firing, pay, promotion, and work load to the foreman in charge of each department or shop. Typically, the foreman's decisions on these matters were final. His task was to maximize production at minimum unit cost. To accomplish this, the accepted method was the "drive system." The drive system entailed constant supervision by the foreman and the use of profane language and verbal abuse to induce the employees to work harder. The factors that made the drive system an effective device to elicit work effort was the threat of dismissal from the job—a threat made credible by the existence of numerous job seekers outside the plant gate. Although employers generally found the "foreman-in-charge" method of personnel administration and the drive system of employee motivation to be cost-effective, these practices nevertheless created considerable tension and dissatisfaction among employees as a result of the welter of pay differentials among workers performing relatively similar jobs, the frequent occurrence of favoritism by the foreman in hiring and firing decisions, the lack of an appeals process and machinery for administration of due process in the plant, and the autocratic, insensitive attitude exhibited by all ranks of management (see Williams 1920).

MOVEMENT FOR REFORM

Beginning in the mid-1880s, a groundswell of opinion developed that favored reform of the employment relationship. This movement gained speed from 1900 to 1914, in the period known as the Progressive era (Hoffstadter 1963).

The movement for reform came from a variety of sources. Industrial engineers such as Frederick Taylor promoted scientific management as a way to resolve labor problems,[7] while industrial psychologists, such as Hugo Münsterberg and Walter Dill Scott, sought to use new psychological concepts and methods to increase industrial efficiency and the worker's satisfaction with the job. Institutional labor economists, such as John R. Commons and Robert Hoxie, analyzed the economic basis of labor problems and the role of labor unions and government regulation as a means to resolve the problems. The actions of progressive business leaders, who voluntarily instituted various employee welfare measures (e.g., company lunchrooms or safety directors) or installed some form of employee representation plan, also greatly helped the movement, as did trade unionists and their supporters, who saw unions and collective bargaining as the most effective way to eliminate various industrial evils such as low wages and unsafe job conditions. Support for reform also came from progressive-minded civic and religious organizations, such as the Civic Federation and the Quakers, as well as from socialists and other left-wing political and economic groups that constantly called attention to the deplorable conditions in industry and the depredations of the business class. Finally, several government commissions materially advanced the campaign by exposing the many abuses and hardships experienced by workers. Among these were the United States Industrial Commission (1898–1902) and the Commission on Industrial Relations (1913–15).

WORLD WAR I: THE CATALYST FOR CHANGE

Before World War I, most employers treated the reform movement with indifference or hostility. The reasons included resistance to change, the continued effectiveness of traditional methods of labor recruitment and management, and the gradual erosion of the union threat after 1904. As long as only progressives and liberals advocated reform, and in the absence of government action, little headway was likely.

The situation changed dramatically, however, as a result of the economic and political events during World War I (Slichter 1919a; Douglas 1919, 1922; Jacoby 1985). War production soon brought on a labor shortage, compounded in 1917 by the draft. The result was a serious disruption of old methods of personnel administration. With numerous job opportunities, labor turnover (already quite high) increased dramatically. Further, work effort and productivity declined significantly. The drive system performed reasonably well when backed up by the fear of unemployment, but it lost its effectiveness when workers no longer feared for their jobs. Finally, the surge in inflation and low unemployment brought on a resurgence of union organizing, wage demands, and strikes.

World War I also led the federal government to become more interested in reform. The Commission on Industrial Relations had been appointed to determine the origins of labor problems, but its liberal leanings had caused Congress to ignore its opinions (Harter 1962). The exigencies of World War I, however, increased the interest in labor problems. During the Wilson administration, policies favorable to organized labor were promulgated, most particularly by the War Labor Board, which encouraged companies in war-related industries to recognize unions voluntarily and to sign collective bargaining contracts. The impetus for these pro-labor policies came partly from ideological convictions and partly from a pragmatic desire on the part of government officials to minimize strikes and disruptions to production (a goal that was only partially achieved).

The net outcome was that by the end of World War I all the major parties to the employment relationship had concluded that workplace reform was in their self-interest, although considerable controversy remained as to its precise nature. It was out of this push for reform that the new field of industrial relations was born.

ESTABLISHMENT OF INDUSTRIAL RELATIONS AS A FIELD OF STUDY

During World War I the term *industrial relations* began to appear with greater frequency in the popular and trade press as citizens, practitioners, and policy makers debated the causes and cures of the breakdown in employer-employee relations.[8] Given the severity of the labor problems at this time, the widespread interest in employment reform, and the absence of organized research and teaching on the subject of the employment relationship, the term soon came to describe a new subject area or field of study. The focal point of this new field was the employment relationship and, in particular, the causes of labor problems and their resolution through improved methods of administration and organization.

The birth of industrial relations as an independent field of academic study was marked by the establishment in 1920 of the Bureau of Commercial and Industrial Relations in the extension division of the University of Wisconsin and of a "course" (area of specialization) in industrial relations in the Department of Economics, under the direction of John R. Commons (U.S. Department of Labor 1921). This specialization was, as far as I can determine, the first academic program of study in industrial relations at an American university. Students taking the specialization enrolled in four subjects: labor legislation, labor history and industrial government, labor management, and causes and remedies of unemployment.

The new field of industrial relations was soon introduced at other major universities. In 1921, the Industrial Research Unit was established at the Wharton School of Business and Commerce of the University of Pennsylvania to promote research on the problems of industry (Wharton School 1989). For the first decade research conducted by the unit was focused almost exclusively on industrial relations topics. In later years, several studies on the economics of the mining, metals, and textile industries were also published.

The first academic unit devoted specifically to industrial relations was created in 1922 by Princeton University with the establishment of its Industrial Relations Section in the Department of Economics (Industrial Relations Section 1986). The purpose of the section was to foster research on industrial relations, principally through published reports and monographs by the faculty associated with the section and the development of a comprehensive library of industrial relations materials. At Harvard University industrial relations appeared in 1923 when the Jacob Wertheim Research Fellowship for the Betterment of Industrial Relations was established. Finally, in 1925, the University of Chicago promoted Paul H. Douglas from associate professor of economics to professor of industrial relations (Douglas, Hitchcock, and Atkins 1925: frontispiece).[9]

Among practitioners, three events helped establish a separate identity for industrial relations. The first event was the publication in October 1919 of the monthly periodical *Industrial Relations: Bloomfield's Labor Digest*, by Daniel and Meyer Bloomfield, two prominent writers and consultants to business on the subject of employment management.

The second event was the formation of the Industrial Relations Association of America (IRAA) in 1920. The IRAA had formerly been the Employment Managers' Association and was composed largely of business people with an interest in personnel work. The association had more than two thousand members and several dozen local chapters in its first year.[10] Among its activities, the IRAA published a monthly journal entitled *Personnel.* Financial distress associated with the severe recession of 1920–21 forced the dissolution of the association in early 1922. Its activities were absorbed by a new organization, the National Personnel Association, which in 1923 changed its name to the American Management Association (Lange 1928).

The third event was the passage of the Kansas Industrial Court Act of 1920, which established the Kansas Court of Industrial Relations, the first such court in the nation. The court was authorized to settle labor disputes in the state through binding arbitration (see Feis 1923).

INDUSTRIAL RELATIONS DEFINED

What was this new field of industrial relations that had suddenly given birth to a new professional organization in industry and a course of study and area of research in academe? A review of the early literature of the field reveals that the answer had several parts.

Every field of knowledge is directed at the study of certain key forms of behavior. Economics, for example, focuses on the operation of markets and the determination of market outcomes such as wage rates and employment levels, while sociology examines social groups and behaviors such as status differentiation and mobility across social classes. Industrial relations was thought to focus on the employment relationship and, in particular, on the relationship between employers and workers and the labor problems that grow out of this relationship.[11]

This conceptualization of the field was most clearly enunciated in an internal research report prepared by the Social Science Research Council (1928) entitled *Survey of Research in the Field of Industrial Relations*. The report was written by Herman Feldman, a professor of industrial relations at Dartmouth College, with the assistance of a twelve-person advisory committee composed of academics, including John R. Commons, George Barnett, and Joseph Willits, businessmen, trade unionists, and government officials. The report states (p. 22), "The only satisfactory basis of distinguishing a body of knowledge from another is in the problems studied." It goes on to say that labor problems provide the focal point of investigation for industrial relations. Specifically, it defines the field as "including those problems of human behavior involved in the reciprocal relations of the worker with four types of situations: his work; his fellow-worker; his employer; and the public."

Industrial relations was also seen at the time as a multidisciplinary field of study, rather than as a distinct discipline of its own.[12] An academic subject area is considered a discipline if it focuses on a conceptually unique or distinctive form of behavior and possesses a theoretical framework for organizing and investigating the activity in question. Based on this criterion, industrial relations was not thought to qualify as an academic discipline since the study of the employment relationship, and the labor problems therein, was based largely on knowledge and theories from existing disciplines rather than on a knowledge base and theoretical framework unique to industrial relations.

The multidisciplinary character of industrial relations, as seen by the field's leading participants in the 1920s, is vividly illustrated by the disciplinary "map" of the field contained in the report of the Social Science Research Council (see fig. 1-1).[13] Across the top of the map are the four employment relations that are the focus of the field, while vertically are listed more than a dozen disciplines or fields of study that in some way contribute to the study of these relations. The cells of the map give examples of subjects from each discipline that are relevant to the respective employment relation. As figure 1-1 suggests, industrial relations in the 1920s was defined very broadly, both in terms of the employment relation studied (e.g., vertical "man-boss" relations within a firm; horizontal worker-worker relations both within a firm and across firms) and the disciplines that were considered part of the field.

Industrial relations was also depicted in the early literature as an exercise in both "science-building" and "problem-solving."[14] Science-building is concerned with the advancement of knowledge for its own sake. The development of theory is critical to science-building in that a theoretical framework is essential for formulating a research design, deducing hypotheses, and providing a consistent, unifying explanation for the behavior under study. In contrast, problem-solving has a more applied, empirical, and normative orientation. The goal is to identify the root cause of the problems under study and how they might best be resolved. Although early scholars in industrial relations saw science-building as part of their goal, their involvement in the field was animated principally by a desire to achieve more scientific, equitable, and humane employment practices through both progressive labor legislation and improved methods of employment management in industry (Derber 1967). Indicative of this applied orientation is the statement by John Calder (1924:vii) that "the term 'Industrial Relations' . . . now signifies a body of definite, liberal policies and practices dealing chiefly with the common economic interests of the employee and employer" and, in a similar vein, the statement by Gordon S. Watkins (1928:5) that "industrial conflict is often characterized as the greatest problem of industrial civilization, and that scientific administration of industrial relations is described as its most imperative need."

Finally, scholars in every academic field wish to use the theories and facts they develop to promote or advance the economic and social interest of the nation. According to early writers on the subject, the discovery and implementation of successful methods of industrial relations would lead to three such benefits: greater efficiency in production; greater equity in the distribution of economic rewards, the utilization of labor, and the administration of employment policies in the workplace; and greater individual happiness and opportunities for personal growth and development (Tead and Metcalf 1920:2–3; Watkins 1922:5–6; Scott and Clothier 1923; Furniss 1925:534–35).[15] Industrial relations was to lead to increased efficiency through such means as improved production methods, motivation, supervision, and cooperation between management and workers. Greater equity in pay, working conditions, and authority was to be achieved through such means as improved compensation systems, workman's compensation laws, and works councils or trade unions. Finally, a greater personal sense of well-being on the part of workers and managers was to be achieved by promoting due process in plant administration, enhanced individual dignity and respect

FIGURE 1.1   Map Suggesting the Field of Research in Industrial Relations

I. Sciences Nearest Related to Studies of Factors in Human Behavior	II. FACTORS IN HUMAN BEHAVIOR With special reference to industry	III. Illustrative Problems Arising in Industry Affecting THE WORKER IN RELATION TO HIS WORK (Objective conditions of the job, personal condition of the worker, attitude towards task)

Geography
  Anthropo-geography
  Anthropology
Physics and Engineering
  Illuminating Engineering
Chemistry
Agricultural Economics
  Mining and Metallurgy
  Transportation Economics
  Mechanical Engineering
  Safety Engineering
  Industrial Engineering
	EXTERNAL PHYSICAL ENVIRONMENT
	A. Climate in general (Temperature, sunlight, altitude)
	
	B. Natural resources and nearness to food supply
	
	C. External physical hazards
		(1)
		A. 1. Effects of seasons on man
		   2. Improvement of external aspect of workplace environment (Ventilation, lighting, noise and vibration in the purely technical aspects)
		B. 1. Availability of free land for cultivation
		   2. Distance from plant and difficulties of getting to work. (Probably belongs in Box 13 or 16)
		C. Traumatic hazards of the job
		   1. Natural—cave-ins, floods
		   2. Artificial—explosions, collapse of walls, etc.

Biology, Biophysics, and Biochemistry
 	
Anatomy
Physiology
  Endocrinology
  Bacteriology
  Neurology
Anthropology
	BODILY (PHYSICAL) CAPACITIES
	A. Bodily capacities
	  1. Physique
	  2. Physiological functioning (glandular activity, stamina, etc.)
	  3. Neurological endowments or defects (genius, feeble-mindedness)
	
	B. Inherited racial characteristics (not including nationality)
	
	C. Inherited sex characteristics
		(5)
		A. Medical problems of worker in a job
		  1. Physical fitness for the job
		  2. Posture, pace, physical fatigue
		  3. Change of physical power with age
		  4. Occupational diseases and general infections
		
		B. Fixed racial traits (if any) affecting work, viz: alleged laziness of negro
		
		C. Sex disabilities, physical and mental Special problems of women in industry

Psychology
  Employment Psychology
  "Industrial Psychology"
 	
Psychiatry
 	
Mental Hygiene
 	
Social Psychology
	INDIVIDUAL MENTAL RESPONSES
	A. "Mental" traits
	  1. Instincts and impulses
	  2. Mental capacities
	    a. Alertness, dexterity, intelligence, etc.
	    b. Special talents
	
	B. "Personality" traits
	  1. Emotional bias
	  2. Habits
	  3. "Drive"
	    (Courage, ambition, perseverance, initiative, will-power, etc.)
	
	C. Mental conflicts and control
	  1. Reaction to anxieties and strains
	  2. "Compensations," complexes, neuroses, etc.
	  3. Adaptation to environment
	
	D. Social sensitiveness
	  1. Behavior patterns and acquired attitudes
	  2. Susceptibility to mob or social pressure
		(9)
		A. Vocational guidance and employee selection
		  1. Psychological tests
		  2. Capacity for transfer, training, and promotion
		B. Detection and appraisal of personality traits
		  1. Discovery of potential leaders
		  2. Promotion problems; college men in business
		C. Psychological and psychiatric problems of work, such as
		  1. Monotony, fatigue, rest periods, hours of work
		  2. "Floaters," labor turnover
		  3. Interest in work, incentives, methods of wage payment
		  4. Tools and methods of work
		  5. Reaction to insecurity, thrift plans, stock ownership, personnel work, scientific management, etc.
		  6. Mental factors in accidents and inefficiency
		  7. Obsessions, neuroses, and other mental hygiene problems
		D. 1. Conscious restriction of output
		   2. Dissatisfaction due to fancied injustices, etc.

Figure continues on pp. 16–17.

IV. Illustrative Problems Arising in Industry Affecting THE WORKER IN RELATION TO HIS FELLOW-WORKER (At his side, in his plant, in his union, in his community or in the world at large)	V. Illustrative Problems Arising in Industry Affecting THE WORKER IN RELATION TO HIS EMPLOYER (Foreman, manager, owner, employing class, investor, capitalist, banker)	VI. Illustrative Problems Arising in Industry Affecting THE WORKER IN RELATION TO THE PUBLIC (Consumer, semi-public agencies, police, government, legislatures, courts, commissions)
(2) A. 1. Fights in plant, grievances, irritability, due chiefly to changes in climate (?)	(3) A. 1. Greater difficulty of maintaining discipline in certain seasons (?) 2. Employer's responsibility for good physical environment B. 1. Physical layout of mining camps (?) 2. Industrial housing (?) C. Mechanical engineering aspects of safety for which employer may be held responsible	(4) A. Sanitary regulations and industrial code. B. 1. General housing problem 2. General transportation problem of workers living at distance from plant C. Safety codes and legislation for building construction, mechanical equipment, etc.
(6) A. Contagious diseases B. Racial conflicts among workers (?) See Box 14, below C.	(7) A. Medical work of the employer 1. First aid, health activities, etc. 2. Hours of work and rest periods 3. Finding jobs for older employee 4. Eradication of occupational diseases B. Possible adaptation of type of discipline to race problems involved C. Sex relations as a factor in personal relationships in industry	(8) A. 1. General community health burden 2. Regulations of working periods 3. General community old age problems 4. Special regulations of certain trades B. C. Protective legislation for women in industry
(10) A. Lack of sympathy or cohesion between highly efficient or highly skilled worker and the mediocre or unskilled B. Exploitation of workers by other more dynamic workers, existence of "agitators," "firebrands," etc. C. Personal traits of leaders of workers (paralleled with qualities of outstanding executives?) D. 1. Effect of group payment plans on relationships of workers to each other, especially to older and less efficient worker, etc. 2. Effect of trade union benefit plans on worker 3. Relationships of workers with each other in strikes and in unions from standpoint of individual behavior	(11) A and B } Grievances, wage difficulties, conflicts caused by unsuitability of the worker for the job, or personality traits of the worker, involving: 1. Selection procedure 2. Rating, follow-up, promotion, etc. B and C } Discipline problems caused by 1. Poor leadership by foremen, managers, etc. 2. Neuroses of executives ("Mental hygiene of executives") 3. Abuse of wage incentive plans, time study, etc. 4. General "unpsychologic" handling of situations in plant C. Mental hygiene work of employer D. Difficulties and misunderstandings due to different behavior patterns of worker, foreman, employer, banker, etc.	(12) A. Civil Service problems (selection, training, promotion, etc.) B. Accidents and damage caused by improperly selected motormen, taxi-drivers, having personality traits of recklessness, etc. C. Mental hygiene burdens forced on community

FIGURE 1.1 (continued)

I. Sciences Nearest Related to Studies of Factors in Human Behavior	II. FACTORS IN HUMAN BEHAVIOR With special reference to industry	III. Illustrative Problems Arising in Industry Affecting THE WORKER IN RELATION TO HIS WORK (Objective conditions of the job, personal condition of the worker, attitude towards task)
Sociology Ethnology Cultural Anthropology History	GROUP CULTURE AND ORGANIZATION (Combined physical, personal and social circumstances—"environment")	(13) A. Nature of group attitudes, prejudices, etc. affecting worker's attitude towards his work 1. Measurement of morale, etc.
Ethics	A. Beliefs, customs, traditions, structural or institutional attitudes, national traits, etc. (Religious, ethical, social)	B. The effect of different economic systems and industrial organization upon the wage earner, including such elements as: 1. The industrial population and the labor market 2. Mechanization, pace, routine work 3. Insecurity, unemployment, "pre-senescence" 4. Competition and monopoly 5. The wage system and wage scales 6. Insecurity, attitude towards older men 7. Personnel practices and labor turnover 8. Employee ownership of stock or control of plant
Economics	B. Economic organization 1. Ownership and control of industry 2. Technology of industry 3. Distribution of wealth 4. General economic setting	
Political Science Jurisprudence	C. Political organization 1. Legislatures and commissions 2. Laws and courts 3. Police and constabularies	C. Obligation and rights of worker 1. Compulsory labor, peonage, etc. 2. Liability for damages, individual contract, etc. 3. Protection of worker by provisions of law
Education		
Science (Physical, Social) Logic Statistics (Experimental Research)	D. Intellectual organization 1. Educational systems 2. Art, literature, etc. 3. Purposeful research	D. Effect of school system on employee's capacity to work, his attitude, etc.

Source: Social Science Research Council 1928.

IV. Illustrative Problems Arising in Industry Affecting **THE WORKER IN RELATION TO HIS FELLOW-WORKER** (At his side, in his plant, in his union, in his community or in the world at large)	V. Illustrative Problems Arising in Industry Affecting **THE WORKER IN RELATION TO HIS EMPLOYER** (Foreman, manager, owner, employing class, investor, capitalist, banker)	VI. Illustrative Problems Arising in Industry Affecting **THE WORKER IN RELATION TO THE PUBLIC** (Consumer, semi-public agencies, police, government, legislatures, courts, commissions)
(14) A. 1. Racial cohesion or conflict among workers in industry 2. Religious discrimination 3. Prejudices against "scab," etc.	(15) A. 1. Degree to which employers and workers are influenced by fixed ideas, Marxianism, memories of past abuses, traditions, ethical considerations	(16) A. Public opinion as a factor in labor conditions or labor disputes 1. Attitude of individual consumers towards wage increases and other demands 2. Attitude of masses towards child labor amendment, etc.
B. Group relationships in general, such as: 1. Unionism: structure and activities a. Organization for group action b. Craft versus industrial unions c. Jurisdictional disputes d. Intra-union problems of factions, leadership, etc. e. Benefit features, recreation, etc. f. Labor banks and other business activities and their effect on unionism and on leaders and members g. International organization of labor 2. Relations of workers under employee representation plans	B. 1. Employers' organizations: structure, activities; open-shop drives, etc. 2. Absentee ownership, financial domination of labor policies 3. Employers' methods of administration a. Technical and organizing ability b. Wages paid c. Manner of exercising authority d. Policies towards older worker e. Personnel practices, etc. f. Housing provisions g. Shop committees and employee stock plans h. Labor turnover problems 4. Problem of joint control of industry 5. Group relations with employer a. Collective bargaining and cooperation b. Restrictive rules, spying system, etc. c. Attitudes towards discipline, authority, scientific management, wage changes, etc. and whole problem of wage scales d. Strikes, violence, etc.	B. Effect of economic system on social problems 1. Unemployment and insecurity; long range planning of public works, etc. 2. Crime, maladjustment, pauperism, citizenship 3. Leisure time activities of masses 4. Cost of products, burden of taxes 5. Housing and transportation 6. Public personnel practices
C. 1. Rights of workers to organize unions 2. Restrictions on boycotts	C. 1. Law of individual contracts 2. Laws affecting wage payments, etc. 3. Relative strength in influencing government 4. Court decisions	C. Labor legislation and administration 1. a. Restrictive Sherman Act, Clayton Act Individual contract Compulsory arbitration Regulation of immigration b. Protective and facilitative Mechanic's Lien, minimum wage Factory regulation, workmen's compensation Social insurances Employment exchanges 2. Attitude of courts towards labor a. The injunction b. Social outlook of judges 3. Industrial constabulary, police in strikes, etc.
D. 1. Workers education 2. Union activities of cultural type 3. Research work of unions	D. 1. Employers' educational work 2. 3. Employers' or joint research work	D. 1. Educational system in relation to the worker 2. 3. Research agencies, public and semi-public, investigating labor relations

17

in the workplace, and greater opportunities for the development of skills and leadership capabilities.

Given these considerations, a composite description of the field as it was perceived to exist in the 1920s might read as follows:

> Industrial relations is the multidisciplinary study of the employment relationship, with particular emphasis on the relations between employers and workers. It seeks to understand the forces of an economic, social, political, psychological, and organizational nature that affect the employment relationship; the goals, behaviors, practices, and organizations of employers and workers; the causes and consequences of imperfections and maladjustments in the employment relationship that adversely affect economic efficiency, workplace equity, and individual well-being; and the practices and policies that can resolve these problems.

2

THE SCHISM IN
INDUSTRIAL RELATIONS

T HE YEAR 1920 marks the birth year of industrial relations as a
professional field of study and practice, for it was then that a
distinct organizational entity devoted to the subject first appeared
in both academe (University of Wisconsin) and industry (the Industrial
Relations Association of America). What is more important than the
year of the founding of the field, however, is that both the IRAA and
the Department of Economics at Wisconsin were actively involved.

The majority of the members of the IRAA were practitioners who
were involved in general management or personnel work, although some
academics also belonged to the organization. These professionals were
especially interested in the new field of personnel management, a subject
a number of them wrote and lectured about. In contrast, the people
active in the industrial relations program at the University of Wisconsin
were institutional labor economists. Although their intellectual interests
covered nearly all aspects of the employment relationship, the primary
focus of their research and teaching was labor history, the practice of
collective bargaining, labor legislation, and the causes and consequences
of unemployment. Most advocated interventionist public policies to
protect and encourage collective bargaining, establish minimum wage
and employment standards, and provide wage earners and their families
with income security through social insurance programs.

What motivated these two disparate groups to develop a common
interest in industrial relations? One reason could have been a common
intellectual interest in advancing the state of knowledge about various

19

aspects of the employment relationship. In fact, science-building was of distinctly secondary importance. Rather, both groups were primarily interested in problem-solving; that is, the resolution of labor problems through improved methods of workplace organization and administration, the promulgation of progressive public policies, and the thorough application of ethics and moral values to the practice of business.[1]

Both the personnel professionals and academic economists had considerable firsthand knowledge of prevailing business practices and working conditions in American industry and were well acquainted with the substantial waste, inefficiency, human suffering, and conflict that this system entailed. Their interest in industrial relations was thus animated by a common desire to eliminate these evils through the discovery and implementation of modern, progressive production and employment methods.

While the two groups shared a common goal, it was also quickly apparent that fundamental and irreconcilable differences existed between them concerning the most effective way to resolve labor problems and, in particular, the appropriate role to be played by trade unions and collective bargaining.[2] Out of this disagreement was born two factions or schools of thought that have competed for control and dominance of the field of industrial relations from its earliest years to the present day. Given that these schools of thought were focused in the early 1920s on the study of personnel management and institutional labor economics, I have labeled them, respectively, the *PM School* and the *ILE School*. Both schools expanded in later years to include people from a variety of other academic disciplines and fields of study and after World War II gradually metamorphosed into what are today the HR (human resource) and IR (industrial relations) wings of the field.[3] Despite the change in labels and affiliated fields of study, the basic perspective of the two schools on the causes of labor problems and the resolution thereof have remained remarkably similar over a seventy-year period.[4]

The remainder of this chapter describes the intellectual origins of each school of thought and their early theoretical points of view on the causes and resolution of labor problems. Later chapters describe the evolution and development of these schools from the 1930s to today.

Personnel Management School

The practice and academic study of personnel management (or employment management as it was originally known) emerged at about the same time as industrial relations.[5] The first university textbook in personnel, for example, by Ordway Tead and Henry C. Metcalf, was published in 1920. Industrial relations was viewed as broader than personnel management in that IR encompassed the entire employment relationship and gave equal weight to the activities and organizations of *both* employers and employees, while PM focused largely on the management side of the employment relationship and, in particular, on the practices and procedures used to recruit, select, train, compensate, motivate, and communicate with employees. Personnel management was therefore seen as a subfield of industrial relations, just as labor relations (union-management relations) was so conceived.[6]

Given that personnel management represented only one part of the subject area of industrial relations, its proponents had little intellectual grounds for claiming sovereignty over it. Yet, as indicated earlier, the impetus behind the rapid spread and popularization of industrial relations after World War I had less to do with IR as an intellectual construct than with IR as a means to achieve improved employer-employee relations. The proponents and practitioners of PM believed they were the principal claimants to industrial relations since, in their view, personnel management offered the best means to achieve IR's end goal—improved efficiency, equity, and human well-being in the workplace.

The manner in which PM was to achieve this goal is discussed later in this chapter. This task requires, in turn, a brief consideration of the evolution of thought and practice in personnel management in its formative (pre-1930) years.

EVOLUTION OF PERSONNEL MANAGEMENT

Personnel management began in the World War I period as a fusion of two separate movements in industry: scientific management and welfare work (Lescohier 1935; Eilbirt 1959; Ling 1965; Wren 1987). The field evolved further in the 1920s with the emergence of the human relations movement (the practitioner, pre-Hawthorne version). A brief consideration of these theoretical developments is necessary to identify and appreciate the perspective of PM with respect to the causes and solutions of labor problems.

Scientific management was born shortly before the turn of the twentieth century. Its most important proponent was Frederick Taylor, although disciples such as Henry Gantt and Harrington Emerson also made contributions (Hoxie 1915; Haber 1964). Taylor's focus of attention was on plant management. He argued that labor problems and the adversarial relation between labor and capital arose from defective organization and improper methods of production and distribution in the workplace. Production and distribution, he contended, are governed by immutable natural laws that operate independently of human judgment. The object of scientific management is to discover these laws and to apply the "one best way" to selection, promotion, compensation, training, and production.

Taylor advocated using time and motion studies to determine the most efficient method for performing each work task, piece-rate systems of compensation to maximize employee work effort, and the selection and training of employees based on a thorough investigation of their talents and skills. Taylor also advocated changes in the organizational structure of the business firm, such as replacing the single foreman in charge of all aspects of production and personnel management in a given department with several foremen, each of whom would be trained in the knowledge and skills of a specific functional activity (e.g., production, machine repair, and so on.) The end result of these reforms in organization and methods would be the elimination of labor problems and the adversarial relation between labor and capital. This would be accomplished because all matters concerning production and distribution would be made on the basis of natural law and the one best way, thus eliminating disputes arising from errors and biases in human judgment. Increased efficiency would result in higher profits *and* higher wages, causing workers and employers to recognize that the employment relationship involves a mutuality of interests, not a conflict of interests.

Industrial welfare work was introduced before the turn of the century, grew in popularity up to the beginning of World War I, and then fell into disfavor thereafter as an independent employment practice (Ling 1965:80). Welfare work consisted of a variety of activities, sponsored and financed unilaterally by individual companies, the aim of which was to improve the home and working life of the companies' employees. Companies installed employee washrooms and lunchrooms, provided the services of a company doctor or nurse, built various recreational facilities, offered financial assistance for home purchases, and sent company welfare representatives to employees' homes to check on the sick or advise on nutritional and hygiene matters. In some cases companies undertook welfare work out of philanthropic motives; others did it as a way to forestall unionism or as a substitute for direct cash compensation. Most often, however, the motive was the belief that welfare work was "good business" because it helped foster loyalty and improved employees' morale.

By the start of World War I a small minority of companies had implemented at least some of the activities or principles associated with scientific management and welfare work (Jacoby 1985). But in most of these firms, to say nothing of the great majority of industry, the main personnel functions of recruitment, hiring, compensation, training, and discharge of employees still remained in the hands of the shop foremen or other line management, and the foremen continued to use the drive system as the principal mechanism for motivating employees. According to the advocates of PM, the labor problems of the war era occurred because the traditional system of personnel management was unscientific and inhumane. The solution, in turn, was to take the personnel function away from line management and vest it in a new staff function called personnel management, where trained experts could devise and implement a set of uniform, progressive policies and practices.

Some of these new personnel policies and practices were direct descendants of scientific management. Thus, firms stripped the individual foreman of the ability to hire at the plant gate and centralized this activity in the personnel department, which developed formalized selection procedures using written employment histories and aptitude tests. Other practices were direct descendants of welfare work, such as providing services or benefits that fulfilled various personal and work-related needs of employees. Thus, the duties of the company welfare worker, such as management of the lunchroom or home visits, were also centralized in the personnel department and transformed from a sideline activity smacking of heavy-handed paternalism to a modern business practice that was an integral part of the management of labor.

Several other personnel principles and practices emerged in the 1920s as reactions *against* some of the perceived shortcomings of scientific management and welfare work (Milton 1960). The two most important came under the headings "human relations" and "industrial democracy."

By the start of World War I, several defects of Taylor's system of scientific management had become apparent (Hoxie 1915). First, the system tried to mold the worker to the needs of the job rather than designing jobs to workers, leading critics to charge that the commodity concept of labor had been replaced by a machine concept. The result for employees was monotonous specialization and a loss of creativity and skill. Second, employers had used scientific management as a ruse to speed up work. Third, it had proved impossible to determine objectively the one best way to determine compensation, promotion, and so forth. Fourth, and finally, employees perceived scientific management to be undemocratic since it was unilaterally implemented and administered by management.

The basic cause of all of these shortcomings, critics argued, was that Taylor and his colleagues had ignored the "human factor." Writing in 1922, Gordon S. Watkins (1922:476–77) states, "The old scientific management failed because it was not founded upon a full appreciation of the importance of the human factor. It was left for the new science of personnel management to discover and evaluate the human elements in production and distribution." The incorporation of the human factor into scientific management soon became synonymous with the term *human relations.*

Although the term *human relations* is widely credited as originating with the Hawthorne experiments at the Western Electric Company in the late 1920s and, more particularly, with the writings of Elton Mayo and his colleagues at Harvard University, it was actually used quite frequently a decade earlier by nonacademic writers.[7] In the preface to the first edition of their personnel text, for example, Tead and Metcalf (1920) state, "The purpose of this book is to set forth the principles and the best prevailing practice in the field of the administration of human relations in industry."[8] Not only was the term used widely before Hawthorne, but many of the basic ideas of the Hawthorne version of human relations can be found, albeit in somewhat impressionistic form, in practitioner-authored articles and books of the early 1920s (see Williams 1920; Lewisohn 1926; Houser 1927).[9] For the most part, these works were largely ignored by later academic writers (a point noted by Wren 1985).[10]

The essence of the pre-Hawthorne human relations perspective was that through effective motivation, communication, and leadership in the workplace it is possible to create an organizational climate that promotes a mutuality of interests between management and labor and high levels of job satisfaction and productivity among employees. Following Taylor, the proponents of PM and human relations in the 1920s maintained that the root cause of labor problems and an adversarial relationship between labor and capital does not reside in any inherent defects of capitalism but, rather, in the organizational and administrative practices of management (Lewisohn 1926).[11] Labor problems are thus a management problem and improved industrial relations is a management responsibility. A common refrain of PM professionals was that only good management practices could *prevent* labor problems, while other proposed solutions to the labor problem (e.g., collective bargaining) were at best palliatives (Bloomfield 1931). The advocates of PM differed fundamentally from Taylor, however, regarding the best approach to eliminate the defects in management practice. Both groups agreed that perfection in organization and administration required the application of scientific principles to management, but Taylor looked to the field of engineering for the solution while the advocates of human relations looked to the new science of psychology.[12]

According to the proponents of human relations, good industrial relations depends on establishing a mutuality of interests between workers and employers. Both groups, it was argued, want the same things from work—maximum satisfaction and financial return—but they perceive themselves in conflict in the attainment of these goals (Filene 1919). The key to successful industrial relations, therefore, is to operate the firm in such a way that attainment of the organization's goals simultaneously fulfills the goals of workers, thereby creating a sense of partnership and an environment conducive to cooperation, trust, loyalty, and hard work (Follett 1925; Tead 1929, 1931).[13] The needs, aspirations, and attitudes of workers, however, are unknowable a priori and can be discovered only through the science of psychology. Hence, the first step in successful PM is to use psychological investigation to discover what workers want from work and the second step is to operate the organization and design its personnel practices in a way that is congruent with these needs.

During the 1920s there was an outpouring of books and articles by psychologists, business practitioners, and consultants on "what the worker wants" (Williams 1920; Thorndike 1922; Tead 1929). Typically, what the worker was thought to want was economic security, respect and fair dealing from supervisors, opportunity for advancement, and effective leadership from the firm's managers. Although much of this work was based on relatively unscientific methods, it nevertheless developed several themes that later proved quite important in PM.

One such theme concerned economic versus noneconomic determinants of employee work behavior. Classical economics and scientific management both used a model of "economic man" in that they presumed employees were motivated primarily by economic considerations.[14] Management writers in the 1920s took the first step in replacing economic man with "social man." Numerous writers (e.g., Thorndike 1922; Lewisohn 1926) argued that workers value such nonpecuniary rewards as status, justice, security, and advancement. Ordway Tead (1929:132) went one step further and, in anticipation of later theories of motivation by Abraham H. Maslow and Frederick Herzberg, argued that economic needs have to be met first but that worker loyalty and satisfaction ultimately depend on the fulfillment of such noneconomic needs as security, justice, and self-worth. The displacement of economic man by social man in the PM literature was important because it provided an intellectual justification for the abandonment of drive methods of motivation that relied on fear and intimidation and the adoption of positive employment methods (e.g., supervisor training, employment security, profit sharing) that not only encouraged hard work by linking personal gain with corporate gain but also fostered an atmosphere of fair treatment and personal growth.

The role of managerial leadership also became an important theme. Writers on PM noted that corporate managers were prone to devoting most of their attention to the "business" side of the firm and to neglecting the "people" side (e.g., firms had created staff departments for the finance, production, and accounting functions long before personnel departments). The proponents of PM claimed that the most important determinant of profitability was the way firms treated their employees (Lewisohn 1926; Spates 1937; Hicks 1941). It was crucial, therefore, for both improved industrial relations and firm performance that managers take a progressive, forward-looking approach to labor. Toward that end, PM treatises of the 1920s expounded the benefits to managers and their organizations of progressive, humane personnel policies and identified the traits of successful leadership so that managers might more effectively deal with employees and earn their loyalty and support (Craig and Charters 1925). The job of the manager had changed from commanding employees to perform certain tasks to enlisting their cooperation, something that could only be done successfully with good interpersonal skills and a sound knowledge of what motivates work effort. The emphasis on leadership thus reinforced the shift of attention in PM away from earlier views of labor as a commodity or a machine to a conception of workers as human beings who, with the right management practices and work environment, could become satisfied, productive members of the company team. This emphasis on the role of managerial leadership also imparted a unilateral, paternalistic tone to PM since it tended to locate all responsibility for improved industrial relations in the hands of management.

The organizational goals of the firm were yet another area of importance. Proponents of PM argued that a congruence of interests between the organization and its employees could be obtained only if the firm pursued goals that were salient to workers (Tead 1931:33–36; Hicks 1941:167–69). Strict adherence to a goal of profit maximization was likely to perpetuate an environment of conflict and mistrust because it emphasized the role of labor as a cost of production and subordinated employees' interests to those of absentee shareholders. Successful industrial relations required, therefore, that managers pursue multiple goals that would satisfy the needs of various stakeholders, including workers. Although this strategy might reduce profits in the short run, the proponents of PM argued that it increased profits in the long run by leading to reduced absenteeism, greater work effort, and less conflict.

The human relations perspective provided one of the fundamental pillars of thought in PM in the 1920s; the concept of industrial democracy provided another. The term *industrial democracy* had been popularized by Sidney and Beatrice Webb of Great Britain in their landmark book *Industrial Democracy* (1897). The Webbs were Fabian socialists and ardent supporters of trade unions. They argued at length that the traditional master-servant relationship in industry was incompatible with democratic principles because workers had neither a formal voice in the determination of wages and other terms and conditions of employment nor protection from arbitrary and/or discriminatory decisions of management with regard to discipline, discharge, and other such matters. From the Webbs' point of view, trade unions were the major instrument by which to introduce democracy into industry because they provided workers with an independent source of representation vis-à-vis the employer.

Proponents of PM in the 1920s were in most cases steadfastly opposed to labor unions and collective bargaining in practice, if not in principle. Some PM writers admitted that labor unions were justified in situations where the firm operated in an autocratic, exploitative manner (Hicks 1941:67–77). Some also allowed that labor unions could play a constructive role in labor relations and that firms might actually benefit from having a union organize its workers (Tead and Metcalf 1920:446– 80). Most PM writers, however, remained steadfastly opposed to labor unions and collective bargaining in practice (McCone 1920; Catchings 1923; Follett 1926). As they saw it, union leaders were driven to promote adversarialism and conflict to justify the unions' existence and thus unions were inimical to achieving the desired mutuality of interests between workers and employers. The proponents of PM also opposed unions on efficiency grounds because they claimed they foisted numerous restrictive practices on management, forced employers to pay inflated wages, disrupted production with strikes and slowdowns, and protected loafers and malcontents from dismissal. Finally, the proponents of PM claimed that unions were the enemy of true industrial democracy because they stifled individualism and were run by autocratic union bosses who were largely unaccountable to the membership.

While the advocates of PM opposed labor unions and collective bargaining, they believed that alternative forms of industrial democracy or "joint representation" could materially advance the interests of both employers and workers (Rockefeller 1923; Lewisohn 1926; Tead and Metcalf 1933; Holliday 1934). The practice of human relations, they said, could not create a mutuality of interests as long as the power and status of workers were so clearly inferior to those of managers. Joint representation was thus seen as a way to equalize power in the organization and foster constructive employee attitudes such as loyalty, commitment, and initiative. It also contributed to greater efficiency in production because it promoted greater employee morale and work effort, provided an escape valve for frustration and discontent, and increased the flow of information to upper-level management concerning conditions and problems on the shop floor. Further, joint representation fostered greater employer-employee cooperation by forcing management to give stronger consideration to the interests and concerns of workers. A final benefit was that it could possibly forestall unionization.

Given these many benefits, it became an accepted axiom of progressive management thought in the 1920s that an employee representation plan was an essential ingredient of good industrial relations. Although the structure and function of nonunion plans varied, the basic features were similar: the plans covered only the employees of a particular plant or firm; workers elected representatives who met with company officials to discuss issues of mutual concern; most plans mandated only that management meet and confer with the employee representatives; the right to strike was prohibited; and the company paid the costs associated with operation and administration of the plan (Carpenter 1926; Tead and Metcalf 1933; Nelson 1982).

In summary, the proponents of PM in the 1920s had worked out a coherent though somewhat heuristic explanation for the cause of labor problems and the best approach to resolving them. Their major goal was to achieve a congruence of interests between employers and workers, for out of such a congruence would flow both greater efficiency and employee happiness. The achievement of improved industrial relations required both the scientific application of engineering and management principles to the organization and administration of work and the incorporation of human relations and industrial democracy into the management and utilization of labor. Given the focus on integrating scientific principles of management with the practice of human relations, PM necessarily drew most of its intellectual inspiration from the fields of engineering, management, and psychology (industrial sociology was not yet a recognized academic field) and approached the study of industrial relations from an internal or intraorganizational point of view centered on the interaction between individual workers and managers within the plant.[15] Ideologically, PM was progressive in its approach to the management of people (relative to prevailing practices of the day), conservative with respect to property rights and government regulation of business, and hostile to labor unions.

INSTITUTIONAL LABOR ECONOMICS SCHOOL

Like personnel management, institutional labor economics did not cover all aspects of the employment relationship in its intellectual domain. Rather, the emphasis of ILE was on the impact of organizational or "institutional" forces (e.g., unions, government, family, social custom, law) on the employment relationship and the operation of labor markets (Commons 1934b). But, like the proponents of PM, the adherents of ILE believed they had the most accurate diagnosis of the causes of labor problems and the most efficacious solution to these problems.

ORIGINS AND THEORETICAL PERSPECTIVE

It is useful to discuss briefly the origins and theoretical perspective of institutional labor economics before embarking on a more detailed analysis of the point of view of ILE concerning labor problems and their resolution.

Institutional economics (IE) was born in America shortly before the turn of the twentieth century. Its intellectual roots came primarily from the German historical school of economics, although the writings of Karl Marx and the Webbs also exerted some influence (Dorfman 1959, 1963; McNulty 1980; Jacoby 1990). Thorstein Veblen, John R. Commons, and Wesley C. Mitchell are generally credited as the founders of IE. Commons, however, had by far the greatest impact in the area of labor, and, indeed, his point of view is sufficiently distinct from that of the others that it is useful to label his branch of the field as institutional *labor* economics.

The economics that dominated American thought in the latter part of the nineteenth century was based on the writings of various classical and neoclassical economists from Great Britain, including Adam Smith David Ricardo, John Stuart Mill, and Alfred Marshall (Ross 1991).

Adam Smith's *The Wealth of Nations* (1776) and later classical and neoclassical writings on economics worked out in some detail the economic and social virtues of free and unfettered competition in product and labor markets. A system of free exchange, Smith claimed, provides maximum individual liberty for employers and employees, reconciles conflicting interests into a harmony of interests, organizes production in the most efficient manner, and results in a just distribution of income to labor and capital. A free labor market maximizes the liberty of employees, for example, because it allows them the greatest choice of their employer, occupation, and location of work and permits the worker to quit one firm and seek a job at another whenever the terms and conditions of employment are judged to be unsatisfactory. Likewise, although employers and employees are nominally rivals in the labor market, the process of competition and free exchange leads them to seek out and voluntarily consummate mutually advantageous trades, leading to a "win-win" outcome and a harmony of interests in the long run. Competitive markets also result in the most efficient production of goods and services since prices (including wages, interest rates, and so on) accurately reflect the opportunity cost of scarce resources and the profit motive, combined with competition, motivates firms to employ more of these resources only as long as the additional gain in economic value to society from the goods and services produced is greater than the economic cost. A corollary of this point is that competition also leads to full employment in the labor market since wage rates will rise or fall until the demand for labor equals the supply. Finally, a competitive market system also gives rise to a just distribution of income in that employees are paid a wage equal to their contribution to production (implying zero exploitation of labor).

Disenchantment among American economists with the classical and neoclassical school emerged in the 1870s and gradually grew into a full-scale rebellion under the label of institutional economics (Dorfman 1959; McNulty 1980). Leading the rebellion was a group of graduate students that included Richard Ely, John Bates Clark, Henry Carter Adams, Simon Patten, and Edwin Seligman, who went to Germany in the mid-1870s to study under several prominent economists who were members of the German historical school (Ely 1938). These economists heavily criticized the classical and neoclassical theory of the British and Americans because, in their view, it represented a sterile exercise in deductive logic based on purported "natural laws" that were either conjectural or widely inconsistent with observed facts. In its place, the Germans advocated that economics be constructed as an inductive science in which assumptions and axioms would be adduced from the careful historical study of economic behavior. Furthermore, they placed much greater emphasis on the positive effects of state regulation and management of markets and on the constructive role labor unions could play in improving the conditions of labor.

When the Americans returned to their home country, they set out to develop a new, or at least greatly modified, economics that borrowed

31

heavily from the teachings of their German professors.[16] The result, as later refined and developed by Veblen, Commons, and Mitchell, was institutional economics.

Institutional economics in the 1920s contained several core propositions that distinguished it from the classical and neoclassical theory (Dorfman 1959; Dickman 1987; Ross 1991). The proponents of IE maintained that the crucial defect in the classical and neoclassical theory was that it presumed that product and labor markets were highly competitive (consumers and workers faced numerous alternative sources of products and jobs). Based on empirical and historical research, the institutionalists concluded that in reality product and labor markets were very imperfect and that business firms thus possessed some monopoly power with which to exploit consumers and workers.

Given the unequal plane of competition, institutionalists argued that free markets and laissez-faire were inimical to individual liberty and created a conflict of interests. Liberty, the institutionalists said, meant the ability to choose one's employer freely and to quit working for that employer when one desired. Free markets, however, imposed a tyranny on workers because the lack of alternative employment (because there were few firms in the local area and/or substantial unemployment) and the costs associated with labor mobility (e.g., loss of seniority rights, loss of income until a new job is found) coerced workers to accept wages and working conditions that they would not voluntarily choose given other options. Likewise, conflict is inevitable when economic circumstances allow the employer to take unfair advantage of workers.

The institutionalists also argued that a free market system was not only inimical to individual liberty but detrimental to the achievement of economic efficiency and growth. The low wages and high prices associated with business monopoly result in inadequate income and consumption spending and a consequent tendency to stagnation and unemployment, for example, while the volatility of wages and prices in a competitive market exacerbate the economy's boom and bust cycle.

CAUSES OF LABOR PROBLEMS

Ely (1886:100) claimed that three "peculiarities" of labor accounted for the worker's disadvantageous position in the labor market: labor's inequality of bargaining power, management's authoritarianism in industry, and the workers' economic insecurity. Later institutional writers amplified on these themes.[17] Each is briefly considered below.

A central tenet of institutional thought is that many workers suffer from an inequality of bargaining power under a nonunion system of individual bargaining (Webb and Webb 1897; Commons and Andrews 1916; S. Perlman 1928; Slichter 1931). The labor problems that result include exploitative wages, substandard working conditions, and labor unrest and conflict. The essence of the idea is that most labor markets contain imperfections that bias the wage determination process against workers. In a perfectly competitive labor market, the individual worker and employer would approach wage bargaining with an equality of power since the employer could not force the worker to accept less than the going rate given the numerous other job opportunities available and the worker could not force the employer to pay more than the going rate given the employer's ability to find numerous replacements. Labor would thus be paid the competitive wage, which would be equal to its contribution to production.

The case studies and investigative surveys conducted by the institutionalists led them to conclude that workers in many labor markets were at a distinct disadvantage in bargaining power vis-à-vis employers. They identified several reasons for this disadvantage, including the presence of substantial involuntary unemployment in normal times; conditions of monopsony and oligopsony (only one or several employers) in the labor market; collusive agreements among employers (often enforced through employers' associations); discrimination against minorities, immigrants, and women; and restrictions on worker mobility because of the loss of seniority or other rights (see Kaufman 1989a; 1991a). The effect of all these conditions was that employers were able to provide less than competitive wages and working conditions because workers were forced into a "take it or leave it" situation by the lack of alternative job opportunities and discriminatory or collusive practices.[18]

The second cause of workers' employment problems that Ely identified was management's authoritarianism in industry. Although workers had won full political rights in the nineteenth century, the employer-employee relationship remained of the master-servant type. This situation created an inequality of political power and due process inside the plant that paralleled the economic inequality of power in the external labor market. Ely identified this lack of industrial democracy as causing several labor problems, including low employee morale and work effort, frequent turnover, and strikes and other forms of conflict.

The third cause of workers' problems that Ely identified was economic insecurity, a theme later stressed by Commons (1926:263–72) and Selig Perlman (1928). As long as a person's labor is regarded as a commodity, Ely claimed, the worker's livelihood is tied to the vagaries of the labor market, the goodwill of the employer, and the uncertain occurrence of sickness and accidents. The worker's existence is thus filled with daily stress and anxiety, for his ability to earn an income to feed, clothe, and shelter his family are dependent on events largely outside his control. In reaction, workers take various steps to protect themselves, such as restricting their rate of output and the employer's ability to hire non-union workers, that are harmful to efficiency and act as catalysts for conflict with employers.

From the diagnosis of these economic and social ills flowed the solutions. The solution to labor's inequality of bargaining power, the institutionalists said, was to eliminate the problem by leveling the plane of competition. This was to be accomplished by what the Webbs (1897) called "the Device of the Common Rule." The Webbs noted that no matter how well intentioned an employer might be, competitive pressures during a recession, or from rivals whose labor costs are somehow lower (e.g., because they use child labor), inevitably force the firm to cut wages, lengthen hours, and speed up the work. To eliminate the downward pressure on wages and labor standards, the Webbs argued, it was necessary to place a floor under labor standards below which no employer could go. This "common rule" could be accomplished by either "the Method of Collective Bargaining" or "the Method of Legal Enactment" (i.e., protective labor legislation).

According to the Webbs, collective bargaining stabilizes wages and working conditions in two ways: first, the union acts as a countervailing power that offsets the weakness of workers in a system of individual bargaining and, second, by organizing all the employers in the product market and establishing uniform labor costs across them, the union takes wages out of competition. Government legislation such as a minimum wage law or a maximum hours law performs much the same function. The Webbs advocated setting the "common rule" at the level that would have occurred had the labor market been competitive and at full employment, thus leading to an increase in both efficiency and equity.

The solution to management authoritarianism, the institutionalists claimed, was industrial democracy, or joint determination of the terms and conditions of employment and the provision of due process in the settlement of disputes over rights. The institutionalists regarded nonunion employee representation plans as a step forward, particularly if they provided employees with independent decision-making power and protection from arbitrary discipline and discharge. The fundamental weakness of such plans, however, was that they were created by a unilateral act of management and just as easily could be abolished or ignored (Douglas 1921). For this reason the institutionalists advocated trade unions as a complement to employee representation plans and viewed unions as the long-term solution to industrial democracy. Union bargaining power, they said, provided workers with both voice and protection that was independent of the goodwill of the employer (Commons 1920; Leiserson 1923, 1929).

Eliminating the insecurity of the worker involved both micro- and macro-level changes (Commons 1921, 1926:263–72). At the plant level, it required a philosophical commitment by management to provide employment security; improved production and marketing methods to reduce seasonal and cyclical fluctuations in employment; and a system of employee representation to provide protection against arbitrary dismissal and discipline. At the economywide level, it required stabilization of the currency by the Federal Reserve Bank, a negotiated or legislated floor under wages and working conditions so that recessions and depression would not lead to a general liquidation of labor standards, and the creation of social insurance programs (e.g., workmens' compensation, unemployment compensation, social security) that would provide both tax incentives to firms to regularize employment and income support to workers who for reasons outside their control were unable to work.[19]

POINTS OF AGREEMENT AND DISAGREEMENT BETWEEN THE SCHOOLS

POINTS OF AGREEMENT

The overarching issue that united both the PM and the ILE schools was the need for employment reform. The traditional way of managing workers in American industry resulted in unacceptable waste, inefficiency, and human suffering. Progressives such as John R. Commons and Clarence J. Hicks sought to reduce and then eliminate these conditions. Both men, and the schools of thought they represented, also had similar views on the essential elements of reform.

Both agreed on the need to apply scientific principles to the organization of production and the management of work. Scientific management was not the *sole* answer to the elimination of labor problems, as Frederick Taylor had believed, but it was an important part of the solution. Both men also recognized the importance of the "human factor" in structuring and managing work. The source of many labor problems was the tendency for managers to treat employees as commodities, when in fact these "commodities" came to the workplace with a full range of human emotions and needs. Thus, the proponents of both the PM and the ILE schools advocated new personnel policies and practices to ensure employment security, respect on the job, and fair treatment. Another area of agreement concerned the importance of replacing the autocratic, master-servant type of employer-employee relationship with one that provided employees with representation rights and due process in the workplace. Finally, both men agreed on the importance and desirability of maintaining the basic institutions of capitalism, including private property and free labor markets.

POINTS OF DISAGREEMENT

In general, the proponents of the ILE school were academically trained economists, while the early writers in the PM school tended to come from the ranks of management in industry (as did many of the teachers of personnel courses in business schools of the 1920s). The two groups inevitably looked at the causes and solutions of labor problems from different perspectives.[20] It was evident to both that the business organization was the place to begin the investigation of labor problems, for that was where the inefficiency in production, the low work effort, and the conflict occurred. When it came to identifying the underlying causes of the problems, however, the two sides diverged. The economists tended to give far greater weight to the external economic, legal, and technological environment, such as business cycles, labor market imperfections, and the legal rights and protections given to employers and employees. In contrast, the management practitioners tended to focus

36

on the internal organizational, social, and psychological environment of the firm, including managerial leadership, methods of compensation, and other motivational devices, and on the organizational climate engendered by management (e.g., degree of trust and goodwill between the firm and its employees). Out of this difference grew some fundamental disagreements about the causes of labor problems and their resolution.

One such disagreement concerned whether a conflict of interests is inherent to the employment relationship. As noted earlier, proponents of the PM school readily admitted as an empirical fact that conflict is rife in many employment relationships. They denied, however, that conflict is inevitable. Hicks (1941:65–79), for example, identified three types of employment relationships: "autocratic," "two antagonistic parties," and "unity of interests." Because the employment relationship is structured as a zero-sum game (what one side gains is at the expense of the other), the first two relationships (the traditional master-servant relationship and the union-company relationship) inevitably exhibit a large degree of adversarialism. Using human relations and industrial democracy, however, one could achieve the third type of employment relationship. In this case, the employer and the employees perceive themselves to be partners in a common enterprise, giving rise to a mutuality of interests and a sense of shared purpose. Because organizational success benefits both sides, the employment relationship becomes a positive-sum game, motivating employees to work diligently for the firm's success.

The institutionalists had a substantially different view. As they saw it, the employment relationship has a fundamentally mixed-motive nature in that it contains significant elements of both cooperation and conflict. An incentive for cooperation exists, for without the participation of both parties to the employment relationship, the firm will not be a viable concern and neither profit nor wages will be earned. Thus, outside limits exist with respect to the level of the wage rate, working conditions, and work effort that the workers and firm wish to obtain. Within these limits, however, an adversarial relationship exists. One dimension of this relationship is economic in that the additional profit earned by the employer from lower wages, a reduced expenditure on working conditions, or a greater pace of work necessarily comes at the expense of workers, and vice versa (Hansen 1922). Another dimension of this relationship is social in nature and involves the frictions and resentments that inevitably arise between order givers (management) and order takers (employees) (see Douglas 1921). While employers may attempt to reduce the adversarialism inherent in the employment relationship through human relations practices, a certain core amount of conflict always exists in that the employer's control of the workplace and drive for greater efficiency and profit necessarily collide with the workers' desire for independence from managerial subordination, employment security, and a higher standard of living.

These alternative views on the adversarial nature of the employment relationship gave rise to alternative views of the efficacy of conflict in the employment relationship. From the point of view of the institutionalists, a certain amount of conflict is a normal by-product of the employment relationship and, indeed, frequently plays a constructive role to the extent that it vents repressed frustrations, resentments, and grievances. Good industrial relations, therefore, is not synonymous with an absence of conflict, for often this indicates complete domination of the relationship by the employer. Rather, good industrial relations requires equalizing the bargaining power of labor and capital both inside and outside the plant and letting them voluntarily negotiate a mutually satisfactory outcome.[21] Thus, the watchword of the institutionalists is *compromise.*

From a PM point of view, however, conflict of an ongoing, substantive nature is undesirable because it is destructive of the trust and shared purpose that are essential to unlocking employee commitment and hard work. The presence of conflict is thus a signal that the management and organization of work continue to suffer from fundamental defects and that additional management action is needed. The end goal, therefore, should be the integration of employer and employee interests and the elimination of conflict (Follett 1926; Hicks 1941). Rather than compromise, which the PM school sees as doing nothing to remedy the underlying sources of conflict, the watchword of the PM school is *cooperation.*

The disagreement between the PM and the ILE schools then moved to the issue of how best to induce firms to adopt the necessary changes in management practices required for harmonious relations. Commons (1926:263) estimated that between 10 and 25 percent of firms in the 1920s used "best-practice" labor relations policies, a figure the proponents of PM did not dispute. The issue for employment reform, then, was how to get the other 75 to 90 percent (the laggards) up to the same level of accomplishment.

The basic approach favored by the proponents of the PM school was to use education, persuasion, and patience. As noted earlier, they believed that a mutuality of interests could be attained by adopting progressive personnel policies, particularly human relations and industrial democracy. The challenge was to induce firms to adopt these practices. The PM school believed a two-prong strategy would work best (Milton 1960:129–40). The first prong involved an appeal to the employer's sense of ethics and Christian duty; that is, convincing the laggards that they had a moral responsibility to improve their treatment of employees. The second prong involved business education; that is, convincing employers that improved management practices were also good for their bottom line.

The early proponents of PM believed that employers would adopt progressive personnel practices if they perceived the benefits to be greater than the costs. Thus, a fundamental axiom of PM is that progressive personnel practices are not only right from a moral and ethical point of view but also more than pay for themselves in the form of increased profit (Tead and Metcalf 1920:9). The problem is that many employers have a difficult time seeing the validity of this proposition because, on the one hand, the costs of improved personnel practices tend to be readily quantifiable and incurred in the short run (e.g., salaries of personnel staff, additional payroll costs associated with employment security), whereas the benefits are often difficult to measure and often do not become evident until well into the future (e.g., increased productivity through higher morale, lower chances of unionization). The result is that many employers mistakenly believe that good labor relations policies are a "luxury" that only profitable firms can afford and thus do not undertake them. The proponents of PM believed that the only way to counteract this view was through education, both on the new techniques of personnel administration (e.g., employment tests, employee representation plans) and on their benefits to the firm (Kennedy 1920; Tead and Metcalf 1920:15–16; Houser 1927:202–18).

From the ILE point of view, these positions were not so much wrong as seriously incomplete. Commons, for example, agreed with the contention that progressive personnel policies could reduce labor problems and that educational activities could make a significant contribution to promoting the adoption of such policies. The major theme of his book *Industrial Goodwill* (1919), for example, was that the cultivation of employee goodwill paid off for business firms. From his perspective, it was a vain hope, however, to believe that education and moral suasion could ever induce the great majority of firms to adopt best-practice personnel policies voluntarily.

The critical flaws in the PM point of view were twofold. The first was that human relations and industrial democracy required managers to relinquish a portion of their unilateral power and control, an idea that was anathema to many managers regardless of its salutary effect on profits. The second flaw was that the PM view did not sufficiently recognize that the incentive for firms to adopt progressive personnel policies was contingent on the state of the economy.[22]

According to Commons (1921), full employment, not education, is the most effective way to promote the adoption of progressive personnel practices in industry. The reason is that full employment creates conditions in the labor market and workplace (e.g., labor shortages, labor turnover, reduced work effort, more strikes) that make it plainly in the self-interest of employers to practice better labor relations. In effect, he says, only when labor is scarce will employers be induced to treat labor as a human resource rather than as a commodity. When the economy operates at less than full employment, the abundance of labor removes much of the incentive on management to adopt progressive measures since it is easy to replace disgruntled, uncooperative, or injured employees with other willing hands. Further, the competitive pressure in a slack market to cut costs forces first financially weaker firms and then their stronger competitors to cut labor compensation and increase work effort (see Douglas 1921, 1922). Thus, from the ILE perspective, the fundamental source of labor problems is not at the individual plant in the form of inhumane and/or unscientific management practices per se but, rather, at the level of industry and the economy, where involuntary unemployment and idle plant capacity make such policies both profitable and necessary (Commons 1921:4, 1934a:190). It follows, in turn, that the most effective means to spur the adoption of progressive personnel policies is to pursue a full-employment monetary policy by the Federal Reserve Bank.[23]

Another source of disagreement between the PM and the ILE schools concerned the role of labor unions and collective bargaining in promoting improved industrial relations. As noted earlier, most PM advocates held labor unions in low regard. While they were prepared to admit that workers are all too often driven to seek a union by autocratic, exploitative employers, they thought unions are not only incapable of solving the underlying problem (poor management) but often saddle the firm and workers with restrictive work rules, inflated wage demands, strikes, and internal political intrigues. More important, nearly all PM advocates objected strongly to the demand of unions for the union or closed shop, on the grounds that no person should be denied employment on account of his or her union status. They also believed that labor unions are run by outsiders whose self-interest is served by fomenting conflict, given that workers desire a union and pay union dues only if they feel dissatisfied with the terms and conditions of employment (Catchings 1923:486).

Proponents of the ILE school took a different view of unions. Some firms, they admitted, are so well managed and pay sufficiently high wages that the workers have no need for a union. The personnel practices of the majority of firms, however, lag behind, either because of poor management or low profits. For this group of firms, unions have a constructive role to play that should be encouraged by public policy.[24] It is true that labor unions typically increase the labor costs of employers, both directly through wage demands and indirectly through restrictive work practices, strikes, and other such practices. While employers understandably resist unions for these reasons, the ILE school maintained that from a social point of view the benefits of having unions clearly exceed the costs. Wage gains secured by unions, for example, are socially useful because they eliminate the low wages forced on workers by labor's inequality of bargaining power; union wage gains motivate management to operate the firm more efficiently, leading to offsetting gains in productivity (the "shock" effect); and union wage gains bolster household income and help promote aggregate demand and full employment.

With regard to restrictive work practices, the institutionalists argued that the obvious costs to employers must be weighed against the benefits to workers and society.[25] Trade unions, they said, are inherently restrictive in nature since their purpose is to prevent certain employment practices that the pressures of competition force employers to adopt. Many of these practices (e.g., twelve-hour workdays, excessive line speed, lack of elementary safety equipment) are clearly injurious to both workers and society and their elimination through collective bargaining is thus to be desired. While individual firms may be put at a competitive disadvantage to the extent that restrictive union practices raise labor costs only at those firms, the solution to this problem is best met by taking labor costs out of competition by organizing all firms in the relevant product market and imposing common labor standards on them.

The institutionalists also favored labor unions as the primary vehicle to achieve industrial democracy. Company unions, works councils, and other employer-sponsored forms of employee representation do not provide industrial democracy in the true sense of the term, since they are created by management and give workers little or no independent power to negotiate improved terms of employment or protection from arbitrary management decisions on discipline and discharge. True democracy means that decisions are reached only with the consent of the governed, implying that workers must be able to elect representatives of their own choosing, engage in collective bargaining over wages and other conditions of employment, and go on strike if an agreement cannot be reached. Industrial democracy also implies that unions have a legitimate right to demand the union shop or closed shop, for, just as all citizens in the nation are bound to abide by laws adopted by the majority, so too should all employees belong to and support the union if it has been freely chosen by a majority in the plant.

Finally, institutionalists were strong advocates of economic and political "pluralism" and saw unions as essential parts of such a system. Business firms, they thought, had a power advantage over workers and consumers because the latter were unorganized and could not effectively represent their interests. The solution was a pluralistic network of organized interest groups, such as labor unions, political parties, church groups, civic associations, and so on, each of which would represent their respective constituencies. This conception of society led the institutionalists to stress a "tripartite" approach to the resolution of labor disputes, in which tripartite meant collaboration, consultation, and compromise between representatives of labor, management, and the public.[26]

For all of these reasons, the proponents of the ILE school saw unions as a desirable, albeit imperfect, instrument to promote improved industrial relations. In contrast, the advocates of the PM school saw unions as an impediment to efficiency and as an abridgement to individual freedom, and, accordingly, they resisted them strongly. As shall become clear in succeeding chapters, the split between the PM and the ILE schools over the issue of unionism would prove to be an enduring feature of the field of industrial relations and one with far-reaching consequences.

3
INDUSTRIAL RELATIONS IN THE INTERWAR YEARS

THE DEVELOPMENT of industrial relations in the years between the world wars is one of the most interesting yet least explored chapters in the history of the field. Industrial relations made slow but perceptible progress over this twenty-year period in carving out an identity as a distinct subject area of teaching and research. Most noteworthy in this regard was the establishment at six universities of IR units or sections dedicated to the promotion of research and, to a lesser degree, teaching in industrial relations. Equally important, the field continued to attract the active participation of persons from both the ILE and PM wings. Although the two sides looked at the causes of labor problems from different perspectives and promoted different policy programs for resolving these problems, as an intellectual concept and academic field of study, industrial relations possessed a sufficient degree of elasticity during this period to accommodate these divergent views and interests. As we shall see, this was not to be the case two decades later.

ESTABLISHMENT OF INDUSTRIAL RELATIONS UNITS
The first independent unit at an American university dedicated mainly, if not solely, to the study of industrial relations was the Industrial Research Department, established in 1921, in the Wharton School of Commerce and Finance of the University of Pennsylvania. (The department's name was changed in 1953 to the Industrial Research Unit.) The first director of the department, Joseph Willits, was trained as an economist but was interested primarily in personnel and employment

management, as indicated by both his professional writings and his participation in programs sponsored by the Industrial Relations Association of America and its successor, the American Management Association (Willits 1931). Under Willits, the department published a number of articles and monographs on IR topics during the 1920s. The PM orientation of its research program is evident in the topics of these articles: promotion, training, attendance, labor turnover, and labor mobility. The Wharton IR unit has maintained its management orientation to the present time, making it the oldest IR unit in the PM branch of the field. Reflecting the unit's PM heritage, its name was changed in 1990 to the Center for Human Resources.

The other five IR units established before World War II were at Princeton University, Stanford University, the University of Michigan, the Massachusetts Institute of Technology, and the California Institute of Technology. Like the IR unit at Wharton, these were all affiliated with the PM school of industrial relations.

The person responsible for the establishment of these units was Clarence J. Hicks (see Hicks 1941:140–52). Hicks had a long career in industry as both an executive and a management consultant on industrial relations matters. One of his earliest and most important assignments was for John D. Rockefeller, Jr., who hired Hicks in 1915 to establish and administer an employee representation plan at one of his companies, the Colorado Fuel and Iron Company.[1] Hicks went on to become the executive in charge of industrial relations at Standard Oil (New Jersey); chairman of the board of trustees of Industrial Relations Counselors, Inc., the most prestigious IR consulting firm of its time; and a member of the National Labor Board, which was created in 1933 to adjudicate disputes arising from Section 7(a) of the National Industrial Recovery Act.

In his memoirs, *My Life in Industrial Relations,* Hicks (1941) describes his dissatisfaction with what he perceived to be the one-sided, pro-union point of view that college students received in their labor courses.[2] To help promote a more balanced view, Hicks helped organize industrial relations units at the five major American universities cited above.[3] He also helped found a sixth unit at Queen's University in Canada (see Kelly 1987).[4]

The first unit Hicks helped establish was the Industrial Relations Section at Princeton, established in 1922 with the help of a generous financial gift from Rockefeller. The purpose of the section was to collect and disseminate information on industrial relations topics, sponsor IR research, and organize conferences and training classes for industrial relations practitioners (primarily upper-level managers). The section was organized as a subunit of the Department of Economics, although the approach to industrial relations was intended to be multidisciplinary (Brown 1976). Given Hicks's philosophical position on the practice of industrial relations and the apparent triumph of welfare capitalism and defeat of unionism in the 1920s, it is not surprising that the early research output of the section had a heavy PM flavor. The first five publications, for example, dealt with employee stock ownership plans, corporate training programs, labor turnover, absenteeism and tardiness, and group insurance.

The four other U.S. IR sections Hicks organized were similar to the one at Princeton. Of these units, the one at MIT has made the most impact on the field.[5] Established in 1937, it was started as a subunit of the Department of Economics and Social Science (McKersie 1990) but was later transferred to the Sloan School of Management. The section initially had three faculty members, Rupert Maclaurin (economics), Douglas McGregor (psychology), and Charles Myers (economics/personnel), each of whom served at some point as section director. The research output of the section during its first decade was eclectic but was weighted toward local labor market studies, human relations topics, and personnel management.

INDUSTRIAL RELATIONS IN ACADEMIC CURRICULA

In the period from 1920 to 1941, no American university or college had a separate degree program or department explicitly devoted to the subject of industrial relations.[6] Several universities offered a major or area of concentration in industrial relations, however, including Wisconsin, Columbia, Michigan, and Missouri.

A concentration in industrial relations was offered at Wisconsin as part of the major in economics. Students were required to take course work in labor legislation, labor history and industrial government, unemployment, and labor management. At Columbia University, an informal Department of Industrial Relations was established in the School of Business sometime in the late 1920s (U.S. Department of Labor 1930; Van Metre 1954). The faculty included Paul Brissenden (economics),

Ordway Tead (personnel management), and A. T. Poffenberger (psychology). The department offered four courses—labor administration, law of the employment of labor, adjustment of labor disputes, and personnel and employment problems. Other examples include the University of Michigan and University of Missouri. The former offered a major in industrial relations in the MBA program (Industrial Relations Counselors 1949), while the latter had an IR major in the undergraduate business program (Bossard and Dewhurst 1931:306).

Although only a handful of American universities had any formal curriculum in industrial relations in the pre–World War II period, the subject was nevertheless taught at nearly all major state and private universities (Bossard and Dewhurst 1931:429–30). The most common vehicle was a survey course in labor problems, offered through an economics department; a second but somewhat less frequently encountered approach was to offer a course in personnel management, generally in a school of business or commerce.

The labor problems course was the intellectual forerunner of what is today called labor economics, although the theoretical and topical orientation of the two subjects is quite different. A typical labor problems text was divided into four sections (Persons 1927; Estey 1928; Daugherty 1936; Watkins and Dodd 1940). The first section was devoted to various labor problems or "evils," such as the insecurity of employment, low wages, industrial accidents, and child and female labor. The second, third, and fourth sections were devoted to a discussion of "solutions" to labor problems. Typically, one section was devoted to *workers' solutions*, another to *employers' solutions*, and a third to the *community's solutions*. These solutions involved, respectively, trade unions and collective bargaining, personnel management (including scientific management, human relations, and employee representation), and protective labor legislation and social insurance programs.

Most of the texts identified the discovery, implementation, and practice of these solutions as the subject matter of industrial relations (Watkins and Dodd 1940:10–11). The different solutions, in turn, represented the policy programs of the PM and ILE schools of thought—the ILE school advocated the first and third solutions (collective bargaining and protective labor insurance legislation and social insurance), and the PM school advocated the second (personnel management). The labor problems texts represented, therefore, the 1930s' version of what today would be called an IR theory text.

Several features distinguish the labor problems courses of the 1930s from a post-1970 labor economics course. First, the emphasis on labor problems gave the course of the 1930s a critical and reformist tone— critical because it suggested that the capitalist system was prone to serious maladjustments and defects that accounted for the "evils," and reformist because it focused on changes in the organizational, economic, and political status quo to solve these evils (Estey 1928; Yoder 1931). In contrast, modern labor economics generally gives the market system high marks for its allocative efficiency and for that reason tends to emphasize the virtues of competition in free markets and the harmful effects of institutional interventions (e.g., unions, minimum wage laws). Second, labor problems texts were generally descriptive and written largely from a historical and sociological point of view; they gave scant attention to the operation of labor markets and the manner in which demand and supply determine outcomes such as wages, hours of work, and so on.[7] Present-day labor economics texts are in many ways the opposite. Finally, the labor problems texts spent several chapters analyzing personnel management, including topics such as the philosophies and goals of management; personnel practices, such as hiring tests, compensation systems, and techniques of performance appraisal; and methods for dispute resolution. Modern labor economics texts generally exclude these subjects altogether.

RESEARCH IN INDUSTRIAL RELATIONS

A review of industrial relations research during the interwar years is complicated by the uncertain definition of what distinguishes IR from non-IR research. The most narrow approach is to limit the focus to those articles and books that have the term *industrial relations* in the title. By this standard relatively little IR research was published during this period. A bibliographic computer search keyed to the term produced references to fifteen published works in the United States between 1930 and 1939. The majority of these references were to short bulletins published in the Personnel Series of the American Management Association (Sokolsky 1936; Miller 1937; Spates 1937, 1938; Stoll et al. 1937; Chester 1939). Multiple references were also found to short studies produced by the industrial relations sections at Princeton University (Industrial Relations Section [IRS], Princeton 1930, 1939; Baker 1939), the California Institute of Technology (IRS, Cal Tech 1939), and the National Industrial Conference Board (NICB 1931; Walter 1934). Other significant references include a large PM-related monograph entitled *Executive Guidance of Industrial Relations*, by C. Canby Balderston (1935) of Wharton's Industrial Research Unit, and two case studies of labor-management relations in the building trades: William Haber's (1930) *Industrial Relations in the Building Industry* and Frederick Ryan's (1936) *Industrial Relations in the San Francisco Building Trades*.

There is also a paucity of IR-labeled research in the articles published in major IR-related journals. Between 1930 and 1939, the *American Economic Review* and the *Quarterly Journal of Economics* each contained one article (Slichter 1939; Gulick 1932) with *industrial relations* in the title, while the *Personnel Journal* contained two such articles (Brown 1935; Tead 1938) and the *Journal of Applied Psychology* contained one (Schultz and Lynaugh 1939).

By this criterion it would seem that industrial relations had a relatively minor presence in academic research of the period. A different criterion of what comprises industrial relations research leads to a significantly different conclusion, however. For example, if one uses the term *industrial relations* as it was originally conceived, as pertaining to research on any aspect of the employment relationship, there is suddenly a great abundance of research, including studies by industrial psychologists on employment tests, by historians on the origins and development of labor unions, and by economists on wage determination. The problem then is how to organize this mass of research so that it has some intellectual coherence and point of reference.

The most noteworthy attempt in this regard was made by Delbert C. Miller and William H. Form (1951) in the first edition of their text *Industrial Sociology*. They presented a comprehensive bibliography of research on industrial relations dating from the turn of the century to 1950. This bibliography was divided into eleven sections, based on their judgment that research in the field came from eleven distinct disciplinary or theoretical points of view. They represented the family tree of IR research in a remarkable diagram, which is reproduced here as figure 3.1. The names attached to each branch are the authors listed in the eleven sections of Miller and Form's bibliography.

One may quarrel with specific aspects of the figure, but it nevertheless provides an accurate portrayal of the development of IR research in the years before 1940.[8] As the figure indicates, IR research spanned a wide range of academic fields and included a very heterogeneous mix of topics. Economics, sociology, anthropology, engineering, personnel management, and psychology all contributed to the field. Topics investigated included union history, wage determination, the practice of collective bargaining, government regulation of the employment relationship, working-class social structures and values, restriction of output by employees, preemployment hiring tests, attributes of effective leadership, determinants of employee motivation and morale, and methods of industrial governance and conflict resolution.

As the figure also illustrates, from its earliest days, IR research was composed of both behavioral and nonbehavioral science wings. The nonbehavioral wing was represented by economics and industrial management (i.e., scientific management). The behavioral wing was initially (1920s) represented by the discipline of psychology, both directly through industrial psychology and indirectly through the psychological component of personnel management. In the 1930s, the behavioral side of IR research expanded greatly with the addition of several new branches of thought, including industrial sociology, applied anthropology, and what Miller and Form called the "Harvard Graduate School of Business Administration" (the writings of Elton Mayo, T. N. Whitehead, and Fritz J. Roethlisberger and William J. Dickson). The involvement of all three fields was the result of a common catalyst, the research findings of the Hawthorne experiments at the Western Electric Company, conducted between 1924 and 1933. For this reason, all three branches are commonly combined under the label of "human relations." Since the human relations movement (the academic version, that is) did not emerge with full force until the publication of Roethlisberger and Dickson's monumental study, *Management and the Worker*, in 1939, a full discussion of this aspect of IR research is postponed until the next chapter.

Figure 3.1 also clearly reveals the presence of what has been called here the ILE and PM schools of thought in industrial relations. The ILE school was composed of the institutional economics and industrial and labor economics branches on the lefthand side of the figure. Initially, the PM school was composed of the fields in the three most righthand

FIGURE 3.1. Outlines of the Streams of Industrial Relations Knowledge

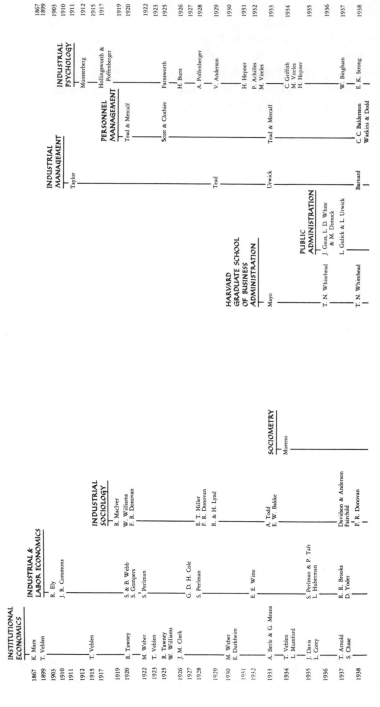

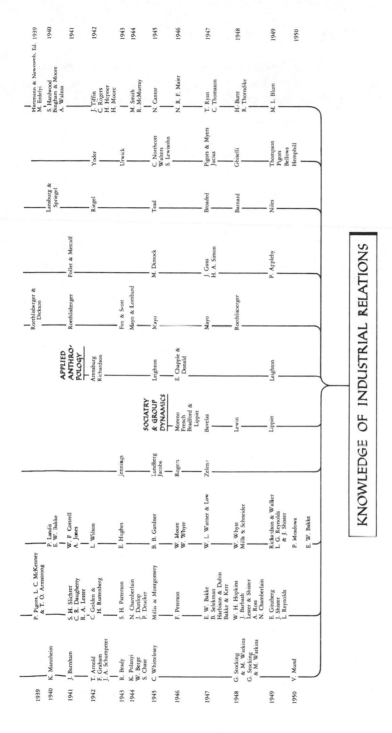

KNOWLEDGE OF INDUSTRIAL RELATIONS

Source: Miller and Form 1951.

branches, industrial psychology, personnel management, and industrial management. Later, the PM side was augmented by other behavioral science fields, such as anthropology and industrial sociology, in the middle of the figure.

A Correction of the Historical Record

In their discussion of the pre–World War II period of industrial relations, Strauss and Feuille (1981:86) claim that "economics is industrial relations' 'mother discipline', and for many years industrial relations and labour economics were viewed as virtually synonymous." They also say (p. 77) that "Commons and his colleagues and students at Wisconsin, especially Selig Perlman and Edwin Witte, comprised the Wisconsin school, which together with colleagues with similar interests, such as Harry A. Millis and Robert Hoxie at Chicago, defined the nature of the field and the chief questions that it has considered over the years." Barbash (1984:4) makes a similar claim: "In an earlier period industrial relations would have been just about the same as institutional labor economics, founded by John R. Commons and the Wisconsin school."

It should be clear from the preceding discussion that assertions such as these are significantly wide of the mark in that they neglect altogether the existence of the PM school of industrial relations and that this stream of thought is grounded largely in management and the behavioral sciences. Since the viewpoint expressed by the quotations cited above is frequently encountered, one must ask why this misinterpretation has gained such a widespread following.

To begin, there can be no gainsaying that the institutional economists were the first academic group to begin serious research in the field of labor problems (McNulty 1968). It is also indisputable that the most influential writer and teacher in the early years of industrial relations in North America was John R. Commons, a fact that legitimately earned him the title "father of industrial relations."[9] Thus, given the early involvement of the institutionalists in the development of the field of industrial relations and the preeminent role played in the birth of the field by Commons (the leading exponent of institutionalism), it is appropriate that writers would emphasize the strong relationship between institutional economics and the development of industrial relations.

To say that institutional labor economics and industrial relations were virtually one and the same is, nevertheless, far from the truth. Several reasons most likely account for this confusion.

It is not always recognized that in the 1920s–30s the discipline of economics, and labor economics in particular, contained an extremely heterodox group of scholars. Some of these scholars were truly economists in that they were conversant with economic theory and interested in economic subjects per se. Others, however, had much greater expertise in related fields, such as personnel management, labor history, sociology, and law. Before World War II, for example, most of the influential academic writers on personnel management, including Paul Douglas, Sumner Slichter, Gordon Watkins, and Dale Yoder, had degrees in economics. Similarly, labor history was dominated by economists, including Commons, Selig Perlman, and Phillip Taft.

In both cases, at least some of these people (e.g., Watkins, Perlman) were not economists as defined above, although their doctoral degrees were in economics. Most schools of business in the pre–World War II period considered personnel management and other business-related subjects to be "applied economics" and included them under the curricular umbrella for the doctoral degree program in economics (Gordon and Howell 1959:400–402).[10] Furthermore, labor economics during this period was construed broadly to encompass nearly all subjects pertinent to the employment and utilization of labor, including personnel management and trade union history, which today would be considered the province of other fields of study (McNulty 1980:156–59). Thus, even though a significant number of the early writers in industrial relations were "economists," this does not mean that economics, at least as the discipline is conceived today, was the principal intellectual wellspring of the field.

Another potential source of confusion concerning the roots of industrial relations involves the labor problems courses offered during the period. The labor problems course was the closest equivalent to an IR theory course in that it focused squarely on the causes and resolutions of labor problems. It was also in the labor problems texts where the most frequent mention of the term *industrial relations* was found. Because these courses were nearly always taught by economists, particularly institutional economists, it is not surprising that scholars concluded that institutional economics was the major intellectual wellspring of industrial relations. Such an inference, however, founders on the fact that nearly every labor problems text featured *both* the PM and the ILE perspectives on labor problems (the employers', workers', and community's solutions to labor problems) and provided extensive coverage of personnel management and employee representation plans. These subjects, it will be recalled, were the mainstays of the PM approach to improved industrial relations; were based heavily on knowledge derived from the fields of engineering, administrative science, and psychology; and had been written about principally by persons with a management background. Thus, on the one hand, the labor problems texts undeniably had a heavy institutional flavor, as one would expect given the disciplinary background of the authors, but, on the other, these texts also made a concerted attempt to present both the ILE *and* the PM perspective.

Yet another source of the confusion pertains to the undeveloped nature of institutional economics. As envisioned by Commons, institutional economics was to be a new approach to the study of the fundamental questions of economics—the allocation of resources and determination of output, prices, and the distribution of income. Toward that end, he attempted to construct a theoretical model based on concepts such as a volitional theory of value, transactions, reasonable value, and property rights, with heavy emphasis on the role of law and judicial opinion (Commons 1924, 1934b, 1950). Unfortunately, his foray into theory was largely unsuccessful; neither his fellow economists nor his students could understand what he was driving at, and his conception of economics was so expansive that his writings had more in common with law and sociology than with economics per se. Given the failure of Commons and his students to develop institutional theory, institutional labor economists fell back on a largely historical, descriptive, multidisciplinary analysis of labor problems and institutional solutions to those problems.[11] This approach was largely coterminous with the subject of industrial relations, however, a fact that made the two subjects seem as if they were one and the same. In practice, they *were* largely one and the same, but only because the institutionalists failed to develop theory.

Another probable reason for the confusion is that contemporary chroniclers of industrial relations tend to ignore the extensive literature of the 1920s–30s authored by nonacademics, most of whom were busi-

nessmen or consultants who approached the subject of industrial relations from a management and behavioral science perspective.[12] Several
authors of the PM school were affiliated with universities, including
Mayo (1929, 1933), Stone (1932), and Balderston (1935), but most
PM writers in the 1920s–30s were businessmen or consultants. Meyer
Bloomfield and Daniel Bloomfield, for example, together or individually
authored numerous articles and edited several books in the 1920s on
employment management, personnel management, and industrial relations (D. Bloomfield 1919, 1920, 1931; M. Bloomfield 1923). Another
example, from the 1930s, is Thomas Spates, who was vice-president for
industrial relations at the General Foods Corporation, a staff member
of Industrial Relations Counselors, and, later in his career, a professor
of personnel administration at Yale University. Spates wrote several
articles on industrial relations (Spates 1937, 1938, 1944), most for the
Personnel Series of the American Management Association.

   Two business-sponsored research organizations also did pioneering
research on industrial relations that was noneconomic and nonacademic
in nature. The most noteworthy was Industrial Relations Counselors
(IRC). Founded in 1926 with financial assistance from John D. Rockefeller, Jr., the IRC was a nonprofit research and consulting service to
industry, the purpose of which was to promote improved relations between employers and employees (Teplow 1976). In addition to Clarence
Hicks, who served as chairman of the board of trustees of the IRC for
several years, other members of the firm included Arthur Young, at one
time a vice-president of the United States Steel Company, a vice-
president of the Industrial Relations Association of America, and a
member of the faculty of the Industrial Relations Section at the California Institute of Technology, and Bryce Stewart, who Commons
(1934a:200) labeled "the leading authority in the country on unemployment insurance." Under the auspices of the IRC, fifteen research
studies on industrial relations topics were published between 1930 and
1939. These studies were widely regarded as of equal or better quality
than anything done in academia at that time.[13] The IRC was also
involved in industrial relations research sponsored by the International
Labor Organization in Geneva, Switzerland.

   The business-sponsored National Industrial Conference Board (today
called the Conference Board) also published various IR-related studies.

Two studies, for example, were on industrial relations practices in small manufacturing plants (NICB 1929) and experiences with employee representation plans (NICB 1933).[14]

Finally, it is probable that the heavy emphasis put on the role of institutional economics stems in part from the intellectual and ideological background of the persons who have been the primary chroniclers of the field's history. As discussed in detail in later chapters, for the last thirty years most of the academic writers in industrial relations have been associated to one degree or another with the ILE school. It is not surprising, therefore, that historical accounts of the field give considerable weight to the contributions of the institutional economists and their point of view, particularly given the preeminent role played by Commons in the early days of the field, that economists were the first group among *academics* to write extensively about industrial relations topics, and the lack of participation by members of the PM school in industrial relations in recent years.

4

THE INSTITUTIONALIZATION OF
INDUSTRIAL RELATIONS

I NDUSTRIAL RELATIONS was born out of the crises in the workplace
engendered by World War I, but its growth and development was
sufficiently slow that twenty years later there was still no formal
degree program devoted explicitly to the study of industrial relations in
an American university. From 1940 to 1950, however, the field under-
went a fundamental transformation from which it emerged as a highly
visible, rapidly growing area of research and teaching. Three events
symbolized this transformation: the founding of IR schools and institutes
at major universities; the founding of a new professional association,
the Industrial Relations Research Association; and the founding of the
first academic journal in America devoted to industrial relations, the
Industrial and Labor Relations Review. This chapter first reviews the economic and political events that precipitated this transformation and
then examines in more detail these three key developments in the field.

PIVOTAL ECONOMIC AND POLITICAL EVENTS
Research and teaching in industrial relations, as in every field of study,
are significantly influenced by events and developments in the economic,
social, and political spheres. This is particularly so for industrial relations, given its applied, problem-solving orientation. The sudden popularization of industrial relations after World War II cannot be
understood without giving some consideration to these developments.

The 1920s were a highly favorable period for the PM school of industrial relations in that it saw the birth and spread of welfare capitalism
as a number of medium- and large-sized companies instituted various

progressive personnel practices, including paid vacations, pensions, supervisor training, improved working conditions, and employee representation plans (Stewart 1951; Bernstein 1960). Although these measures smacked of paternalism and unilateralism, workers seemed willing to accept management's control of the workplace as long as the companies delivered on their promise of providing job security and a steady increase in pay. The success of welfare capitalism in the 1920s, coupled with the economic prosperity and politically conservative, pro-business climate of the period, dramatically undercut the appeal of labor unions, as witnessed by a drop in union membership of more than 1 million during the decade.

The challenge for nonunion employers, as Commons noted, comes in periods of recession and depression, for it is then that competitive pressures lead managers to search out ways to cut costs and increase productivity. Frequently these goals are accomplished at labor's expense, through layoffs, wage cuts, longer hours, or a speed-up of the work. Workers in this situation suddenly discover that the presumed mutuality of interests has been replaced by a conflict of interests, bringing with it a struggle over the terms and conditions of employment. Given workers' unequal power position with respect to both authority and pay, it is not surprising that union representation also becomes more attractive.

This scenario was vividly played out in the Great Depression (Bernstein 1970). With the onset of the depression in late 1929, America's corporate leaders pledged to hold the line on labor standards and avoid the liquidation of labor and personnel programs that had occurred in the previous business downturn of 1921–22. This pledge was largely honored until the fall of 1931, when the economic decline intensified and first marginally profitable firms and then their stronger competitors were forced to implement wage cuts, layoffs, and speed-ups. Once the dam was breached, a downward spiral in labor standards ensued until the nadir was reached in early 1933. By then, money wages had been reduced by nearly one-third and 25 percent of the work force was unemployed (including more than half of those employed in durable manufacturing). The net outcome of this debacle was a serious demoralization of both employers and workers, a growing mood of discontent and bitterness among workers over the perceived injustices associated with the downward spiral of wages and working conditions, and the discrediting of the PM school and its ethos of individualism, competition, and enlightened paternalism (Brody 1980).

The strategy adopted by the Roosevelt administration to revive the economy was largely institutional in inspiration (not Keynesian as often alleged).[1] The plan was to short-circuit the decline of wages and prices caused by destructive competition, either by restricting competition (cartelizing markets) or establishing negotiated or legislated minimum wage and price floors, and then to restore purchasing power and demand by redistributing income from the rich, whose propensity to spend is low, to the working class, whose propensity to spend is high.

With respect to the labor market, three methods were used to accomplish these objectives: to substitute collective bargaining for individual bargaining, to use legislation to establish minimum labor standards (e.g., minimum wages, maximum work hours), and to establish social insurance programs (e.g., unemployment compensation, Social Security) that provided income security and purchasing power to wage earners and, in the case of unemployment compensation, incentives to employers to minimize layoffs.

It is still a matter of debate among economists whether these policies helped bring the country out of the depression. There is no debate, however, that they fundamentally transformed the nature of the employment relationship across a wide swath of American industry. Most important in this regard was the passage of several pieces of labor legislation, including the National Industrial Recovery Act, the National Labor Relations Act, the Fair Labor Standards Act, and the Social Security Act. Of these, the most important for industrial relations was the National Labor Relations Act (Wagner Act), enacted into law in 1935. The act declared that the goal of public policy was to encourage the practice of collective bargaining, both to eliminate labor's inequality of bargaining power and to introduce democratic rights of independent representation and due process into industry (see Keyserling 1945).[2] The act established the union representation election process, proscribed a series of "unfair labor practices" (e.g., discharge of union activists), and established the National Labor Relations Board to administer the act.

In the early 1930s, union membership was about 10 percent of the work force and was concentrated in a handful of industries, such as construction, railroads, the needle trades, and coal mining. By 1940, however, union membership had tripled, and it now represented almost 30 percent of the nonagricultural work force, with much of the gain in the previously unorganized mass-production industries, such as automobiles, steel, rubber, meatpacking, and electrical equipment. While the passage of the Wagner Act was probably the single largest impetus to union growth, the formation of the Congress of Industrial Organization (CIO) and the rivalry between the CIO and the American Federation of Labor (AFL) were also significant.

Accompanying the meteoric growth in union membership was a similar surge in strikes, picket-line violence, and bloodshed as workers aggressively fought to secure union representation and collective bargaining while the broad mass of employers fought back equally hard to keep unions out of their plants. The level and intensity of conflict were such that Sydney Lens (1974) aptly called the strikes of this period "labor wars."

The events outlined above catapulted collective bargaining and labor-management conflict to the forefront of public concern. The entrance of the United States into World War II further heightened this concern. It was essential that employers and unions hold wages and prices in check to prevent inflation from spiraling out of control and that the issue of union recognition and bargaining disputes be speedily resolved lest strikes and labor unrest disrupt war production. To enforce "responsible" behavior on the part of both parties, the federal government created the War Labor Board and gave it authority to administer wage and price controls and to investigate and resolve labor disputes (Rayback 1966). The latter was done through tripartite commissions composed of representatives of labor, management, and the public that held hearings, attempted to mediate a resolution of the dispute, and, failing that, rendered a binding arbitration award.

Although the Board largely succeeded in stabilizing labor-management relations during the course of the war, paradoxically its activities increased the probability of conflict after the war. Many companies thought they had been pressured by the Board to recognize unions, sign collective bargaining contracts, and agree to new or expanded contract provisions that they otherwise would not have done. Once the war was over, these companies were intent on recapturing their losses. Many unions also looked forward to the end of wartime controls, for they too were intent on making up for lost bargaining opportunities, particularly with regard to wages, which had badly lagged behind both prices and corporate profits. The prospect, therefore, was for renewed labor-management conflict at the end of the war on a scale as large or larger than when the war began five years earlier. (This prospect became a reality in 1946 when the economy experienced a strike wave of unprecedented proportions.)

From the perspective of 1945, then, employer-employee relations, and labor violence and unrest in particular, was suddenly the number-one domestic issue confronting the nation. Just as the labor conflict engendered by World War I precipitated the birth of the field, the labor conflict of the Depression and World War II years led to the emergence of industrial relations as a widely recognized, fully institutionalized academic field of study.[3] Industrial relations had come of age.

NEW INDUSTRIAL RELATIONS PROGRAMS

Given the relative paucity of research centers and degree programs in industrial relations in the pre–1945 period and the magnitude of the labor problems facing the country, it is not surprising that legislatures and state university systems quickly acted to fill the gap by creating new units expressly dedicated to research and teaching in industrial relations. Among the most important of these programs were those at Cornell University (1945), the University of Chicago (1945), the University of Minnesota (1945), the University of California (1945), Yale University (1945), the University of Illinois (1946), Rutgers University (1947), the University of Wisconsin (1948), New York University (1948), and the University of Hawaii (1948).[4] A number of Catholic colleges and universities were also in the forefront of establishing IR programs, although these were generally smaller and emphasized teaching over research. Examples include Rockhurst College (Kansas City), Loyola University (Chicago), Manhattan College (New York City), Seton Hall (New Jersey), and St. Joseph's (Philadelphia) (see Graham 1948; Justin 1949).[5]

The organizational structure and functions of these programs varied greatly. The most comprehensive and prestigious program was the New York State School of Industrial and Labor Relations at Cornell University. The school was an autonomous unit of the university, had forty faculty (as of 1949), offered a full range of resident instruction programs (i.e., a four-year undergraduate degree, a two-year master's degree, and a doctoral degree) and numerous extension courses off campus for both union and management groups, and conducted extensive research on all aspects of industrial relations. Graduate students could choose a major or minor field of concentration in collective bargaining, mediation, and arbitration; human relations in industry; industrial and labor legislation and social security; labor market economics and analysis; labor history, organization, and management; personnel management; or industrial education.

Most other universities followed the Cornell model in that they housed their industrial relations programs in a free-standing administrative unit, as opposed to a subunit of an existing department (e.g., economics) such as had been done at Princeton and MIT. The most common designations given to these units were school, institute, and center.

Some of the units were in business schools, but this was not the preferred approach. Rather, the more common arrangement (Rezler 1968a) was to house the program in a nonbusiness division of the university, such as a graduate school or a college of arts and sciences or social sciences; to make the unit an autonomous division of the university; or to divide administrative control of the unit among several departments or schools, emphasizing interdisciplinary control and coordination.

Placing the IR unit outside the business school facilitated the recruitment of a multidisciplinary faculty from all the major divisions of the university, ensured that the unit's intellectual and ideological neutrality on labor-management issues was not compromised, and allayed fears among organized labor that the units would become tools of the business community. An additional consideration at some universities was that the business school was hostile to the concept of a joint labor-management program.[6]

Placing the units outside the business school also created "turf" problems, however, since both the IR units and the business schools claimed jurisdiction over personnel and human relations subjects. Some universities (e.g., Illinois) resolved the conflict by permitting both the IR unit and the business school to hire faculty and teach courses in these areas.[7] This arrangement was satisfactory for the IR units because it allowed them to offer management-related subjects. In addition, the personnel and human relations area in business schools was underdeveloped and represented little effective competition, particularly since relatively few students majored in personnel at the time.[8] Thirty years later, however, the shift in student demand from labor relations to personnel and human resources significantly increased the competition between the IR units and the business schools, often to the detriment of the former. (This subject is discussed further in chapter 7).

Wide variation also existed among the units with regard to their functions and activities (Rezler 1968a). A minority were "full service" in scope, in that they offered their own courses, on-campus degree programs, and off-campus extension classes for management and labor groups and promoted an active faculty research program. The more common practice was for the unit to offer one or more of these activities but not all.[9] Some offered both undergraduate and graduate IR programs, but most offered graduate-level (master's) programs only. Only two universities in the 1950s offered a Ph.D. degree in industrial relations, Cornell and Wisconsin.[10] Finally, some IR units had their own full-time faculty and administrative control over courses, while others shared faculty (generally on a joint-appointment basis) and courses with other departments in the university.[11]

An important part of the mission of many IR units was to provide labor education courses to unions in the local area. Unions generally found this service, offered on an extension basis, more valuable than the academic degree programs offered through resident instruction (Ruttenberg 1958). Involvement in labor education brought with it both benefits and costs. On the benefit side, it strengthened ties between the academic community and the labor movement, provided an important educational service to a constituency that otherwise would not have had the opportunity to obtain university instruction, and provided a valuable bridge between theory and practice for faculty. On the cost side, the involvement of the IR units in labor education caused many business leaders to regard them as pro-labor, created internal cleavages between faculty who specialized in resident instruction and research and those who specialized in extension education (the latter were viewed as less prestigious and were generally compensated accordingly), and caused numerous administrative headaches with regard to promotion and tenure (see Derber 1987). Some IR units decided that the benefits were worth the costs and maintained their labor education activities, while others phased out their extension work or transferred extension activities to a separate administrative unit (e.g., a labor studies department).

A significant degree of standardization existed among IR units with respect to their curricula. Martin Estey (1960), who conducted a survey of IR curricula, found, for example, that four courses comprised the "core" of most IR programs: personnel management, labor economics, labor law, and collective bargaining. Among the other courses that were frequently taught were human relations in industry, trade unionism and union government, industrial sociology, industrial psychology, social security, and comparative labor movements (also see Schnelle and Fox 1951). These courses corresponded closely to the major areas of concentration in Cornell's program. Other IR programs could not match the breadth and depth of the courses offered by Cornell, but they nevertheless offered concentrations in a number of the same areas. The Illinois program, for example, had four areas of concentration: labor economics (including collective bargaining, labor legislation, mediation and arbitration, and social security), human relations in industry, labor union organization and administration, and personnel management.

Finally, the names attached to the units varied in some interesting ways. Most included the term *industrial relations*, either alone or in combination with some other term. Examples of the former include the Institute of Industrial Relations at Berkeley and the Industrial Relations Center at Minnesota; examples of the latter include the School of Industrial and Labor Relations at Cornell and its near equivalent, the Institute of Labor and Industrial Relations at Illinois; and the Industrial Relations Research Institute at Wisconsin. Several programs did not use *industrial relations* in their titles: the Labor and Management Center (Yale), the Institute of Management and Labor Relations (Rutgers), and the Institute of Labor Relations and Social Security (New York).

Several aspects of these new IR programs are important. First, the goal of the new units was to promote both problem-solving and science-building, but problem-solving was the first priority. The legislation that established the School of Industrial and Labor Relations at Cornell, for example, stated that the unit's mission was "to improve industrial and labor conditions in the State through the conduct of research and dissemination of information in all aspects of industrial, labor, and public relations, affecting employers and employees" (quoted in Adams 1967:733).

Second, in keeping with the original conception of the field, the new units were also explicitly organized on a multidisciplinary basis. Thus, all the units brought together faculty and course subjects from the several disciplines that touched on the employment relationship and, more specifically, on the pressing labor problems of the times. The intellectual rationale (strongly believed at that time by most in the field) was that the study and resolution of labor problems would be materially advanced by an interdisciplinary melding and integration of ideas and research methods, an intellectual cross-fertilization that would take place only if faculty from the various disciplines were brought together in one administrative unit so they could interact on a personal and daily basis.[12]

Third, the new units contained faculty and courses that represented both the ILE and the PM schools of industrial relations. The ILE school in the late 1940s–early 1950s had broadened beyond its base of institutional labor economics to include academics from labor law, labor history, and political science. The PM school had likewise expanded from its base of personnel management and industrial psychology to include faculty from human relations, industrial sociology, management, and anthropology. Thus, the ILE wing of the field was represented in the Cornell program by courses and faculty in such subject areas as collective bargaining, mediation and arbitration, industrial and labor legislation and social security, and labor market outcomes and analysis, while the PM perspective was provided in human relations in industry, personnel management, and industrial education.

Every large IR program (including the institutes devoted solely to research) contained a disciplinary mix of faculty, although the relative weight given to particular disciplines and the overall ILE versus PM orientation of the programs differed. In general, the units had a strong ILE flavor (about 7 to 8 on a scale of 1 to 10, with 10 being complete ILE). The Cornell program was close to the average.[13] The Minnesota program, in contrast, was more PM-oriented, a reflection of the strong interest in personnel administration among three of the unit's well-known faculty, Dale Yoder, Herbert Heneman, Jr., and Donald Patterson. Yale's Labor-Management Center (a subunit of the Institute of Human Relations) also had a relatively strong PM perspective, whereas the programs at Illinois, Wisconsin, and Michigan State were above average in their ILE focus.[14]

The ILE orientation of most of the new IR programs was attributable to several factors. One was the impact of current events. Given the meteoric rise of unionism, collective bargaining, and strikes in the decade after 1935, it was not at all surprising that most of the new programs had an ILE orientation. After all, labor-management relations was the number-one domestic problem facing the country. Another was that economists had historically been the group most actively involved in research and teaching in the area of labor-management relations, so it was to be expected that they would be disproportionately represented in the new IR programs and bring an ILE perspective to them. Also contributing to the ILE orientation was public sentiment, which was relatively favorable toward unions and collective bargaining. This fact was mirrored in the values and beliefs of most IR academics of the period regardless of discipline. Finally, in contrast to the ILE side, the subject areas on the PM side of industrial relations either lacked academic respectability or were relatively new and underdeveloped. Personnel management, for example, had an atheoretic, cookbookish, practitioner flavor, whereas industrial sociology, human relations, and administrative science and organization theory were still in their infancy.[15] In addition to its intellectual shortcomings, personnel management suffered a significant image problem because of the public's perceptions that it was often used by companies as a manipulative, stop-gap device to keep out unions (Yoder 1952).

The fourth notable aspect of the new IR units was that they were controversial, particularly with regard to their perceived pro-labor tilt. Research and teaching resources had for years been devoted to the study of business. From the point of view of the backers of the new units, it was only fair that the same should be done for blue-collar workers and labor unions. Thus, many IR units established boards of advisers that included representatives of both management and labor, brought both union and company officials to campus for lectures and seminars, and sponsored off-campus extension classes for management and union members on subjects such as supervisor training and handling grievances.

This attempt at evenhandedness was only partially successful. Many employers' groups strongly resisted the establishment of the new IR units. One significant reason was the basic incompatibility of viewpoints. The

IR units took the existence of unions and the necessity (if not the virtue) of collective bargaining as "givens" and thus saw their mission as promoting dialogue and accommodation between labor and management. Many employers remained steadfastly anti-union, however, and thus saw the attempt at dialogue as a thinly disguised attempt to promote collective bargaining.

Other considerations also came into play. The creation of the IR units increased substantially the amount of teaching, research, and university resources devoted to the organized labor movement, a movement many employers saw as threatening their economic position and power. Many employers also believed that the faculty of the IR units were ideologically pro-union and thus were inculcating students with biased, antibusiness viewpoints. They also charged that the units were agents of socialism and communism, given their alleged bias in favor of collectivist solutions to labor problems. As a result of all of these pressures, many unit directors had to beat back attempts by employers and their allies in the university system to eliminate the programs.[16] The IR units also found that many employers were very reluctant to participate in classes or conferences or to be on advisory boards if representatives of organized labor were also participating.

While the primary threat to the new IR units came from the employer side, they did not escape attack and criticism from labor. Many officials of organized labor were suspicious of the programs since universities in the past had been largely antagonistic to the aims and methods of the labor movement. Labor leaders were also skeptical about becoming involved with intellectuals, who often promoted goals or methods that were not grounded in the pragmatic experience of trade unionism (Ware 1946). For these reasons, some center directors had to fend off attempts by trade union leaders to purge the programs of management courses and management representatives, which, if successful, would have turned the units into labor education programs. The universities resisted these lobbying efforts, as well as those of management, thus preserving at least a modicum of balance in both IR research and teaching.

FOUNDING OF THE IRRA

Until the founding of the Industrial Relations Research Association (IRRA) in late 1947, the only other professional association to bear the name *industrial relations* had been the short-lived Industrial Relations

Association of America. With its demise in 1922, no professional group in America existed for the next twenty-five years for either academics or practitioners that made industrial relations the focal point of its programs and activities.

The IRRA had its genesis in January 1947.[17] At the annual meeting of the American Economic Association (AEA), Richard Lester of Princeton University, with the assistance of William McPherson of the University of Illinois, organized an informal meeting of about thirty labor economists to discuss the need for and feasibility of creating a learned society in the field of industrial relations. A twenty-person organizing committee was created, and in late 1947 a constitution and set of bylaws were adopted and a slate of officers was elected. The first president-elect was Edwin Witte, an institutional labor economist from the University of Wisconsin and a former student and colleague of John R. Commons.

By late 1948, the IRRA had almost one thousand members, drawn from academe, industry, and government. At its first annual meeting, held in late December 1948, in conjunction with the meetings of the AEA, five paper sessions were included on the program: "Collective Bargaining, Wages, and the Price Level"; "Disputes That Create a Public Emergency"; "Developments in Social Security"; "Collective Bargaining and Management Rights"; and "The Role of Various Disciplines in Industrial Relations Research." The IRRA continued to grow rapidly, reaching a membership of sixteen hundred four years later.

Like the academic IR programs, the IRRA endeavored to be inclusive in both disciplinary representation and ideological beliefs. Its track record in this regard has been mixed, however, and it has certainly fallen short of the record in IR teaching. As a matter of policy, the IRRA has been committed to preserving and promoting the multidisciplinary character of industrial relations and, in particular, to bringing members of both the PM and the ILE schools into its ranks. The constitution of the IRRA states that one of the purposes of the association is "the encouragement of research in all aspects of the field of labor—social, political, economic, legal, and psychological—including employer and employee organizations, labor relations, personnel administration, social security, and labor legislation." The organization also adopted a position of neutrality regarding issues of ideology and public policy, particularly with regard to trade unionism. Thus, the constitution says that "the

Association will take no partisan attitude on questions of policy of labor, nor will it commit its members to any position on such question."

As shall be discussed in more detail in later chapters, the IRRA has never fully lived up to its good intentions. An examination of the organization's founding and early activities, for example, clearly reveals that it was largely composed of, and controlled by, ILE-oriented labor economists. Lester and McPherson were members of this group, as were three-quarters of the members of the organizing committee. The ILE orientation is also evident in the people who have served as the organization's president. Edwin Witte, the first president, was the closest surviving heir to the institutional tradition of Commons and the Wisconsin school. The next twelve presidents were Sumner Slichter (1949), George Taylor (1950), William Leiserson (1951), J. Douglas Brown (1952), Ewan Clague (1953), Clark Kerr (1954), Lloyd Reynolds (1955), Richard Lester (1956), Dale Yoder (1957), E. Wight Bakke (1958), William Haber (1959), and John Dunlop (1960). All of these men had disciplinary backgrounds in economics (broadly defined), most were of the ILE school (Yoder and Bakke were the closest to the PM school; no one was a neoclassical economist), and all were ideologically supportive of the New Deal system of collective bargaining (or at least none went on record as opposing it).

Finally, the ILE orientation of the IRRA is indicated in the program topics selected for the annual meetings. Of the eight to ten sessions at the winter meetings during the 1950s, about two-thirds were devoted to unionism and collective bargaining and labor legislation topics (the two principal solutions to labor problems of the ILE school) and one-fourth to topics of a more pure economics nature (e.g., wages and prices, labor mobility). In some years the program included one session that was devoted to a personnel or human relations topic, while in other years no PM topics were included on the program.

FOUNDING OF THE *ILR REVIEW*

Another significant event of the postwar period was the establishment of the *Industrial and Labor Relations Review*, the first scholarly journal in America devoted specifically to IR. Sponsored by the School of Industrial and Labor Relations at Cornell University, the journal appeared for the first time in October 1947. Its editor was Milton Konvitz, a well-known authority on labor law.

The *Review* had a significant influence on the field in that its editorial policy (choice of paper topics, authors, and books to be reviewed) helped define both the intellectual boundaries and center of gravity of industrial relations. Like the IRRA, the *Review* clearly recognized that industrial relations was multidisciplinary and addressed subject areas in both the PM school (personnel management, human relations) and the ILE school (labor-management relations, protective labor legislation). This fact was most clearly illustrated by the broad and relatively well-balanced selection of books chosen for inclusion in the book review section.

The same balance was not achieved in the articles, however. Like the papers in the proceedings of the IRRA, the great majority of the papers published in the *Review* were written by economists and dealt with trade unions, the process and outcome of collective bargaining, labor legislation, and labor market issues. Of the twenty-six articles published in the first four issues of the journal, for example, twenty dealt directly with unions, collective bargaining, and labor legislation, while only two pertained to personnel management or human relations topics in nonunion workplaces.

To a significant degree the preponderance of ILE-related research was a reflection of both the nature of the research being done at the time and the choices authors made regarding the journals to which they submitted articles, rather than any explicit editorial policy of the journal itself. Labor unions and collective bargaining were, after all, *the* research topics in the late 1940s, labor economists had historically represented the largest disciplinary contingent in IR, and relatively little academic research of intellectual substance was being done in personnel management at that time. Likewise, most IR scholars in those PM-related fields where significant research was taking place (e.g., human relations, industrial sociology, management, industrial psychology) submitted articles to journals in those fields rather than to the *Review*.

But the ILE tilt of the journal also reflected to some degree the underlying value system of the School of Industrial and Labor Relations and the editorial board of the journal. In the foreword to the first issue of the *Review*, for example, Edmund Day (president of Cornell University) wrote, "The establishment of the *Industrial and Labor Relations Review* is a logical extension of the function which higher education is assuming in the area of labor-management relations." The use of the term *labor-management relations* was important in that it immediately narrowed the domain of research to one subset of industrial relations—unionized employment situations. Likewise, it is instructive that Edwin Witte was chosen to be the author of the lead article for the first issue. (The title of his article was "The University and Labor Education.") Finally, if the editorial board of the *Review* could find numerous books on PM subjects to include in the book review section of each issue, one must wonder why there were not at least a few PM-related articles.

5

THE GOLDEN AGE OF
INDUSTRIAL RELATIONS

T HE "GOLDEN AGE" of the field of industrial relations spanned a ten-year period from 1948 to 1958.[1] This period was the high point for the field both because of the public attention given to the subject of employer-employee relations and because of the quality and volume of academic research on this topic. These favorable conditions were reflected in a strong growth in student enrollments, a continued increase in the number of IR programs, and, most important, an unprecedented involvement in IR research by top-flight scholars from a wide variety of academic disciplines.[2]

The flowering of multidisciplinary industrial relations research in American universities was the result of both intellectual developments in the disciplines associated with industrial relations and the unsettled, sometimes tumultuous state of labor-management relations in the nation. The most important impetus for the widespread involvement in industrial relations research by scholars from disciplines as disparate as anthropology, law, sociology, economics, and psychology was the sudden spread of unionism across the mass-production industries of the country and the surge in strikes and labor violence that accompanied it. When trade unions represented only a small proportion of the workers in a handful of industries, the topic of unions and collective bargaining was of sufficiently small social and economic significance that few scholars other than labor economists gave it much attention.

The situation changed dramatically after World War II, however, as unions organized more than half the work force in manufacturing, industry after industry experienced long and bitter strikes, and the public debate over the Taft-Hartley amendments to the Wagner Act heated up to the boiling point. Suddenly, topics such as union growth, union governance, the collective bargaining process, strikes, the impact of collective bargaining on the management and performance of firms, and the macroeconomic impact of collective bargaining on wages, prices, and productivity were in the forefront of academic and public attention. In response, a large number of scholars from not only economics but a wide range of other disciplines were drawn into the study of industrial relations.

The push of current events toward greater involvement in industrial relations research was abetted by the pull of intellectual developments in both the behavioral sciences and the field of management. The major development that precipitated the participation of behavioral science researchers was the emergence of the human relations movement, spawned by the experiments at the Hawthorne plant of the Western Electric Company in the late 1920s–early 1930s. (Recall that this movement was distinct from the one that originated in the early 1920s among personnel practitioners.) In the short run (pre–1960), the impact was positive in that the human relations movement contributed to a substantially increased involvement in IR research by behavioral scientists, thus strengthening not only interdisciplinary research but also the attachment of those researchers to the field. Over the longer run, however, the movement also contributed to the breakup of the PM and ILE schools, an event that was to have very negative consequences for the field.

To appreciate this sequence of events, one must understand the origins and development of the human relations movement and the evolution of thought in labor economics during the same period (1930–50).

The Human Relations Movement

The human relations movement emerged as a distinct area of academic study and investigation in the late 1930s, reached a peak of influence during a ten-year period stretching from roughly the mid-1940s to the mid-1950s, and then went into decline, eventually to be absorbed by the new field of organizational behavior in the early 1960s. The widespread consensus is that the human relations movement (and the related field of industrial sociology) was born as a result of the series of industrial experiments conducted at the Hawthorne, Illinois, plant of the Western Electric Company from 1924 through 1932 (Miller and Form 1964; Whyte 1965, 1987).

The Hawthorne experiments started as a straightforward exercise in scientific management (Greenwood and Wrege 1986; Wren 1987). The issue investigated was the impact of different levels of illumination on worker productivity. The results, however, were quite surprising: the rate of output of the workers in both the control group and the test group increased regardless of the level of lighting.

In 1927, the illumination tests at Hawthorne were replaced by a set of experiments involving five relay assemblers. Initially, to establish a baseline for comparison, the work performance of the assemblers was monitored for two weeks in their regular department. They were then isolated in a separate room with their own supervisors and observers. Various changes in the work environment were introduced, such as differences in the incentive pay system, the number of lunch breaks, and the work hours. After a year of experimentation, all the work conditions were returned to their original level. The results that emerged baffled the company officials: the assemblers' productivity had increased steadily over the year, and at the end of the experiments it was considerably higher than at the beginning.

The assistant plant manager, George Pennock, presented these anomalous results to several faculty members at MIT and Harvard for their analysis. Three of these people were Elton Mayo, T. North Whitehead, and Fritz Roethlisberger, all of whom were in the industrial research department at Harvard. (Two other faculty members of this department also published significant work in human relations, George Homans and Benjamin Selekman.) The professors found the results intriguing and decided to conduct further investigations. One line of activity they pursued was a large-scale interviewing program in which employees were encouraged to tell a counselor what was on their minds. A second line of investigation was the observance of the interpersonal and social dynamics of workers in a small-group setting. In this experiment, a small group of bank wiring workers was isolated in a separate room and their behaviors and interrelationships recorded. Unlike in the relay assembly experiment, the supervisors and observers did not interact and become friendly with the workers. Although the output of the relay assemblers had increased significantly over the course of the experiment, the same did not occur with the bank wiring workers. In fact, these workers deliberately restricted output through informal group norms and sanctions.

The first extensive description and interpretation of the experiments at Hawthorne was by Mayo in *The Human Problems of an Industrial Civilization*, published in 1933. Six years later, Roethlisberger and William Dickson (chief of the employee relations research department at the Hawthorne plant) published what is still considered a monumental work on the Hawthorne experiments, their six hundred–page book *Management and the Worker* (1939). Both sets of writers identified several general lessons to be learned from the experiments.

As they saw it, "a remarkable change of mental attitude" was the key factor in explaining the increase in productivity of the relay assemblers (Mayo 1933:71). The variations in the external work conditions, such as the lighting, incentive rates, and rests, were, they believed, minor influences on the work performance of the employees. Far more significant was the positive impact the experiments had on the psychological state of the workers and the social environment of the shop.[3] An important finding, for example, was that the relay assemblers experienced a significant increase in morale and interest in their job, attributable in part to the friendlier, more relaxed style of supervision and the greater opportunity to provide suggestions and feedback on the organization and performance of their work.

The researchers reached another important set of conclusions from the interview program; namely, that an employee's work performance is significantly affected by his or her general emotional state and specific attitudes or "sentiments" regarding work, the work environment of the plant, and his or her coworkers and superiors. They found that these sentiments are critically influenced by psychological and social relations affecting the employee both inside and outside the plant and that these relations (such as desiring to gain the social approval of workmates) often lead to "nonlogical" forms of behavior (i.e., behavior that does not maximize the economic gain of the individual), such as deliberate restriction of output.

Finally, from the bank wiring room experiments, Mayo and his collaborators discovered that even the smallest workshop has a complex, informal social system with a well-defined set of status hierarchies, rituals, customs, norms of behavior, and sanctions. This social system, they found, exerts a powerful influence on the performance of work and the tenor of workplace relations.

Roethlisberger and Dickson provided massive documentation of the data collected from the Hawthorne experiments and drew a number of implications from them. It was Mayo, however, who fashioned from these implications an overarching theory or "world view" of man, the nature of industrial society, and the successful integration of man into society (Mayo 1945; Roethlisberger 1977). Further, it was Mayo's theory, and the policy implications and social and political philosophy that accompanied it, that proved to be the most controversial.

Mayo's point of view regarding industrial relations was grounded in several fundamental tenets. He believed, for example, that people have a strong emotional need to integrate themselves into a larger social group to give purpose and structure to their lives. When such a social order is absent, individuals develop emotional ills such as anomie (feelings of disorientation and isolation), depression, and frustration.[4] As he saw it, much of the waste and conflict in industry was attributable to these psychological maladjustments, brought on by the disorganization of traditional society because of rapid industrialization and the emergence of a new social system based on competition and individualism (the antithesis of a stable social structure). Accordingly, the route to greater productivity and harmony in industry was to create a social structure and set of human relations in the plant that fostered teamwork or, in his words, "spontaneous collaboration" (such as he thought existed among the relay assemblers) by providing workers with a sense of community and shared purpose and thereby eliminating the feelings of anomie, frustration, and so on.[5] The responsibility for unleashing the spontaneous collaboration of workers rested, in Mayo's view, with management, for only the managerial elite in a capitalist society had the power and authority to reshape the social environment of the workplace. To do so, managers needed to abandon their preoccupation with technical skills and instead cultivate social skills, such as interpersonal communication, effective leadership, and an understanding of worker motivation and attitudes.

The work of the Harvard group provided a great stimulus to behavioral science research in employer-employee relations for three reasons. First, it seemed to provide considerable support for the view that psychological factors are important determinants of employee productivity and worker-management relations. Although the earlier generation of human relations writers (the practitioners of the 1920s) had given great weight to the "human factor," it was only after the Hawthorne experiments that detailed scientific evidence was advanced to support this proposition. Second, the Harvard group called attention to the important impact of informal social organization and social interaction on productivity and the tenor of workplace relations. The significance of the social dimension of employer-employee relations was largely neglected in the writings of the earlier generation of human relationists and thus its discovery in the Hawthorne experiments represented a true advance in knowledge.[6] Third, and finally, the Harvard group demonstrated the relevance of anthropological and sociological research methods to the problems of industry.

The publication of *Management and the Worker* in 1939, as well as Mayo's book, precipitated great interest among both practitioners and academics in the Hawthorne experiments and the new subject of human relations. Interest was further fueled by the largely independent work of Kurt Lewin on "group dynamics" (Roethlisberger 1977; Wren 1987). Lewin, a psychologist who had been trained in Germany, came to the United States in the 1930s and took a professorship at MIT. His research focused on the behavior of individuals in small groups, a phenomenon that he concluded was heavily influenced by social pressures and symbolic interactions. His theory of group dynamics, and its applications to topics such as organizational change and climate, was highly complementary to the research findings of Mayo and the Harvard group and contributed additional synergy to the development of human relations.

Because of these and other developments, human relations research in American universities became a hot topic in the 1940s. Indicative of this interest, several interdisciplinary university programs were created to conduct human relations–style research. The first such unit was the Committee on Human Relations in Industry at the University of Chicago, created in 1943. The program was directed by W. Lloyd Warner, an anthropologist.[7] Other members included Burleigh Gardener and William Foote Whyte, both sociologists. Whyte later (1948) moved to the School of Industrial and Labor Relations at Cornell and became the leading voice in industrial relations of the human relations school.

Another important institutional development was the creation in

1944 of the Labor and Management Center at Yale University. The center was a unit of the Institute of Human Relations and was under the directorship of E. Wight Bakke, a sociologist turned economist. This eclectic background helped Bakke establish an interdisciplinary research record that was an exemplar in industrial relations. One of Bakke's major collaborators at the center in the 1950s was Chris Argyris, author of the influential book *Personality and Organization* (1957) and a major contributor to the development of the field of organizational behavior.

Yet another important behavioral science research center was the Research Center for Group Dynamics at MIT, established by Kurt Lewin in 1945. After Lewin's death in 1947, the center was moved to the University of Michigan, where it continued to sponsor important research in group training (T-groups) and organizational change.

Michigan was also home to the Institute for Social Science Research, established in 1946 by Rensis Likert, a psychologist. The institute pioneered in the collection and analysis of attitudinal data, while Likert became one of the foremost advocates of participative management. His pathbreaking book on the subject was *The Human Organization* (1967).

The human relations movement was at the apogee of its influence and prestige for roughly a ten-year period beginning in the late 1940s and extending to the late 1950s. Research in human relations proceeded along several fronts as a result of both the emergence of various theoretical subschools within human relations and the diverse disciplinary backgrounds of the people involved.[8] The psychologists, for example, were heavily involved in studies of the determinants of employee morale and motivation (Maslow 1954; Herzberg, Mausner, and Snyderman 1959; McGregor 1960) and leadership styles and effectiveness (Lewin, Lippitt, and White 1939; Tannenbaum and Schmidt 1958; Likert 1961); the management theorists examined the conflicts between employees' psychological needs and work in large organizations (Argyris 1957); the sociologists examined bureaucracy in business firms (Gouldner 1954), social hierarchies, and relations in offices and factories (Gardner 1946; Whyte 1948), and workers' adaptation to assembly-line production methods (Chinoy 1952); while the anthropologists investigated patterns of human interaction (Chapple 1949, 1952) and the development of social systems in factories (Warner and Low 1947).

The initial wave of human relations research largely bypassed the subjects of trade unionism and collective bargaining, in part because the Hawthorne experiments had taken place in a nonunion plant. This omission generated considerable criticism (e.g., Hart 1948; Bendix and Fisher 1949), which in turn precipitated psychological and sociological studies on various aspects of labor-management relations, including industrial conflict (Homans and Scott 1947; Whyte 1951b; Kornhauser 1954; Dubin 1960), the dynamics of labor-management relations at the plant and company level (Bakke 1946; Harbison and Dubin 1947), the leadership and internal dynamics of union locals (Sayles and Strauss 1953), and the role of psychological factors in the bargaining process (Stagner 1948; Haire 1955).

In the academic world, human relations represented a new and distinct area of study vis-à-vis personnel management. The former was more theoretical and research-oriented and focused on the underlying determinants of individual and group behavior in the workplace, while the latter had a heavy vocational orientation and emphasized specific techniques and practices useful to various personnel tasks such as employee selection, compensation, and performance appraisal. Human relations, therefore, was more intellectually substantive than personnel management and, consequently, was held in higher professional esteem.[9]

At the time, human relations was widely seen as a subfield of industrial relations and part of the PM school. Elton Mayo, in turn, was widely regarded as the intellectual father of human relations and thus one of the preeminent figures in industrial relations. Because these links between Mayo, human relations, and industrial relations are often slighted in present-day discussions of IR theory and research, it is worth documenting them more thoroughly.

There are several compelling pieces of evidence that Mayo's contemporaries considered him a participating member of the field of industrial relations. For example, in 1928, Harvard University invited Mayo to present a lecture as part of its recently created Wertheim Lectures on Industrial Relations. His paper (Mayo 1929) was published with five others, including one by John R. Commons. Mayo's connection to industrial relations was reaffirmed two years later when the Harvard Business School published his article "A New Approach to Industrial Relations" (Mayo 1930), which described the Hawthorne experiments then under way.[10] Two other testimonials to Mayo's influence on industrial relations are a statement in *Fortune* (1946:181)—"One of the most challenging views in the turbulent field of industrial relations today is held by Elton Mayo. . . . Indeed, many believe that Mayo holds the key to industrial peace"—and a claim in *Time* (1952:96) that Mayo was "the father of industrial human relations." Finally, the first sentence in a biography of Mayo (Trahair 1984:1) states, "George Elton Mayo pioneered in the field of industrial human relations and for that work deserves a place in business history."

Considerable evidence also indicates that human relations was commonly perceived to be a subfield of industrial relations by people in both the PM and the ILE wings of the field. In a review article on individual and group behavior in organizations, for example, Conrad D. Arensberg (1951), a leading behavioral science researcher, discussed three commonly used names to describe this area of research—human relations, industrial sociology, and industrial psychology—and rejected all three as unduly narrow in perspective. He went on to state (p. 330), "The best common description of the field, then, is the historical one: scientific study of the sources of unrest in labor and management relations, that is, the study of the problems of *industrial relations*" (emphasis added).

Looking at the subject from an ILE perspective, labor economist Lloyd Reynolds (1948:285) stated: "The problems [of human relations in industry] range over the whole field of labor and industrial relations. . . . The phrase "human relations in industry" connotes not a separate subject matter speciality, but a different point of view and method of approach. In a later article, Reynolds (1955:2) amplified on this theme: "The study of industrial relations needs to be conceived in very broad terms. People concerned with curriculum construction are perhaps forced to draw fine lines between 'industrial relations,' 'labor relations,' 'labor economics,' 'human relations,' 'personnel management' and so on. This fragmentation should not veil the fact that we are integrally involved in all the phenomena surrounding the use of human effort in production."

The IRRA's 1957 research volume, *Research in Industrial Human Relations* (Arensberg et al.), provides additional evidence. The editors state in the preface (p. vii) that "human relations in industry has become both the label of a group of studies of people at work and the slogan of a movement of thought and action in American industrial relations."

Finally, one of the branches of IR's intellectual family tree, shown in figure 3-1, is the human relations movement (what Form and Miller labeled the "Harvard Graduate School of Business").[11]

LABOR ECONOMICS: FROM LABOR PROBLEMS
TO LABOR MARKETS

The emergence of the human relations movement strengthened the PM side of IR research considerably. A similar transformation in the field of labor economics had equally far-reaching consequences for the ILE school.

In the 1920s and 1930s, the emphasis in the field of labor economics was far more on the first word of the term than on the second. Thus, the text *Labor Economics*, the first book to use the term in the title, published in 1925 by Solomon Blum (McNulty 1980:127), contained twenty-one chapters, seventeen of which were devoted to labor legislation, labor unions, and collective bargaining. The other four were on the more economics-related subjects of the business cycle, wage theories, unemployment, and the mitigation of unemployment. The presentation was entirely descriptive (no demand-supply diagrams were used), was critical of orthodox (neoclassical) theory, and was generally supportive of collective bargaining and protective labor legislation. [12]

Blum had a broadly institutional perspective on labor economics that was not only critical of orthodox theory and the operation of free markets but also heavily interdisciplinary in its approach. As Blum's book exemplifies, labor economics in this period was largely estranged from its mother discipline and had as much in common with law, history, and sociology as with economics per se. [13] This difference in perspectives, in turn, led to a considerable rift between the institutional labor economists and the neoclassical theorists, who dominated much of the rest of the discipline.

The neoclassical school was the more narrowly construed in that it took the institutional structure of the economy as a "given" and focused instead on the operation of markets, used deductive logic to derive a large body of formalized economic theory to explain the operation of markets (e.g., marginal utility and marginal productivity theory, supply and demand curves), generally assumed markets operated in a competitive and efficient manner, and thus arrived at policy conclusions that favored minimal government or trade union intervention in the economy.

The institutionalists looked with disdain on the work of the theorists because, they claimed, it was based on a set of assumptions that were manifestly at odds with reality and thus led to incorrect explanations or predictions of economic phenomena and pernicious policy conclusions. In contrast, the neoclassical theorists claimed that the institutionalists did not understand economic theory and thus that their criticisms were either misdirected or mistaken and that their economic analysis was not a scientific endeavor per se but a thinly veiled attempt to provide a justification for trade unions and government intervention in the economy.

Partly in reaction to the neoclassical critics, Commons attempted to develop a theoretical base for institutional economics. His major efforts in this regard were two books, *The Legal Foundations of Capitalism* (1924) and *Institutional Economics* (1934b). As noted in chapter 3, neither of these books had much impact on the field, in part because few economists could understand what he was trying to say and in part because his theoretical framework was so expansive that it went far beyond the bounds of economics as most people perceived the subject.[14] Not only was Commons unsuccessful in developing institutional theory, but so were his students and other institutional labor economists of the period.

The field of labor economics in the 1930s was thus largely isolated from its mother discipline.[15] This situation began to change late in the decade with the entrance into the field of a new generation of labor economists (McNulty 1980; Kaufman 1988, 1993; Kerr 1988). Important names among this new generation were John Dunlop, Clark Kerr, Richard Lester, Lloyd Reynolds, Arthur Ross, and Charles Myers.[16] These economists turned labor economics away from a historical, descriptive analysis of labor problems and toward an analytical study of labor markets.[17] They were clearly in the neoclassical tradition in that they sought to refashion labor economics so that it would more nearly resemble other areas of economic analysis. At the same time, they continued to have many links with the institutionalists, particularly in their use of the case study, inductive method of research; their focus on the pervasiveness and importance of imperfections in the labor market; their favorable view of collective bargaining and protective labor legislation as ways both to offset employer market power and to introduce industrial democracy into the workplace; their belief in the social and economic efficacy of pluralism; their skepticism of the microeconomic model of the firm (particularly the profit-maximization assumption); and their desire to broaden economic theory beyond the study of market forces by bringing in nonmarket considerations from other disciplines.[18]

Three major events shaped this blend of perspectives. The first was that these economists had received a heavier dose of economic theory in their doctoral studies than had the earlier generation of institutionalists. Much of this theory was imported from England, which up to that time had produced far more able economic theorists than had the United States. Doctoral students in economics, for example, were required to master Alfred Marshall's *Principles of Economics* (1920), a pioneering text that developed the competitive model of demand and supply in product and factor markets, albeit with numerous qualifications to take into account institutional realities. (Calculus was used in footnotes and appendixes). Another required text for labor students of the 1930s was John R. Hicks's *The Theory of Wages* (1932). This book was an exact antithesis to institutional works such as Blum's *Labor Economics* (1925) in that Hicks applied neoclassical competitive theory thoroughly and unflinchingly to the labor market. Hicks (particularly in chapter 1) largely omitted the qualifications Marshall thought were important on the grounds that they had little impact in the long run on the pattern of wages and employment. Other important English contributions to economic theory in the 1930s were Joan Robinson's *The Economics of Imperfect Competition* (1933), which developed models of imperfect competition, such as monopsony (one buyer of labor) and oligopsony (several buyers of labor), and J. M. Keynes's *The General Theory of Employment, Interest, and Money* (1936), which purported to show that the macroeconomy could become mired in an underemployment equilibrium.

The second event that significantly influenced these labor economists was the Great Depression (Kerr 1988; Reynolds 1988). The Depression seemed to provide overwhelming evidence that the market mechanism did not work as effectively or as automatically as predicted by competitive theory. According to competitive theory, wages and prices are supposed to rise and fall to maintain an equilibrium between demand and supply. The assumption is that if people remain unemployed for long, it is through choice or laziness. For the new generation of labor economists, the persistence of mass unemployment during the 1930s, and the large-scale human suffering that accompanied it, were convincing evidence that the cause of the unemployment problem was defects of the market, not defects of the unemployed.

Another development of the Depression years that influenced their perspective was the surge in union membership and the spread of industrial unionism. As collective bargaining replaced individual bargaining across a wide swath of American industry, it seemed clear that institutional forces were increasingly supplanting market forces as determinants of wages, hours, and conditions of employment.

The third event that fundamentally shaped the research and policy perspective of this new generation of labor economists was their involvement during World War II in the wage stabilization and dispute resolution activities of various government agencies, most particularly the War Labor Board (WLB). Dunlop, Kerr, Lester, Reynolds, and others were plucked from their academic jobs and assigned leading administrative and research positions with various branches of these organizations. Their jobs intimately involved them in the process of wage determination and collective bargaining, for a principal activity of the WLB was controlling wages to prevent wartime inflation and resolving disputes over wage differentials and wage increments that might provoke work stoppages and threaten war production. The immersion of these young academics in the real-world operation of unions, firms, and labor markets profoundly affected their approach to labor economics after they returned to academe at the end of the war (Kerr 1988). They began to question the relevance of orthodox competitive theory (such as contained in Hicks's *The Theory of Wages* [1932]), for labor markets seemed to operate with considerably less efficiency, and collective bargaining with considerably less harm, than standard theory predicted (Kerr 1950; Lester 1951). The experience also impressed upon them the need to make economic theory more realistic by broadening it beyond a narrow study of supply and demand in competitive markets (Dunlop 1944:5). It also stimulated their interest in public policy issues related to labor.

After the war, many of the new generation of labor economists began to produce a great volume of research on labor markets and collective bargaining. This research was distinctive in that it represented a willingness and an ability to develop and use economic theory, a focus on the operation of labor markets, a skepticism of the ability of competitive theory to explain labor market outcomes such as wage differentials and weekly hours of work adequately, and a desire to broaden economic analysis of the labor market to include social, psychological, and institutional conditions.[19]

The hallmark studies of this era were Dunlop's *Wage Determination under Trade Unions* (1944), Arthur Ross's *Trade Union Wage Policy*

(1948), several studies by Lester on wage diversity (1946b, 1952), Kerr's article (1954a) "The Balkanization of Labor Markets," Reynolds's New Haven labor market study *The Structure of Labor Markets* (1951), and the local labor market study by Charles Myers and George Shultz (1951). The message of these and other studies was severalfold: the structure of wages in nonunion labor markets diverges significantly from the level predicted by competitive theory; labor markets contain significant imperfections such as limited information and restrictions on worker mobility that provide employers with market power over wages; firms do not always maximize profits; collective bargaining often is benign or even helpful in its impact on economic efficiency; and quite apart from economic efficiency, collective bargaining is desirable because it provides industrial democracy and due process in the workplace.

Given the institutional nature of labor economics, until the late 1930s, the academic study of industrial relations and labor economics were closely intertwined. With the rise of the new generation of labor economists and the reorientation of the field from labor problems to labor markets, industrial relations and labor economics began to grow apart and develop distinct intellectual identities. The ties between labor economics and industrial relations remained close, however, and labor economics continued to be the dominant source of intellectual inspiration for academic IR. This was partly because of the continued influence of the institutional tradition in labor economics and partly because of the dual interests of the new generation of labor economists and their uneasy relationship to the broader discipline of economics. This latter reason requires additional discussion.

Although the new labor economists were trained as economists and published a wide range of research on labor economics subjects, they were also seriously interested in the field of industrial relations. Indeed, as we have seen, many of the directors of the new IR institutes and centers were labor economists from this group, as were the prime movers in the establishment of the IRRA. In effect, these economists had dual intellectual interests—the operation of labor markets (labor economics) and the study of employer-employee relations (industrial relations).[20] They were able to straddle this intellectual divide successfully because their perspective on the operation of labor markets, and the policy conclusions derived therefrom, dovetailed with the ILE perspective in industrial relations on how best to resolve labor problems and promote improved employer-employee relations.

While the new labor economists started out as economists first and became committed to industrial relations only later, it is clear from their research record and professional activities that by the late 1950s industrial relations had become their de facto home.[21] Important in this process was the hostile reception their research and policy program received from neoclassical price theorists, with the result that many of the new labor economists felt a sense of estrangement and alienation toward the economics discipline. When the new labor economists started their careers, they perceived themselves as neoclassical reformers in that they used the Marshallian model of demand and supply as their basic theoretical tool but sought to broaden it to take into account the market imperfections and noneconomic factors that Hicks had omitted from *The Theory of Wages* (Kerr 1988). To their dismay, not only was their effort at revisionism poorly received by the "ruling elite" in economics (microeconomic price theorists), but it was frequently dismissed with contempt as "mere sociology" (Reynolds 1988). A defining moment in this regard was the publication of Lester's (1946a) article "Shortcomings of Marginal Analysis for Wage-Employment Problems" in the *American Economic Review*. Lester's article attacked the relevance of the marginal analysis contained in neoclassical theory to explain the determination of wages and employment levels. The hostility of the theorists was evident in the counterreplies by Fritz Machlup (1946) and George Stigler (1947), who conceded nothing to Lester and argued instead that either he did not understand the implications of neoclassical price theory or his data did not prove what he claimed it did.[22]

Differences in policy perspectives furthered the rift between the neoclassical price theorists and the new group of labor economists. The new labor economists were generally predisposed to favor collective bargaining and protective labor legislation such as the minimum wage (Lester 1947a; Reynolds 1957, 1988). Their position was built on the view that nonunion labor markets contain imperfections that give employers some market power over wages and introduce numerous distortions and inequities into the wage structure. Collective bargaining and minimum wage laws, therefore, were seen as useful checks to employer power, a spur to efficient production and improved management methods, and a vehicle for increased workplace equity. The neoclassical theorists (e.g., Stigler 1947; Simons 1948; Lindblom 1949; Machlup 1951), in contrast, took a decidedly negative view of the role and impact of unions and minimum wage laws. Starting from the presumption that labor markets are highly competitive, they argued that unions are a monopolistic source of inflated wages and reduced productivity, while protective labor laws such as the minimum wage not only reduce allocative efficiency in the economy but hurt, rather than help, low-wage workers because of the reduced employment opportunities that result.[23]

Because of these differences in outlook, and the professional antagonisms they engendered, the new labor economists came to feel that they were not entirely welcome or accepted in economics proper and that their research and point of view would not get a fair hearing in the American Economic Association. Thus, in the late 1940s and early 1950s, the new labor economists became involved in industrial relations, first, because they had a genuine interest in the subject and, second, because the field provided a natural focal point for them to discuss and pursue their more institutionally oriented research. These motivations had much to do with the founding of the IRRA.[24] It was not coincidental, for example, that shortly after his rebuff by Stigler and Machlup Lester took the lead in organizing the association. The function of the IRRA as a haven for the new labor economists is also revealed in the preponderant number of institutionally minded labor economists who later served as president of the organization, the disproportionate number of session topics at the annual meeting devoted to economics-related topics, and the fact that its annual meeting was held at the same time and location as the annual meeting of the American Economic Association.

There are clearly several parallels between the development of labor economics and of human relations. Both fields had intellectual antecedents in the 1920s and 1930s but emerged in the early 1940s as distinct subject areas with articulated theoretical frameworks and intellectual boundaries. Both fields also developed a strong affiliation with industrial relations, human relations with the PM wing of the field, labor economics with the ILE wing. The major difference was that the labor economists had been more actively involved and more widely represented in the academic arena of industrial relations before World War II than had the behavioral scientists. Coupled with the surge in interest in unions and labor-management relations after the war, this placed the labor economists in the position to become preeminent in the field during its golden age, in the late 1940s and 1950s.

RESEARCH IN THE GOLDEN AGE

The confluence of current events and intellectual developments outlined above resulted in an unprecedented outpouring of industrial relations research in the 1950s. Noteworthy aspects of the IR research of the period include its volume, disciplinary breadth, and interdisciplinary character.

VOLUME

Industrial relations was without doubt one of the boom areas of research in the social and behavioral sciences in the 1950s. Whereas a computer search for the period 1930–39 turned up only fifteen published works with *industrial relations* in the title, a similar search for the years 1950–59 produced more than sixty. And if one defines industrial relations to include any subject related to the employer-employee relationship, the number of entries is huge. Adding articles published in academic journals and proceedings only reinforces this conclusion, in part because in the 1950s periodicals such as the *ILR Review* and the IRRA proceedings were devoted exclusively to IR research, whereas in the 1930s no such publications existed.

BREADTH

Equally impressive is the disciplinary breadth of the IR research of the 1950s. Economics was heavily represented, of course. The doyens were Sumner Slichter and Edwin Witte. Among the younger generation of economists, several economic theorists (e.g., Paul Samuelson, Milton Friedman, Fritz Machlup, Edward Chamberlain) made contact with the field, as well as a host of labor economists. The labor economists were themselves a heterodox group, represented on one end by people who were more management or union specialists than economists per se (e.g., George Strauss, Frederick Harbison, Milton Derber, George Taylor, James Healy, Dale Yoder), on the other end by people who were applied price theorists and statisticians (H. Gregg Lewis, Martin Bronfenbrenner, Melvin Reder, Gary Becker). In the middle was a large group (John Dunlop, Clark Kerr, Richard Lester, Lloyd Reynolds, Arthur Ross,

Charles Myers, Neil Chamberlain, Albert Rees, Lloyd Ulman, Joseph Shister) who combined both perspectives.

Industrial relations also attracted a large number of researchers from other fields, most notably a group associated (some more loosely than others) with the human relations movement. In addition to the intellectual godfather of the group, Elton Mayo, there were anthropologists (Conrad Arensberg, Eliot Chapple, Lloyd Warner), psychologists (Douglas McGregor, Arthur Kornhauser, Daniel Katz, Mason Haire, Frederick Herzberg, Ross Stagner, Harold Leavitt, Chris Argyris), and sociologists (George Homans, William Foote Whyte, Burleigh Gardner, Melville Dalton, Harold Wilensky).[25] Industrial relations also attracted other noneconomists who were outside the human relations movement, including sociologists (e.g., Reinhard Bendix, Herbert Blumer, Robert Dubin, C. Wright Mills, Wilbert Moore) from the structural-functional school (a school of thought in sociology that was generally hostile to the small-group, internally oriented perspective of human relations), academics from administrative science and management (Peter Drucker, Herbert Northrup), history (Irving Bernstein), law (Benjamin Aaron), political science (Lloyd Fisher, Seymour Lipset), and personnel (Donald Paterson).

As a result of this extensive multidisciplinary involvement, IR research had unprecedented breadth in its topic areas, theoretical perspectives, and research methods.[26] A remarkable but almost completely ignored publication by Harold Wilensky (a sociologist and research associate at the IR center at the University of Chicago) entitled *Syllabus of Industrial Relations* (1954) is the best evidence of this breadth. Wilensky states that the purpose of the syllabus is to offer a "road map" for the study of the field of industrial relations, which he subdivides into five principal areas of study: the characteristics and direction of development of urban industrial society; the organization of work in industrial society (including labor markets and the management of human resources); trade union history, organization administration, and impact; collective bargaining systems, processes, and issues; and public policy.[27] Wilensky then provides a three hundred–page overview of the relevant research and research issues in each of these areas. The expansive nature of industrial relations research as of the mid–1950s is indicated by the names of the academic journals Wilensky cites: *Applied Anthropology, American Economic Review, American Journal of Sociology, Harvard Busi-*

ness Review, Human Organization, Industrial and Labor Relations Review, Journal of Applied Psychology, Personnel, and Social Forces.

INTERDISCIPLINARY CHARACTER

The primary intellectual justification for the creation of the IR schools and institutes, as noted previously, was the belief that the study and resolution of labor problems would be materially enhanced by a collaborative, integrative research design that would draw upon methods and ideas from the various disciplines related to the employment relationship. Using three different approaches, IR scholars in the 1950s made considerable attempts to practice this precept.

The first approach was to conduct cross-disciplinary research; that is, research performed by a person trained in one discipline on a subject traditionally examined by scholars in a different discipline. Several economists, for example, examined aspects of management, such as the impact of collective bargaining on the practice of management (Chamberlain 1948; Slichter, Healy, and Livernash 1960) and specific personnel problems such as job evaluation (Kerr and Fisher 1950) and recruitment and hiring methods (Lester 1954). Among the most notable efforts in this regard were Herbert Simon's book *Administrative Behavior* (1947) and E. Wight Bakke's *Bonds of Organization* (1950) and *The Fusion Process* (1953). Several noneconomists also crossed disciplinary lines. Examples include William Foote Whyte's study of incentive wage systems and employee productivity (1955), Lloyd Fisher's study of the harvest labor market (1953), and articles by Robert Dubin (1949) and Benjamin Selekman and Sylvia Selekman (1950) on the impact of collective bargaining on productivity.

The second approach was to select a particular IR topic and then commission a series of research articles on it by scholars from a wide range of disciplines, with the intent of encouraging a melding of ideas and perspectives. One example is the book *Industrial Conflict* (1954), edited by Arthur Kornhauser (psychology), Robert Dubin (sociology), and Arthur Ross (economics). It contained contributions from more than thirty other scholars, including many of the most prominent participants in industrial relations from economics, sociology, psychology, history, and law. Another noteworthy example is the volume *Causes of Industrial Peace* (Golden and Parker 1955), a series of case studies of collective bargaining relationships sponsored by the National Planning

Association and written by a heterogeneous group of academics and practitioners.

The third and most ambitious approach was for an interdisciplinary team of researchers to carry out a research project. The exemplar of such research is the two-volume series *Labor-Management Relations in Illini City* (Derber et al. 1953), a joint effort by three economists, three sociologists, and two psychologists. The Illini City study is noteworthy in two respects; first, because it remains the most thorough attempt in American industrial relations to conduct truly interdisciplinary research and, second, because it produced such meager returns relative to the massive work that went into it.[28] Although there were several project-specific reasons for this disappointing outcome, many researchers nevertheless viewed it as a sobering lesson on the inherent limitations and pitfalls of the interdisciplinary approach (see Derber et al. 1950; Derber 1967).

Another example of team research that had at least a quasi-interdisciplinary representation of scholars was the book *Industrialism and Industrial Man* by Clark Kerr, John Dunlop, Frederick Harbison, and Charles Myers (1960). The 1950s saw a boomlet in international and comparative IR research, particularly cross-national patterns of industrial relations practices and comparisons of IR structures and outcomes in developed and less developed countries.[29] The most important impetus behind this burst of research was the creation of the Inter-University Study of Labor Problems in Economic Development project. The project was initiated and organized by Kerr, Dunlop, Harbison, and Myers (all were economists, although Myers and Harbison had considerable expertise in the management area) and financially supported by the Ford Foundation. Twelve books and more than twenty articles were published during the 1950s under the project's auspices, with contributions from academics across a wide range of disciplines. The most notable of these studies was *Industrialism and Industrial Man* (1960), by the four project leaders. The heart of the book is a cross-country comparison of the impact of the industrialization process on labor market institutions, the work force, managerial elites, the "rule makers" in society, and the nation's culture and value system. The central conclusion is the "convergence hypothesis"; namely, that as nations develop, the imperatives of the industrialization process are such that the basic features of their social, economic, and political systems converge to a common standard (e.g., an open and mobile society, a reduced level of worker protest and class conflict, increasing government involvement in the labor market).

The book generated considerable professional attention in industrial relations when it was first published, and the authors hoped that it would chart a new direction for research in the field. This hope, as discussed more in the next chapter, has been largely unrealized. The convergence hypothesis, however, remains an actively debated subject, although more in sociology than in industrial relations (see Form 1979; Goldthorpe 1984).[30]

THE BATTLE OVER HUMAN RELATIONS

The research trends discussed above reflected the influence of various centripetal forces that were working to bring together and integrate the various disciplines associated with industrial relations. Unfortunately, centrifugal forces were also at work that were simultaneously weakening the bonds of association among the disciplines. The most visible was the "spectacular academic battle" (Landsberger 1958:1), which developed during the 1940s and 1950s between the proponents and critics of the human relations approach to industrial relations—a division that corresponded closely to the historic division of the field into the PM and ILE schools.

The critics of human relations came primarily from economics and sociology, although a few were from political science and other fields. Human relations found few defenders among economists, and labor economists Clark Kerr and John Dunlop, the most influential members of the ILE school in the 1950s, were two of the most outspoken critics.

While economists were generally united in their opposition to human relations, industrial sociologists were deeply split. One group, what Kerr and Fischer (1957) identified as the "plant sociologists" and Miller and Form (1980) identified as the "interactionists," were among the most vocal proponents of human relations. Members of this group included William Foote Whyte and George Homans. Another group, identified by Miller and Form as "structuralists," were critics of human relations. Included in this group were Herbert Blumer, C. Wright Mills, and Wilbert Moore.

The critics attacked the human relations approach on a variety of grounds (see Bell 1947; Blumer 1948; Mills 1948; Bendix and Fisher

1949; Dunlop 1950; Barkin 1950; Kerr and Fisher 1957; Roethlisberger 1977). Among the more important reasons were that human relations research neglected the influence on IR outcomes of external economic, social, political, and technological conditions and overemphasized the influence of internal social and psychological factors; not only were the independent variables used in human relations research (e.g., sentiments, patterns of interaction, leadership styles) likely to have a small quantitative effect on the dependent variable, but many were not independent in a causal sense and represented dependent or intervening variables; the model of man assumed in human relations research was fundamentally flawed because it overemphasized the role of nonlogical sentiments, feelings of anomie, and needs for stability and group belongingness; the development of a competitive, individualistic society did not threaten social and economic disorganization but rather promoted political freedom and economic growth; human relations underplayed conflicts of interest between workers and managers and promoted the manipulation of workers to achieve management's profit objectives; and human relations was antiunion in spirit and practice.

Several proponents of human relations rebutted the critics and pointed out the weaknesses of the economists' approach to the study of industrial relations (see Arensberg 1951; Whyte 1950, 1959; Arensberg and Tootell 1957). Among their major points were that human relations did not ignore variations in external environmental conditions but, rather, took this variation as a "given" and then proceeded to analyze how the internal social system of the plant adjusted; the internal psychological and social factors stressed in human relations research had a far larger impact on IR outcomes than the critics admitted, in part because the technological and economic system allowed managers significant discretion in how they organized work and managed the work force; economists' theories of industrial relations treated unions and firms as organizational "black boxes" and hence were unable to specify the link by which variations in external conditions give rise to specific IR outcomes; the economists' model of rational, individualistic behavior was seriously in error because it neglected the social dimension of work and the role played by custom, ritual, symbols, group norms, and sanctions; much of the criticism of human relations was fundamentally misdirected because it was aimed at specific hypotheses or positions staked out by Mayo and his close followers and that many human relationists later abandoned or never subscribed to in the first place; and while the aim of human relations was to promote increased employee job satisfaction and cooperation between workers and managers, this did not mean that human relations was inherently anti-union, for its proponents recognized that unions protected employees' vital interests and helped promote a stable social order in the plant.

The debate over human relations had both positive and negative repercussions for the field of industrial relations. On the positive side, the debate encouraged an interchange of ideas between researchers in the various disciplines related to industrial relations, thus helping to break down the walls that separated the economists from the sociologists, the sociologists from the psychologists, the psychologists from the historians, and so on. It also suggested the outlines for a theoretical compromise or *modus vivendi* between the "externalists" of the ILE school and the "internalists" of the PM school.

The nature of this compromise was most clearly spelled out by Charles Myers (1955:46) in a chapter of the book *Causes of Industrial Peace* in which he attempted to summarize and synthesize the conclusions of several authors such as Clark Kerr, John Dunlop, and Douglas McGregor:

> In the preceding chapters we have seen how favorable external environmental factors give to management and the union an opportunity to develop peaceful relationships; and how certain attitudes, approaches, policies, and procedures make it possible to achieve these relationships in specific situations. . . . Environmental factors . . . do not by themselves cause peace. A favorable combination of various environmental factors make it easier for management and the union to achieve a mutually agreeable and noncollusive peaceful relationship, but the parties still have to desire peace and work to achieve it. . . . Environmental factors . . . largely establish a range within which management and the union can largely determine their own relationship.

The compromise Myers offered provided a role to both the external environmental factors emphasized by the ILE school and the internal, social, and psychological factors emphasized by the PM school. In effect, Myers said that environmental factors (e.g., economic conditions, the body of labor law, prevailing social norms) determine the context in which labor-management relations are conducted and place certain bounds on the outcomes, but within these bounds the precise outcomes are a function of the policies, practices, attitudes, and human relations practices of the parties involved.

Unfortunately, neither the ILE nor the PM school took this compromise position to heart. Of the two protagonists in the battle over human relations, the ILE group was the harshest and most uncompromising in its attack on the other. This, in turn, led to the major negative repercussion of the battle over human relations: it seriously exacerbated the intellectual and ideological frictions and antagonisms that separated the members of the PM and ILE schools, heightening the sense among the former that they were not entirely welcome in industrial relations.

As documented earlier in this chapter, in the late 1940s–early 1950s, the human relations group perceived that they had an intellectual affiliation with the field of industrial relations. A decade later, however, it is equally clear that their links to industrial relations had weakened significantly. As detailed in the next chapter, the disengagement of the PM school from industrial relations occurred for a variety of reasons. Clearly, one contributing reason was the intensity and uncompromising nature of the ILE attack on the human relations program.

Dunlop and Kerr, as well as other leading figures of the ILE wing of the field, were highly critical of human relations for both scientific and policy and ideological reasons. From a scientific point of view, they strongly objected to what they regarded as the almost complete neglect of external environmental factors in human relations research and the corresponding overemphasis on internal social and psychological factors. Dunlop (1950:384) stated this position as follows:

> Attention to the internal communications systems of an organization, or the interaction of such systems between unions and managements in collective bargaining, without frequent resort to the environmental setting, can have only limited use as an explanation for industrial relations behavior. From this vantage point the human relations approach must be cut to size—to a minor role—in any full explanation of industrial relations behavior.[31]

The proponents of the ILE school also had fundamental disagreements with the human relations movement on matters of policy and ideology. Dunlop and Kerr, for example, had a strong philosophical commitment to the New Deal system of industrial relations and its support of collective bargaining. They perceived human relations to be another, albeit more sophisticated, attempt at preserving management control of the workplace and keeping out unions and collective bargaining.[32] Human relations, with its emphasis on cooperation and worker-employer integration, also conflicted with the ILE commitment to shared governance and pluralism in the economic, political, and social spheres (Kerr 1954b; Kerr and Fisher 1957).

In response to this antagonistic stance, the members of the PM school felt that they were at best junior members of the field and at worst *personna non grata.*[33] This message was communicated in several ways: by the stridency of the attacks on human relations[34]; by the exclusion of much human relations research from the meetings of the IRRA and the exclusion of prominent scholars in human relations from the presidency of the organization[35]; by the paucity of human relations research reported in the *ILR Review;* and by the cold shoulder given to the PM perspective in Dunlop's influential book *Industrial Relations Systems* (1958). Because of its importance to the subsequent development of the field, Dunlop's book requires more detailed discussion.

DUNLOP'S *INDUSTRIAL RELATIONS SYSTEMS*

Dunlop (1958:vii) states that the purpose of his book is to present "a general theory of industrial relations; it seeks to provide tools of analysis to interpret and to gain understanding of the widest possible range of industrial relations facts and practices." The general theory he proposes involves three groups of actors: workers and their organizations, managers and their organizations, and government agencies concerned with the workplace. The behavior and interactions of these actors is critically affected by the complex of rules (agreements, statutes, orders, regulations, practices, customs, and so on) found in every industrial relations system.[36] The central task of a theory of industrial relations, Dunlop states, is to explain why particular rules are established in particular industrial relations systems and how and why they change in response to changes affecting the system. The key consideration in this regard, according to Dunlop, is the environmental context of the actors, represented by three interrelated factors: technology (the production process, the size of the plant, the required job skills, and so forth); market or budgetary constraints (the degree of competition in the product and labor markets, the characteristics of the work force, the amount of profit or the size of the budget, and so on); and the power relations and statuses of the actors (the laws affecting union organization and bargaining power, the amount of rule-making authority vested in management, and so on). Finally, the last component of Dunlop's model is ideology, the set of shared values and beliefs regarding the interaction and roles of the actors that helps bind the system together.

Several aspects of the book are noteworthy. For example, *Industrial Relations Systems* was the first explicit attempt to frame a *general* theory of industrial relations. Several "partial" theories that focused on specific facets of industrial relations behavior had been advanced earlier, such as Commons's (1909) theory of the extension of markets and trade union development, Perlman's (1922) theory of the labor movement, and Ross's (1948) theory of the trade union as a political institution in an economic environment, but no one before Dunlop had attempted to construct a conceptual framework that integrated and systematized the disparate parts of the field into a coherent whole. In effect, what Dunlop attempted to do was transform industrial relations from a multidisciplinary field of study that drew on bits and pieces of theories from other fields into a unique academic discipline with a broad-based theoretical framework that was capable of generating hypotheses on the full range of behavior found in the employment relationship.

Another notable aspect of Dunlop's book was that it shifted the focus of the field from its institutional-inspired preoccupation with fact-gathering and problem-solving toward a more rigorous science-building approach that emphasized theory construction, the deduction of hypotheses, and the testing of hypotheses. In this regard, Dunlop states (pp. vi–vii):

> The field of industrial relations today may be described in the words of Julian Huxley: "Mountains of facts have been piled up on the plains of human ignorance. . . . The result is a glut of raw material. Great piles of facts are lying around unutilized, or utilized only in an occasional manner.". . . This volume reflects the judgement that far too much of the writing concerned with industrial relations . . . has lacked intellectual rigor and discipline. The need has been for theoretical structure and orientation.

Dunlop's book also gave short-shrift to the PM perspective in industrial relations, particularly the human relations movement. In its almost four hundred pages, the book makes no mention of Mayo, Roethlisberger, Dickson, Whyte, Homans, or other major PM figures (the closest exception is Benjamin Selekman) or of significant research results from the behavioral science side of industrial relations. Likewise, Dunlop's theoretical framework focuses almost exclusively on the external environment and the relations between organizations (firms, unions, associations of firms and unions, government) as the determinants of industrial relations outcomes and almost entirely omits from the theory such staples of the human relations model as leadership and supervisory styles, informal work groups, worker morale, patterns of interaction and sentiments, and organizational integration.[37] In this respect Dunlop more than lived up to his earlier claim that the human relations approach deserved only "a minor role" in a full explanation of industrial relations behavior. Dunlop's position had the effect of accepting human relations as a member of the industrial relations family but rejecting it as of substantive importance. Dunlop was also clearly not willing to accept Myers's proffered compromise.[38]

The final noteworthy aspect of Dunlop's book is that the discussion of industrial relations systems is framed almost entirely in terms of unionized employment situations. The primary reference to nonunion employers is on pages 116–17, where he discusses four models of managerial authority—dictatorial, paternal, constitutional, and worker-participative—of which the first two occur in nonunion situations. Nowhere else in the book are nonunion firms (or these authority models) discussed in any detail; nor are any examples of rules or rule making in nonunion firms provided. This stands in sharp contrast to the extensive discussion given to collective bargaining situations in coal mining, construction, railroads, and automobiles and the dozens of examples of rules negotiated in these industries by unions and firms. One is left with the distinct impression that in Dunlop's mind the subject of industrial relations is largely coterminous with the organized sector of the economy.[39]

Dunlop's book was widely hailed as a major scholarly work and many researchers still regard it as the first and foremost statement of IR theory (see R. Adams 1988; Fiorito 1990; Meltz 1991). From my point of view, the book *has* been immensely influential, but for reasons quite apart from the quality of the scholarship or the merits of the theory per se. *Industrial Relations Systems* marked out a distinct Y in the intellectual road for industrial relations. The Y, in turn, was formed as a result of a fundamental contradiction. Dunlop claimed that the book presented a *general* theory of industrial relations, yet it omitted almost entirely discussion of the PM perspective, research findings from the behavioral sciences, the nonunion (unorganized) sector of the economy, and the organizational structure and internal dynamics of either companies or unions.[40] The book also sought to move industrial relations away from its historic emphasis on applied, problem-solving, multidisciplinary research and toward a more academic, science-building, unidisciplinary orientation.

Thus, Dunlop presented the field with a clear choice. If it followed the model he laid out, it would effectively shed the PM school and its behavioral science disciplines and become a more rigorous but narrowly constituted field oriented toward the discipline of economics (and to a lesser extent law), the study of unions and collective bargaining, and the policy perspective of the ILE school. If it rejected his model, the field would remain as it had been constituted since the 1920s—as a coalition of disciplines from both the behavioral and nonbehavioral sciences, oriented toward a relatively applied, problem-solving approach to research. It would provide relatively balanced coverage of union and nonunion work situations and the structure and operation of firms and labor organizations, using two rival policy perspectives (the ILE and the PM schools) on the resolution of labor problems.

Which fork in the road was chosen? In hindsight, it is clear that the field followed the path laid out by Dunlop, albeit for a variety of reasons, many of which had little to do with him. The year 1958, therefore, marks a symbolic turning point in the intellectual history of industrial relations as a field of study. Why did IR scholars make this choice? The next two chapters provide an answer to this pivotal question.

6

The Hollowing Out of Industrial Relations

O N THE SURFACE, the 1960s and 1970s were a period of expansion and consolidation for industrial relations as a field of study. The number of IR programs in the United States continued to increase so that by 1965 more than forty had been established (Derber 1967:8), and the number continued to grow into the 1970s. New programs were created after 1960 at the University of Oregon, Ohio State, Iowa State, Alabama, Georgia State, Pace, the New York Institute of Technology, North Texas, Xavier, and Cleveland State. The number of Ph.D. programs also grew. Some schools (e.g., Illinois, Michigan State) followed the Cornell model and created separate interdisciplinary Ph.D. programs in industrial relations, while others (e.g., Iowa, Georgia State) established an IR major in an existing Ph.D. program in business administration or economics.

Progress on the research front was less clear cut, but positive signs were certainly evident. For example, the journal *Industrial Relations* was founded in 1961, under the auspices of the Institute of Industrial Relations at the University of California at Berkeley.[1] Substantial bodies of new research were also published on hitherto unexplored topics, such as public sector collective bargaining and manpower programs. Also noteworthy, scholars were making much greater use of mathematics, formal theoretical models, and statistics in research. Finally, academic membership in the IRRA nearly tripled between 1960 and 1979. Based on a survey of IR research completed as of the late 1960s, Herbert Heneman, Jr. (1968:49), was sufficiently impressed to declare (possibly with a degree of overstatement), "The two most important disciplines of the first half of this century were mathematics and physics; beyond reasonable doubt industrial relations is the most important discipline of the second half."

Heneman based his claim on the fact that the field of industrial relations covered all aspects of the world of work and that developments and trends in the world of work had become central, in his view, to the nation's social and economic progress. But, ironically, even as Heneman was writing these words, the core of the field was being seriously eroded, including its hitherto undisputed claim of intellectual sovereignty over the subject of work. In particular, what occurred between 1960 and 1979 was a hollowing out of the field as it metamorphosed from a broad coalition of behavioral and nonbehavioral disciplines devoted to the study of all aspects of the world of work to a much narrower field devoted to the study of unions, collective bargaining, and the employment problems of special groups (e.g., minorities, the aged, the poor) with a core group of committed participants made up mainly of a small and dwindling number of institutional labor economists.

If unionism and collective bargaining had continued to grow in the 1960s and 1970s as they had in the previous two decades, this narrowing of focus might have been both intellectually justified and organizationally viable. As it was, the nonunion sector of the economy became not only the major source of new gains in employment but also the major source of new innovations in employment relations practices (Foulkes 1980; Kochan, Katz, and McKersie 1986). The result was that the preoccupation of industrial relations with unionism and collective bargaining led to its gradual decline as a field of study, a condition partially hidden from view through the 1970s but one that became all too obvious in the 1980s.

This chapter explores both the symptoms and the causes of the hollowing out of industrial relations. Specifically, it examines the debate over the theoretical and disciplinary status of the field in the 1960s; the narrowing of industrial relations from a broad "all aspects of employment relations" definition to a narrow "labor-management" definition; the decision of the PM school to end its association with industrial relations and establish itself as a separate, rival field of study; and the growing estrangement between the fields of labor economics and industrial relations. I then discuss four reasons for the hollowing out: the increased emphasis among academics on science-building and the concomitant downgrading of problem-solving research; the incompatibility of the theoretical models used by the members of the PM and ILE schools; the adverse tide of current events; and the pro–collective bargaining value system of the major academic figures in industrial relations.

Debate over the Theoretical and Disciplinary Status of IR

A palpable sense emerged among IR scholars in the 1960s that industrial relations had lost its intellectual bearings. The result was a large volume of articles and books that took an introspective, often critical look at the field, a mood that seemed strangely at odds with the decidedly upbeat spirit that had prevailed only a few short years ago. The temper of the times was captured by Donald Woods (1968:87) at a conference that had analyzed various alleged problems in IR programs:

> I approach my task this morning with some reluctance for I feel that our discussion is simply a part of a long playing record that has been playing the same old melody and the same old lyrics for many years. If you examine the annual proceedings of almost any industrial relations or personnel association you will find periodic public confessionals decrying the second class status of industrial relations. The theme is always the same—the lack of rigorous theoretical underpinnings, the cleavage between theory and practice, the lack of intellectual cohesion and respectability, whether industrial relations should be a separate discipline in its own right, and whether the subject should be oriented to traditional disciplines or be interdisciplinary in nature.

As Woods suggested, the debate over theory and methods during this period revolved around several related and interconnected themes: whether IR was best conceptualized as an art or a science; whether IR had a theoretical framework and, if it did not, whether such was possible; whether IR was a bona fide academic discipline and, if it was not, whether it was practical and desirable for it to become one; and, finally, among those scholars who believed IR was not a self-contained discipline, whether teaching and research in the field should be organized on a loosely structured multidisciplinary or closely integrated interdisciplinary basis. As shall become clear, IR scholars were in effect arguing over the merits of two very different conceptualizations of the field.

ART OR SCIENCE?

The debate over whether IR was best conceptualized as an art or a science originated in the multiple objectives of the field's founders: the reform of workplace organization and practice, the promulgation of new public policies, and the advancement of knowledge. Before the 1950s, IR was heavily oriented toward the first two goals, which had given the field a distinct applied, problem-solving character. This character was accentuated by the heavy intellectual influence of institutionalism, which favored an inductive, case study, historical approach to research over more formalized, deductively derived theories and frameworks.

The proponents of IR as an art or exercise in problem-solving largely came from the reform, public policy, institutional perspective. Thus, J. Douglas Brown, an early advocate of this position, stated in his IRRA presidential address (1952:6):

> Industrial relations is not a science. Rather it is the study of the values arising in the minds, institutions, and emotions of individuals as these values become embodied in group organization and action. The understanding and solution of problems of group organization and action can never be divorced from the more basic understanding of the values which determine individual behavior. No matter how useful scientific methodology may be along the way, the goal of industrial relations research and practice lies beyond the "timber line" of science.

In a similar vein, Slichter, Healy, and Livernash (1960:6) said: "The factors involved in industrial relations are so numerous and occur in so many combinations and permutations that worthwhile theories are difficult to formulate. What is important is to know what is going on and to see that every industrial relations situation is more or less unique and must be explained as a whole."

Finally, George P. Shultz (1968:1) stated in his IRRA presidential address: "The field of industrial relations, in my view, is problem-based. It is not a discipline in itself but rather draws on many disciplines for theory and techniques to understand and help solve the problems arising in the workplace, the labor market and at the bargaining table."

Other IR scholars had the opposite view. John Dunlop (1958:vi–vii), for example, claimed that the preoccupation of the field with fact-gathering caused it to lack scientific rigor and that the greatest need was for the development of a theoretical structure. Milton Derber, another proponent of the "science" view, stated (1964:604):

> The "art" conception, with its focus on uniqueness, tends, I believe, to have a limiting effect. . . . If every case is unique, why bother to investigate more than a few examples? . . . The social science attitude toward industrial relations research promotes a different climate. It implies first of all a conscious awareness of the scientific method. It impels the researcher to break down his problem in terms of its basic theoretical foundations. It stimulates an interest in study design and in more efficient techniques of data collection. It encourages experimentation with varying observational quantitative tools. It gives the researcher an incentive to view his problem and his data in a broader setting and to develop hypotheses and key questions for further investigation.

THE DISCIPLINARY STATUS OF IR

Another area of debate concerned whether IR had achieved the status of an academic discipline and, if it had not, whether doing so was both practical and desirable. The importance of this issue was attested to by Martin Estey (1960:99) in a report to the IRRA that summarized the results of his comprehensive survey of academic IR programs: "Perhaps the most challenging issue with which educators in the field are grappling is whether industrial relations is, or can become, a discipline in its own right."

A review of the literature of the period reveals that most IR scholars believed the field had not yet achieved status as a true discipline (Tripp 1964; Woods 1968; Shultz 1968; Heneman 1969). Gerald Somers (1969:vii) said, for example, "Even its most devoted supporters must confess that industrial relations has not yet achieved a status comparable to the traditional academic disciplines." Some accepted this lack of status with equanimity, while others believed it to presage the decline of the field. The former view was based on the argument that the multidisciplinary character of industrial relations was a strength because the study of employment issues requires a diversity of theoretical and methodological perspectives (Aronson 1961:42–43; Shultz 1964.). Opponents argued that the multidisciplinary character was a weakness because the lack of a unifying theoretical framework (the sine qua non of a discipline) inhibits rigorous research and thereby encourages scholars to forsake IR for their home disciplines (Somers 1969:40).

IR THEORY

The debate over the disciplinary status of IR was closely tied to the controversy over whether it was possible and desirable to develop a body of IR theory. Most IR scholars were in agreement that, despite Dunlop's best efforts, the field still lacked an integrating theoretical framework (Aronson 1961; Chamberlain 1960; Derber 1964; Heneman 1969; Somers 1969). Controversy raged, however, over the feasibility and desirability of constructing such a framework.

Advocates of developing a body of IR theory cited several reasons for doing so. Theory, they said, was necessary to guide researchers in the selection of topics, the development of hypotheses, and the interpretation of data. Robert L. Aronson (1961:27–28) expressed this view:

> Ideally, our research problems ought to be formulated with reference to a theoretical framework of large scope and significance. That is, we should have constantly before us, so to speak, some kind of intellectual construct that enables us to organize knowledge and to choose between socially relevant research questions and those which, in Merton's terms, are "scientifically trivial." . . . Theorizing of any kind, low or high order, is in fact rather rare in our field. More typically, we seek data first and either ask questions later or hope that, through statistical manipulation, the data will order themselves into useful patterns of relationship. If not logic, then experience will certainly tell us that this kind of naive empiricism is an unrewarding approach to greater understanding.

Another commonly cited problem resulting from the lack of theory was that research in the field shifted from subject to subject as scholars responded to the latest newspaper headlines or shifts in the funding priorities of foundations. Derber (1964:606) stated the problem this way:

> This very incomplete picture of postwar research leads to two conclusions: (a) in a comparatively short period of time (less than two decades) research in industrial relations has fluctuated quite widely among subject areas, and (b) the shifts have been closely related to shifts in contemporary public problems. . . . A certain measure of variety in problems not only is desirable to refresh the typical researcher but may also enrich successive projects. But "following the headlines" or "responding to the lure of foundations" is not the way to construct a reliable body of concepts, facts and principles.

Finally, the advocates of developing IR theory noted that a field built on the findings of case study empiricism (descriptive, statistical, or whatever) was incapable of providing more than ad hoc and ex post diagnoses of the causes of employment problems and suggested resolutions thereof. As Aronson (1961:34) put it, "The lack of a theoretical framework in our field is the explanation of our failure to anticipate and respond to the issues of public policy and concern. This is, perhaps, the ultimate irony: having eschewed theory for empiricism, we are helpless in the face of pragmatic problems."

Other scholars denied that IR theory was either achievable or desirable. Their basic argument was twofold. First, a unique theory of industrial relations was impossible given the nature of the phenomenon (the employment relationship) under investigation. In this vein, Neil Chamberlain (1960:101–3) stated:

> If one stops to consider what constitutes the bond of association between those who inhabit our professional territory, he is driven back on the thin line of defense that it includes all of those whose interests are touched by labor. . . . I have not, however, been able to discover any unifying theme in the study of labor. . . . The word—I cannot even call it a concept, since it represents a bundle of concepts—does not create any unifying or central preoccupation, to give meaning to our association. There is no broad problem which unites all in search for greater understanding it. In each of its many contexts and conceptual forms, "labor" may be an instrument for organizing knowledge, but as a single enveloping interest it is without content and no more useful in organizing knowledge than would be, for example, the effort to relate the study of money in whatever context it is found.

Woods provides another example of this viewpoint (1968:88):

> If our definition [of industrial relations] is so broad as to include the whole range of subject matter related to this field—labor economics, labor law, labor history, human relations, and the behavioral sciences—then we do not have a single, uniform theory covering all of these areas, and we probably never will have one. True, we may develop some broader frameworks for at least better understanding the variables and relationships operating in this field. But this will not provide an integrated body of theory that can be used as an operational, analytical tool.

If the development of IR theory was not achievable, then what was the better approach? The answer, according to this group of scholars, was, first, to recognize that the most rapid theoretical advances would result if scholars specialized in theory development within each of the constituent disciplines of industrial relations and, second, to structure industrial relations as an applied field of problem-solving in which theoretical constructs and concepts could be mixed and matched to suit the topic at hand. Thus, Chamberlain (1960:102–3) stated:

> I am not decrying the importance of understanding and drawing on as many areas and fields of knowledge as a person is capable of assimilating. I am just suggesting that intellectual progress is made up of bits of knowledge, from whatever sources derived, that are put together in meaningful patterns and organized around conceptions and related to central problems. This requirement is the reason, I am sure, why each of us has retained a kind of Oedipal attachment to the discipline which has mothered us. . . . I am suggesting that the relevance of the information which is derived from other fields is enhanced, not lost, by pouring it into the theoretical preoccupations which characterize the individual's home discipline.

Likewise, Woods (1968:88) said:

> If we look at particular areas within the industrial relations field, such as labor economics, then there already is a body of established theory. There are gaps in these theoretical constructs. And we have not exploited these theoretical tools and concepts as rigorously or as broadly as we could. But the solution is not to desert our basic disciplinary base, whatever it may be, but to improve it and make it more relevant for the broader field of industrial relations. It is my view that we have to rely largely on our mother discipline for new theoretical ideas, while at the same time being ready to accept any relevant concepts available in cognate disciplines.

INTERDISCIPLINARY OR MULTIDISCIPLINARY?

Another dimension of the dispute concerned the merits of organizing IR research on an interdisciplinary versus a multidisciplinary basis. Derber (1967:16) framed the issue as follows:

> The relative merits of the interdisciplinary approach are still being debated. Its proponents note that only through the utilization of the concepts and techniques of several disciplines can labor problems prop-

erly be studied and analyzed. By combining the disciplines as dictated by the problems, the research will have the benefit of the most advanced and sophisticated developments in these disciplines. The opponents of interdisciplinary research argue that this approach is unduly time-consuming and that it forces compromises which involve a watering-down of disciplinary standards.

Widespread agreement existed that the amount of interdisciplinary research (i.e., research performed by persons from different disciplines that integrated theoretical concepts and/or methodological tools from these disciplines) in industrial relations had noticeably declined after the mid–1950s (Derber 1967:136; Filley 1968). Controversy remained, however, as to whether this decline was something to be lamented. As Derber suggested, those IR scholars who saw the field as chiefly oriented toward problem-solving favored the interdisciplinary approach. Their major justification was that employment problems almost always contain a mix of economic, social, psychological, legal, and organizational dimensions and, thus, an adequate understanding and resolution of these problems requires a melding of theories and perspectives from all the disciplines germane to the issue (Dunnette and Bass 1963; Shultz 1964).

Other scholars took a different view, however (Somers 1961, 1969; Heneman 1969). As they saw it, the major purpose of research should be to push out the frontiers of knowledge and build industrial relations as a science, implying a major emphasis on constructing theories and testing hypotheses. This group, therefore, was considerably more skeptical about the virtues of interdisciplinary research insofar as attempting to traverse disciplinary boundaries makes theory construction and the derivation of hypotheses quite difficult. For these reasons, they favored one of two approaches: the more preferred was to create a unique theoretical base for industrial relations and make the field a discipline of its own; the fallback was to structure industrial relations as a loose multidisciplinary field, have researchers concentrate on science-building in their respective disciplines, and encourage where possible a cross-fertilization of ideas.

IMPLICATIONS

It is noteworthy that this debate over the appropriate conceptualization of industrial relations did not occur until the 1960s, a full forty years after its founding as an academic field of study. Given that a broad consensus had existed in earlier years concerning the essential features of industrial relations (e.g., Miller and Form 1951; Wilensky 1954; Reynolds 1955), the emergence of this debate must be regarded as strong prima facie evidence that the intellectual foundation of the field had recently shifted or was in the process of being realigned.

Further, these debates clearly represented two opposing views of the nature and the future of the field. The first view was that of the "traditionalists," who desired to preserve industrial relations as a confederation of researchers from a variety of disciplines engaged in applied, empirically oriented, interdisciplinary research on labor problems. The second view was that of the "modernists," who put greater emphasis on the importance of rigorous, scientific research.

The modernists were thus the change agents in industrial relations in that the field as it then existed did not provide what they most wanted—a theoretical framework and the opportunity to pursue "hard" academic research. The drive for such a framework led the modernists in two potentially opposite directions. The preferred direction was toward the creation of a theoretical framework that integrated the various disciplines relevant to the employment relationship, thus establishing industrial relations as a bona fide discipline on a par with economics and sociology. If the effort at integration failed, however, the modernists' quest for theory and science-building would then lead to an entirely different outcome; namely, the breakup and fragmentation of the field as researchers retreated to their home disciplines and the theoretical frameworks therein and as various subject areas of industrial relations were spun off to whatever discipline had the most relevant theoretical framework for the issue at hand. Although the disputants in the debates probably did not fully realize the consequences of the choices being made, these choices were to be momentous for the future of the field.

NARROWING OF THE INTELLECTUAL DOMAIN

While IR scholars were immersed in the debate over problem-solving versus science-building, a second transformation was taking place in industrial relations that was far more profound but much less discussed. This transformation was the narrowing of the intellectual domain of industrial relations from a field that included research on all aspects of the employment relationship, and most particularly on both union and nonunion work situations, to a field focused largely on the study of unionism and collective bargaining.[2]

It is difficult to pinpoint exactly when industrial relations became more narrowly defined. It seems reasonably clear, however, that the process began with the institutionalization of the field immediately after World War II, became evident in IR research in the mid- to late 1950s, accelerated in the early 1960s, and was largely accomplished by the early 1970s.

Up to the mid-1950s, it was accepted without question that industrial relations included both the ILE and the PM schools and thus issues related to employer-employee relations in both union and nonunion and interorganizational and intraorganizational contexts.[3] This definition was clearly acknowledged in both IR academic programs and scholarly research, as documented in the previous chapter. During the 1960s and 1970s, IR academic programs continued to include courses from both the ILE and the PM wings of the field, thus maintaining a fidelity to the original broad, integrative conceptualization of the field. In the area of research, however, the field was caught in a contradiction of growing proportions as IR scholars continued to profess allegiance to the broad conceptualization of industrial relations (Heneman 1969; Somers 1969) while the research they performed had less and less of a management or behavioral science focus and, concomitantly, an ever greater focus on collective bargaining and labor economics.

This narrowing of focus is evident from the topics of the articles published in the *ILR Review* and *Industrial Relations*, the two major academic journals in the field. I examined articles published in the *Review* for two time periods, 1955–59 and 1975–79, and calculated the proportion of those articles that pertained to three broad subject areas: unions and collective bargaining, labor economics, and personnel and organizational behavior (OB).[4] For 1955–59, 68 percent of the articles were related to unions and collective bargaining, 22 percent to labor economics, and 10 percent to personnel and OB. The distribution for 1975–79 was 33 percent, 61 percent, and 6 percent, respectively.

I did the same calculations for *Industrial Relations* but started with the years 1961–65 (1961 was the first year of publication). For the 1961–65 period, 50 percent of the articles were on unionism and collective bargaining, 24 percent were on labor economics, and 26 percent were on personnel and OB. During 1975–79, the figures were, respectively, 51 percent, 36 percent, and 13 percent.

Clearly, by the late 1970s, the major IR journals had become a near exclusive preserve for research on such ILE-oriented subjects as labor markets, collective bargaining, and the employment problems of particular labor force groups. Equally important, the proportion of articles devoted to pure labor economics topics was increasing, particularly in the *ILR Review,* where the share of such research nearly tripled over this twenty-year period. Given the concomitant disappearance in the journals of descriptive case studies and data collected by the participant-observer (two favorite research methods of the institutionalists and behaviorists), by the late 1970s it was increasingly difficult to distinguish IR journals from other applied journals that catered to labor economists.[5]

Another piece of evidence comes from the topical focus of the IRRA's research volumes. During the late 1950s, the IRRA published two research volumes that were clearly consistent with the broad, integrative definition of industrial relations. The first was the 1957 volume *Research in Industrial Human Relations* (Arensberg et al.), which included a number of chapters on management and organizational issues but only four (out of thirteen) on subjects related to unionism. The second was the 1960 volume *Employment Relations Research* (Heneman et al.), which contained six chapters, two devoted to management issues, two to labor economics, and two to collective bargaining subjects.

During the 1960s, by contrast, the IRRA research volumes were devoted entirely to collective bargaining or labor economics topics. The marginal position of management-related subjects in industrial relations was then attested to by George Strauss in the 1970 research volume *A Review of Industrial Relations Research* (Ginsburg et al.). In his chapter, "Organizational Behavior and Personnel Relations," Strauss states (pp. 201–2): "I must predict this may be the last review which deals with OB as a part of industrial relations. Personnel's loss of status means that it can no longer serve as a bridge between the fields. . . . Though IR claims to be multidisciplinary, it is in fact heavily dominated by economists and for many in the field the terms industrial relations and labor economics are interchangeable."

Strauss's prediction proved to be overly pessimistic given the IRRA's subsequent decision to devote the 1974 research volume to organizational behavior. Nevertheless, the increasingly tenuous position of human relations and organizational behavior–type research was attested to in the preface to the 1974 volume: "The question of whether to publish a book devoted to Organizational Behavior (OB) caused strenuous debate within the Executive Board. There was one group which felt that OB did not really belong with Industrial Relations. The other group was willing to provide an opportunity to test OB's relevance." Twenty years earlier such a question never would have been debated.

Three symposia on behavioral research in industrial relations provide further evidence of the transformation of the field. The first symposium, published as a monograph by Industrial Relations Counselors in 1962, was entitled *Behavioral Science Research in Industrial Relations*. In the introductory paper, "A Broadening View of Industrial Relations," Richard Beaumont, director of research for the IRC, states (p. 9) that the purpose of the symposium is to help management in "establishing and maintaining effective human relationships." He cites six issues that are crucial to this task: selection, motivation, evaluation, identification, communication, and organization. The remainder of the volume is devoted to six papers that explore various facets of these issues, authored by such well-known academic members of the PM school as Frederick Herzberg, Chris Argyris, and Leonard Sayles.

This volume is noteworthy in that it provides yet another example of the existence of the PM wing of industrial relations. Further, it documents that as of the early 1960s at least some participants in industrial relations still perceived the field to include academics from the management and behavioral science side of employment relations. The volume is also noteworthy in that it is one of the last collections on human relations and OB topics to be published under the label of industrial relations.

The second symposium, "The Behavioral Sciences and Industrial Relations," was published in 1965 in the *ILR Review*. In the introduction, the journal editor stated that the purpose of the symposium was to "clarify the relationship of the field of organizational behavior to the study of industrial and labor relations as well as applications of behavioral analysis to general and specific industrial relations problems." In the lead article, William Foote Whyte (1965) discussed the origins, development, and current status of the field of organizational behavior. The remainder of the symposium was devoted to five papers by authors from sociology, psychology, management, and economics and political science, four of which were on general management and organizational issues and one of which focused on a specific aspect of collective bargaining, strikes. Like the IRC volume, the authors of the *Review* articles viewed industrial relations as a field that included academic research in the classic PM tradition—the study of organizations and the practice of management using the theory and methods of the behavioral sciences. The symposium also provides clear evidence that behavioral science and management-oriented research had noticeably slipped from being a central part of the IR research program on the employment relationship (as in the early 1950s) to a subject on the periphery of the field. If this were not the case, why would the *Review* have thought it necessary to sponsor a special symposium on the subject?

The third symposium, "Behavioral Research in Industrial Relations," was published in 1983, also in the *ILR Review*. It clearly illustrates the narrowing of the field that took place over the previous fifteen years as IR shed general management subjects and became increasingly associated with the study of unionism and collective bargaining. Thus, of the seven papers selected as examples of behavioral IR research, all were devoted to some aspect of collective bargaining. Even more revealing, although the purpose of the introductory paper by Lewin and Fueille (1983) was to provide a comprehensive review of behavioral research in industrial relations, it focused almost exclusively on behavioral research related to collective bargaining subjects (e.g., union representation elections, bargaining, strikes) and omitted almost all mention of the large body of nonunion-related human relations research of the 1950s or the OB or human resource management (HRM) research of the 1960s and 1970s. Thus, although behavioral science research was still being conducted in industrial relations, the perceived domain of IR research had been narrowed so that it now focused on unionized employment situations and the institutions, practices, and impact of collective bargaining.[6]

Miller and Form's text *Industrial Sociology* (1951) provides yet another piece of compelling evidence of the change in the field. Their "family tree" of industrial relations (see fig. 3.1), in the first edition of their book, clearly reveals that they and other behavioral science scholars considered themselves and their subject area to be a part of industrial relations. This is also suggested by the broad definition of industrial relations implicitly used by Miller and Form in the first chapter of the text, a definition that in effect equated the field with the study of work in all its different dimensions. By the second edition, published in 1964, the family tree had been dropped, along with all mention of the term *industrial relations* in the first chapter. These deletions suggest that Miller and Form no longer perceived industrial sociology to have a close kinship to industrial relations.[7]

A final piece of evidence comes from the observations of historian David Brody. Speaking of the field of industrial relations in the 1960s and 1970s, he says (1989:9):

> There was, at once, a retreat from the interdisciplinary scope and the methodological eclecticism that had for so long characterized labor scholarship. Sociologists, political scientists, and anthropologists lost interest in labor topics, while labor economics took up neoclassical analysis with a vengeance, applying it first to the study of human capital, then to whatever else could be subjected to deductive, individual-level microanalysis. The academic high ground was meanwhile seized by the new discipline of organizational behavior, which had sprung from the human relations strain within the postwar industrial relations field and now pronounced itself a behavioral science capable of conducting rigorous quantitative and theoretically grounded analysis. Industrial relations itself shrank down into a kind of mini-discipline, confined as before to the union sector, but striving belatedly to assert its own credentials as a rigorous social science.

As Brody suggests, the result of the trends outlined above was that industrial relations became, in the view of most academics and practitioners, synonymous with the study of unions and collective bargaining.[8] The outcome was a growing gap between the professed intellectual domain of the field and the actual domain as evidenced in IR research.[9] Thomas Kochan's textbook *Collective Bargaining and Industrial Relations* (1980) provides a particularly clear illustration of this contradiction. In the first sentence of chapter 1, Kochan defines industrial relations as "a broad, interdisciplinary field of study and practice that encompasses all aspects of the employment relationship." In the third sentence, however, he introduces a qualifier that permits him to move swiftly to the narrow definition: "Within this broad field industrial relations professionals have historically given special attention to relations between labor and management." The remainder of the text is then devoted to the theory and practice of union-management relations.

The IRRA's choice of session topics for its annual winter meetings in the late 1970s provides further evidence of the gap between the field's stated ideals and actual practice. As noted earlier, the IRRA was founded with the express purpose of fostering research on all aspects of the employment relationship, including union and nonunion work situations. It is understandable that in the first decade of the organization's existence a large number of sessions would have been devoted to topics pertaining to the union sector, given the meteoric rise of organized labor in the previous two decades and the host of important problems and issues in labor-management relations that demanded attention. By the late 1970s, however, the share of the organized work force had dropped sharply and many of the innovations in employment practices were originating in the nonunion sector. Did the IRRA's selection of session topics reflect this shift? An examination of the proceedings of the winter IRRA meetings for the years 1975–79 reveals the answer is clearly no. They contained twenty-five sessions related to some aspect of union-management relations and only five pertaining to some aspect of nonunion work situations.

THE PM SCHOOL LEAVES INDUSTRIAL RELATIONS

In the last chapter I suggested that Dunlop's *Industrial Relations Systems* effectively defined an intellectual crossroad for industrial relations, with one branch corresponding to the broad conceptualization of the field (the confederation of the PM and ILE schools with a significant representation of behavioral and nonbehavioral and union and nonunion viewpoints) and the other representing the narrow conceptualization (near-exclusive dominance of the ILE school with its economic and institutional disciplinary focus and topical concentration on labor-management relations). The evidence clearly suggests that the narrow definition was chosen. As a result, the field gradually lost its historic claim to cover all aspects of the employment relationship and instead became associated with the study of unionism and collective bargaining. Furthermore, the PM school slowly divorced itself from industrial relations and, by the end of the 1960s, had relatively little interaction with it.

Previous chapters have documented the significant involvement in pre-1960 industrial relations of scholars from the PM school. By the end of the 1970s, George Strauss was the only prominent representative of the 1950s-era PM school who could still be considered a card-carrying member of the field. In part, this trend reflected natural causes, such as death and retirement; however, it also reflected a dwindling of participation per se, particularly in the form of articles published in the major IR journals and involvement in IRRA activities. The falloff in involvement in industrial relations was most marked among sociologists, which was doubly surprising given the large number of sociologists who were active in the field in the early 1950s and the emphasis in both sociology and industrial relations on collective action.[10]

Concomitantly, only a small number of the newer generation of behavioral science and management scholars became active in industrial relations. Of those who did, most wrote on collective bargaining–related topics. The most prominent example of research of this genre was Richard Walton and Robert McKersie's A Behavioral Theory of Labor Negotiations (1965). Other examples include the papers (some by British authors, some by American) in Industrial Relations: A Social Psychological Approach (Stephenson and Brotherton 1979); several articles on strike trends by sociologists (Britt and Galle 1974; Snyder 1977); and a smattering of articles on the determinants of union joining (e.g., Schriesheim 1978).[11]

The number of younger PM-oriented scholars who were active in industrial relations in the 1960s and 1970s and who did non–collective bargaining research was relatively small. Included in this group were Edward Lawler III, Thomas Mahoney, Donald Schwab, Jeffrey Pfeffer, Lyman Porter, and George Milkovitch, all of whom occasionally published in the two major IR journals and participated in IRRA meetings (generally on an invited basis). None, however, was considered a big name in IR research per se, although several had national name recognition in their home fields. Perhaps more revealing is the list of PM-oriented people who were widely recognized for their research on aspects of the employment relationship and yet were not associated with industrial relations. Examples include Richard Steers, David McClelland, Warren Bennis, Stanley Seashore, Jay Lorsch, Paul Lawrence, Victor Vroom, Daniel Katz, and Fred Fiedler.

Of the many reasons that younger scholars of the PM school decided not to become involved in industrial relations, one of the most significant was the birth of the field of organizational behavior and its applied offshoot, human resource management. Before the mid-1950s, the management-oriented academics of the PM school may have been dissatisfied and uncomfortable with the field of industrial relations, but no alternatives existed. The emergence of organizational behavior and human resource management in the late 1950s–early 1960s provided such an alternative.

Organizational behavior developed as the fusion of two streams of thought, human relations and the organization and administration part of management (Landsberger 1967; Strauss 1970, 1992). The subject of management was divided in most business school curricula into several distinct areas, such as production, organization and administration, personnel, and policy and strategy (Bossard and Dewhurst 1931; Gordon and Howell 1959). The organization and administration part developed from the work of Frederick Taylor and was subsequently developed by people such as Henri Fayol, Max Weber, Luther Gulick, Chester Barnard, James Mooney, and Ralph Davis (Wren 1987). It focused largely on issues of organizational structure and efficient administrative practices (e.g., optimal span of control, systems of control and planning).

Until the late 1950s, human relations and organization and administration remained largely separate fields of study. Human relations was largely concerned with face-to-face relations in small group settings and largely abstracted from issues of organizational structure. Organization theory took something of the opposite approach.

Scholars such as Bakke, Argyris, McGregor, Whyte, and Bennis were led toward a fusion of the two areas partly in response to critics (e.g., industrial sociologists) who had charged that human relations ignored organizational and structural influences on in-plant patterns of employer-employee relations.[12] As OB developed, it provided, on several counts, a far more compatible home for members of the PM school than did industrial relations: it included mostly persons from a behavioral science or management perspective, disputes over ideology and anti-unionism could be largely avoided since OB had an avowedly management perspective, and it facilitated the growing specialization and compartmentalization that were developing in all areas of academic research.

The emergence and development of organizational behavior also did much to strengthen the academic fortunes of the field of personnel management, which at the time was viewed as a second-class citizen in academe because of its notable lack of theory and rigor (Gordon and Howell 1959; Dunnette and Bass 1963; Strauss 1970), a fact quickly revealed by a perusal of the field's leading journals (e.g., *Personnel Psy-*

chology and *Personnel*).[13] During the 1960s, however, personnel began to undergo a significant metamorphosis as new theories and concepts discovered in organizational behavior research (and the closely allied field of industrial and organizational psychology) were applied to the traditional personnel topics of compensation, recruitment, selection, performance evaluation, and training. One of these new ideas was to view employees as "human resources" (Miles 1965; Armstrong 1988). According to this view, if managers were to unlock employee commitment and work effort, then the workers had to perceive that they were valuable assets or human resources of the firm, with the implication that in return for their hard work and diligence the employees would share in the long-term economic success of the organization.

This perspective led to a significant shift in both management theory and practice (Lewin 1991). Viewing employees as human resources rather than as personnel encouraged a change from a short-term, expense-oriented, tactical approach to the management of labor to a longer-term, strategic, investment approach. The new field of human resource management, or HRM as it quickly became known, also led to a shift in management practices in industry. Whereas human relations had led managers to emphasize the improvement of interpersonel relations and social conditions in the plant through techniques such as sensitivity training, human resource management encouraged firms to focus on practices and techniques that promoted employee development, such as job enrichment and pay for knowledge.[14] As human resource management gained in popularity in the 1960s, a growing number of companies renamed their personnel or industrial relations departments human resource departments, and increasingly the professionals in these departments no longer engaged in IR but in HR. This change in nomenclature and perspective was to spread to the world of academe a decade later.

ESTRANGEMENT BETWEEN LABOR ECONOMICS AND INDUSTRIAL RELATIONS

The hollowing out of industrial relations was further exacerbated by the weakening of the links between it and labor economics. As we have seen, labor economics entered a second phase in its development in the early 1940s with the shift in focus from the study of labor problems to labor markets. Although this trend caused a growing cleavage between industrial relations and labor economics, the multidisciplinary perspective and practitioner orientation of the labor economists of this period enabled them to straddle the divide and keep one foot in each field. Straddling this divide became increasingly difficult after the mid-1950s, however, as labor economics entered the third phase of its development.

During this phase the shift toward the study of labor markets intensified, while the subjects of labor problems and management's approach to the resolution of such problems were discarded. This in itself further separated industrial relations from labor economics as newly trained labor economists became, in effect, applied price theorists who had little knowledge of or interest in the employment relationship per se and the issues therein.[15] This phase was also marked by a profound transformation in the theoretical, methodological, and ideological approach to the study of labor markets, all of which were antithetical to the perspective and purpose of the ILE version of industrial relations.

Intimately involved with this phase in the development of labor economics was a group of economists at the University of Chicago whom Kerr (1988) has labeled the "neoclassical restorationists." The seminal figures were George Stigler and Milton Friedman (see Reder 1982; Kaufman 1993). Other members included H. Gregg Lewis, Gary Becker, Jacob Mincer, Albert Rees, and Melvin Reder.

The events of the Depression had seemingly discredited competitive neoclassical price theory, a point of view exemplified by the antagonistic attitude of the ILE-oriented labor economists toward it (L. Reynolds 1988). Stigler and Friedman launched a major counterattack on several fronts. In the first, Friedman sought to show, with respect to macroeconomic theory, that the Depression was not the inherent fault of the price system but resulted instead from erroneous policies of government, thus negating the belief that the price system at the aggregate level was dysfunctional (Friedman and Schwartz 1963). The second was the rigorous development of the theory of price determination in competitive markets, thereby providing an analytical framework that the critics lacked (Stigler 1942). The third was the application of the competitive model to a host of new labor market issues, such as hours of work, discrimination, education, and family size. This line of attack was started by Lewis (1956) but was pursued most strenuously by Becker (see Becker 1957; 1976). The fourth line of attack was the methodological attack by Stigler and Friedman on realism in theory (Stigler 1949; Friedman

1953). The ILE-oriented economists had attacked competitive theory because its assumptions were unrealistic (see Phelps 1955:421–45), but Stigler and Friedman argued that the true test of a theory is its predictive ability, not the realism of its assumptions. Finally, the restorationists pioneered the application of statistical methods to the analysis and testing of labor market hypotheses (see Lewis 1963).

These developments had a markedly adverse impact on industrial relations. The rise of competitive theory, for example, struck at both the intellectual and the ideological foundations of ILE-style industrial relations. The intellectual focus of industrial relations is the study of labor problems in the employment relationship and methods to resolve these problems. The assumption underlying this approach is that labor problems are an inevitable by-product of industrialism and the defects and imperfections contained in the market system and that various institutional and administrative reforms are necessary to offset the effects of these imperfections. In contrast, the premise of neoclassical economics is that markets operate relatively efficiently and that competitive forces are an effective guarantor of efficiency in production and equity in the terms and conditions of employment. From the point of view of neoclassical economists, therefore, free markets have no "problem" that needs reform and industrial relations has little intellectual justification, except possibly as a repository for the specialized study of labor unions. Ideologically, the ILE school maintained that unions and protective labor legislation were needed to level the plane of competition, offset market defects such as public goods and externalities, and provide shared governance at the workplace. From a neoclassical perspective, these alleged virtues paled in comparison to the negative consequences that arose from unions and government legislation, such as inflated labor costs, inefficient allocation of resources, reduced productivity, and barriers to competition.

The rise of Chicago-style neoclassical economics also adversely affected industrial relations because of the insularity of disciplinary perspectives that it promoted. As discussed earlier, a major impetus behind the founding of the Industrial Relations Research Association was the desire of labor economists in the 1940s to promote a more inclusive, multidisciplinary style of research on labor markets. Industrial relations, therefore, played an important bridging role as these economists attempted to take the theoretical models from economics and introduce into them social, psychological, and institutional variables. The labor economists of the Chicago school aggressively pursued the opposite tack, however. Their goal was "imperialistic," in that they sought to take the economist's basic model of constrained utility maximization and competitive markets and use it to explain as many different dimensions of human behavior as possible (Becker 1976; Stigler and Becker 1977). As a consequence, economists not only lost interest in integrating theories and concepts from other disciplines into economics but increasingly exhibited a negative attitude toward those who tried. Industrial relations thus lost its appeal to economists as the entree to other disciplines, causing all but those interested in union-related topics to forsake the field.

The net result of all of these developments was that industrial relations gradually lost much of its theoretical and philosophical link to labor economics. The World War II generation of labor economists who had provided the bridge between the two fields ceased to play this role by the early 1960s. Some turned their research interests toward other areas (e.g., economic development), while others went on to highly influential careers as university presidents (Clark Kerr, Arnold Weber, Edwin Young) and secretaries of the Cabinet (John Dunlop, George Shultz, Ray Marshall).[16] The new "restorationists," by contrast, had little interest in industrial relations and were certainly hostile to its pro–collective bargaining perspective. Strauss (1978:535) summed up the situation: "If collective bargaining represents industrial relations' central core, then labor economics has largely divorced itself from that core."

Beginning in the early 1960s, therefore, industrial relations experienced a hollowing out from two sides. On one side the field gradually lost PM scholars from management and the behavioral sciences, while on the other few of the new generation of neoclassical labor economists chose to become active in the field. The residual group of academics who remained active participants in industrial relations was composed of two groups. The larger group was made up of institutionally oriented labor economists, along with a small number of like-minded people from law and history. The smaller group was composed of scholars from the behavioral sciences and management who were interested in unions and collective bargaining. Unfortunately for the field, both of these groups had critical weaknesses as a base for future growth. The problem with the former was that institutionalism was in its death throes in labor economics, thus substantially restricting the supply of new economics-based talent to industrial relations. The problem with the latter group was that it would never attract large numbers of participants, or the best talent, since economists controlled the major journals and professional association and economic theories and statistical methods were the major research tools in the field.

CAUSES OF THE HOLLOWING OUT PROCESS

Up to this point, the chapter has documented the symptoms of the hollowing out process. What was the cause of this process? The answer, I believe, involves four factors.

SCIENCE-BUILDING

The emphasis on problem-solving and policy formulation in the 1920s through the early 1940s imparted several distinctive characteristics to the IR literature of that period. These included a heterodox set of topics, reflecting the diverse range of labor problems encountered by employers and workers; a critical tone regarding prevailing economic and social conditions; a heavily applied, case-oriented research method that eschewed theory development for the collection of empirical facts; a multidisciplinary and often interdisciplinary approach to research; and a strong normative element as researchers not only described "what is" but also "what should be."

After World War II, a movement developed among academics to make research in all the social sciences more scientific, an approach I have referred to as science-building. The hallmark of science-building is the rigorous application of the scientific method to academic investigation, where the scientific method involves development of a body of theory, the use of this theory to generate hypotheses about the causes of some phenomenon or behavior, and the empirical testing of these hypotheses through the collection and statistical analysis of data. The product of such research has several distinctive characteristics, including a much greater emphasis on theory development; the use of deductive reasoning to develop such theory, rather than the inductive approach typically used by problem-solving researchers; research topics in which less weight is given to the needs or problems of practitioners or policy makers and more to methodological considerations, such as whether the problem is amenable to theoretical analysis and whether appropriate data are available for empirical analysis; considerable emphasis on methods and techniques of statistical estimation and hypothesis-testing; unidisciplinary research and a focus on small pieces of behavior; and a sharper separation between positive analysis and normative conclusions.

Both problem-solving and science-building have their strengths and weaknesses. Among the virtues of problem-solving are its relevance, realism, and intellectual holism, while its defects include a tendency to advance causal explanations that are ad hoc, to engage in aimless or unstructured empiricism, and to let a priori normative beliefs influence the research. The strengths of science-building are its rigor, quantification, and ability to be generalized, while its drawbacks include a tendency to become overly "academic" in perspective and thus divorced from real-world concerns of practitioners and policy makers, to emphasize issues of research methodology over practical significance, and to focus on minutiae at the expense of the big picture.

Although both approaches to research co-existed from the earliest years of the field, the problem-solving approach dominated from the 1920s to the early 1940s. From the early 1940s to the early 1960s, the two co-existed in a rough balance. Since the early 1960s, however, the science-building approach has gained increasing dominance (Barbash 1979). This trend explains much about the changing character of IR research and industrial relations as a field of study.

It is not accidental, for example, that in the 1920s and 1930s industrial relations research had a strong applied, interdisciplinary, reformist flavor, for this was the era when the problem-solving approach was transcendent. Likewise, this fact explains both the virtues of the research of that period (e.g., its direct relevance to practice and policy) and its defects (e.g., its atheoretic nature). Similarly, the research during the 1950s was "golden" in part because the academics of the period were well trained in both science-building and problem-solving, a serendipitous combination that led to outstanding research because it was both relevant and theoretically informed. Unfortunately, the equilibrium achieved during the 1950s between problem-solving and science-building was not stable, and both the pursuit of knowledge and the internal reward system in academia pushed IR scholars further and further in the direction of science-building. The inevitable result was a clash between the proponents of the two approaches to research that erupted in the 1960s in the form of the theoretical and methodological disputes reviewed earlier in this chapter.

In hindsight, it is clear that science-building won out. A comparison of articles published in the *ILR Review* and *Industrial Relations* in the early 1960s and in the late 1970s reveals several trends: a sharp decline in case study research, particularly of the old-line institutional variety; the virtual disappearance of interdisciplinary research; a dramatic increase in articles that make use of a formalized theory or model; a concomitant shift in the disciplinary orientation of IR research (narrowly defined) toward economics; a marked increase in the number of articles that derive hypotheses and then test these hypotheses with advanced multivariate statistical techniques; a decline in primary source data, such as obtained from company records, personally administered surveys, or participant-observer techniques, and a marked increase in the use of large data sets obtained from secondary sources, such as government data files; a marked decline in practitioner and policy-relevant research and a noticeable increase in research whose major innovation is theoretical, methodological, or data improvement (e.g., achieving an improved estimation technique or a "richer" data set); a marked loss in historical perspective and awareness of institutional realities; and a narrow focus on a small subset of employment relations issues. (For a similar assessment, see Dunlop 1977; Strauss and Feuille 1981; and Rehmus 1985).

The shift toward science-building entailed both benefits and costs for the field. The largest gains were registered in the empirical area as computers, multivariate statistical techniques, and large data sets enabled researchers to test hypotheses rigorously and to quantify relationships. Significant advances were made, for example, in determining the interactive effect of market concentration and union density on industrial wage levels (Weiss 1966), the impact of employer tactics on union success in NLRB elections (Getman, Goldberg, and Herman 1976), and the efficacy of various methods of third-party dispute resolution (Kochan et al. 1979). Although less far-reaching, theoretical advances were also obtained, such as models of union wage policy (Atherton 1973), bargaining and strikes (Cross 1969; Ashenfelter and Johnson 1969), and the dynamics of arbitrator behavior (Farber and Katz 1979).

Science-building, while arguably a boon to the advancement of knowledge, was unquestionably a detriment to the cohesiveness and organizational vitality of industrial relations as a field of study. Although very dissimilar in their theoretical and topical interests, the members of the PM and ILE schools nevertheless had a common interest in resolving labor problems and advancing the three goals of efficiency, equity, and human well-being. Problem-solving was thus the glue that held the coalition of diverse disciplines together and provided the raison d'être for their interaction. When the objective of the field switched to science-building, the rationale for having a multidisciplinary field of study diminished significantly, for productivity in theorizing and hypothesis-testing was furthered by disciplinary specialization, not interdisciplinary collaboration.[17]

Thus, science-building unleashed strong centrifugal forces that simultaneously weakened the attraction of participation in a multidisciplinary field such as industrial relations and increased the incentives to pursue unidisciplinary research. The result was the hollowing out of the field as scholars in the behavioral sciences, economics, law, history, and the other affiliated disciplines went their separate ways. The only groups that retained an interest in industrial relations were the institutional labor economists, for whom there was no home discipline to return to, and the minority of scholars from various disciplines who were interested in collective bargaining—the residual topic not included in the intellectual domain of the other disciplines.

The decline in the attractiveness of multidisciplinary research had serious negative ramifications for IR doctoral programs. As research was becoming more specialized along disciplinary lines, students in IR doctoral programs increasingly felt they had to pursue such specialization in their course work and dissertations if they were to remain competitive in the job market. IR programs reacted to this threat by permitting students to obtain more depth in one disciplinary area at the expense of cross-disciplinary breadth, but this course of action then called into question the basic rationale for having an interdisciplinary program in the first place, particularly given the administrative and organizational complexities of such programs.[18]

LACK OF IR THEORY

Industrial relations is recognized as a field of study precisely because it focuses on an activity—the employment relationship—that is not the explicit subject of any other academic area. The bane of industrial relations, and the cause of its second-class academic status, is that the activity it has selected for investigation does not contain any common, unifying process or form of behavior around which a unique theory can be built and a set of hypotheses deduced. As aptly expressed in the quotation by Chamberlain cited earlier in this chapter, the employment relationship covers such a wide number of subjects that the only intellectual common denominator is labor (or work). There is nothing intrinsic to the subject of work, however, that provides the basis for a theoretical model per se. This being the case, a process of disintegration takes place as researchers return to their home disciplines where conditions are better for science-building and, simultaneously, the subject area of the employment relationship gets carved up and the pieces transferred to those disciplines with the greatest comparative advantage in theorizing.

A portion of the hollowing out of industrial relations in the 1960s and 1970s was due to exactly this process. The first casualty was the confederation between the PM and ILE schools. As long as members of both the PM and the ILE were engaged primarily in applied research of a problem-solving nature, they had a common reason to work together, despite their divergent disciplinary perspectives. When science-building became the dominant goal of research, however, the gains from joint collaboration were reduced dramatically since the incompatibility of the theoretical frameworks made cross-disciplinary research both unproductive of new hypotheses and very time-intensive.

In some respects, in fact, the theoretical frameworks of the behavioralists and the economists were not only incompatible but also antagonistic from a science-building perspective. As I have argued elsewhere (Kaufman 1989b), the outcomes of the employment relation reflect the interaction of objective, external conditions (technological, economic, legal) and the human response to those conditions, which is shaped by internal, subjective psychological and sociological variables. If a theory is to be a true theory, it must treat one of these two factors as a given so as to derive falsifiable predictions ex ante.

Thus, in behavioral research of the PM school, researchers tend to view the external environment, and variations thereof, as the given and to search for explanations of the change (or level) in IR behavior in internal social, psychological, and organizational conditions (e.g., differences in leadership styles, corporate strategies). The economics perspective of the ILE school pursues the opposite approach. It takes internal social, psychological, and organizational conditions as the given and looks to external conditions (e.g., variations in the rate of unemployment, changes in the technology of production) for the causal or independent variables.

This dichotomy in perspectives was the fundamental source of disagreement in the 1950s between the advocates and critics of human relations. Gerald Somers later gave voice to the intellectual conundrum this opposition of viewpoints creates when he remarked (1969:40) that "the great need is for a vehicle by which the externalists (economics, law, and politics) and the internalists (psychology and sociology) can integrate their efforts" (also see Somers 1972). He failed to grasp the extent of this conundrum, however, for he devoted the remainder of his article to an attempt to achieve such an integrated theory, a task that had he succeeded would have simultaneously neutered the predictive ability of the theory he was attempting to build.

Once science-building became the raison d'être of academic research, it was inevitable that the ILE and PM schools would go their separate ways. Unfortunately, this process occurred not only between the PM and ILE schools but also within them. Just as the theoretical perspectives of economics and psychology were incompatible, so too were the ties between such erstwhile allies as sociology and psychology and economics and law. The result was a progressive weakening of the bonds that held the coalition of disciplines together.

Carried to its logical extreme, the process of science-building will result in the total demise of any multidisciplinary field. The good news for industrial relations is that this process has not happened—yet. Although most of the other parts of the employment relationship were stripped away and appropriated by other disciplines, collective bargaining remained the intellectual property of industrial relations. The bad news is that industrial relations gained jurisdiction over collective bargaining by default; that is, not because IR developed its own theoretical framework to explain collective bargaining processes and outcomes but, rather, because other disciplines were also unable to do so.

It follows from this fact that industrial relations is not secure until it independently develops a theoretical framework that can explain the major features of labor-management relations (or whatever other area is at the core of the field). Lacking such a framework, industrial relations, perforce, will remain a multidisciplinary field of study. This situation is clearly an intellectual weakness, not a virtue, in an environment of science-building. It also explains why industrial relations has had a stronger orientation toward the discipline of economics in the post–World War II period than in earlier years. The reason is that the field's current focus on collective bargaining makes it more amenable to economic theorizing than when the field encompassed the entire employment relationship.

CURRENT EVENTS

The hollowing out of industrial relations that occurred after 1960 was further abetted by the turn of current events.

Part of the perceptible malaise that seemed to descend on the field in the early 1960s was no doubt due to the realization among IR scholars that current events had shoved industrial relations off the center stage of public concern. When the nation's attention was riveted on issues of strikes and union power, as it was in the late 1940s and early 1950s, students and researchers flocked to industrial relations, imparting to it a sense of both importance and excitement. By the early 1960s, however, labor-management relations had gone from being front-page news to being back-page news as collective bargaining became institutionalized and routinized and strikes and other attention-getting forms of conflict dropped to the lowest levels since the early years of the Depression. As the spotlight of public attention shifted to other economic and social problems, IR academics inevitably felt some angst as they contemplated declining student enrollments in graduate programs and a body of research topics that was looking increasingly picked over and pedestrian.

As labor-management relations receded in newsworthiness and policy concern, other labor-oriented issues took their place, including automation and structural unemployment, discrimination and civil rights, job dissatisfaction and alienation among blue-collar workers, poverty, and manpower training programs. All of these issues were labor problems and thus fully in the intellectual domain of industrial relations. They were also well suited to the field's multidisciplinary focus, involving as they did a diverse range of economic, organizational, political, and social influences.

Were industrial relations truly a problem-solving field, it would have gone with the headlines (per the critics' charges) and made these topics the new focal point of research. Efforts were made in this direction, but in the final analysis they did not quite gel. It is certainly clear, on the one hand, that IR academics gave these new labor problems considerable attention in the 1960s and 1970s. For example, the IRRA devoted several sessions at its annual winter meetings to these subjects and published research volumes on adjustments to technological change (Somers, Cushman, and Weinberg 1963), poverty (Levitan, Cohen, and Lampman 1968), manpower training programs (Weber, Cassell, and Ginsburg 1969), and civil rights (Hausman et al. 1977). On the other hand, as the IR literature makes clear, collective bargaining remained the heart and soul of industrial relations. The new issues were the "swing" topics in IR in that they waxed and waned in research importance based on their newsworthiness. Thus, automation was a prominent subject in the early 1960s, while poverty had its day in the late 1960s and early 1970s and then faded from sight. The one subject that was always given attention at every IRRA meeting and in nearly every issue of the IR journals, however, was collective bargaining.

The emergence of collective bargaining in the 1970s as the core subject area of the field was unfortunately timed from the perspective of current events. Just as industrial relations became increasingly associated with the study of collective bargaining, the extent and influence of collective bargaining noticeably began to decline. Union density, for example, dropped from 32 percent of the work force in 1960 to 25 percent in 1980. Further, the bulk of the pioneering innovations in employment relations practices no longer came from the union sector but from a small but growing number of nonunion companies that were successfully applying behavioral science–based human resource and organizational development methods (see Foulkes 1980; Beer and Spector 1984; Kochan, Katz, and McKersie 1986).

Thus, quite apart from the pressures of science-building and the lack of IR theory, industrial relations would have lost some of its organizational vitality as a result of the gradual decline in size and influence of the union sector of the economy. In the late 1970s, these developments did not seem unduly worrisome, however, and there were even reasons for modest optimism. Union representation and power, for example, remained strong in such core areas of the economy as mining, construction, manufacturing, and transportation. Similarly, although union membership as a percentage of the work force had declined, union membership itself had increased by 5 million—hardly the sign of a decaying institution. Finally, one of the major employment relations developments of the 1960s–70s was the spread of unionism and collective bargaining to the public sector. This development created a substantial agenda of new labor problems that needed investigating (e.g., alternatives to the strike as a method of dispute resolution; the juxtaposition of the economic and political power of public sector unions), thus providing IR academics with new grist for their research mills and a renewed sense of purpose for the field.

Current events must be rated, therefore, as a modest cause of the field's hollowing out in the 1960s–70s. As we shall see, however, the 1980s were a far different story.

VALUES

Industrial relations has always been animated by a distinct value system and ideology that have given purpose and direction to the field (Weber 1987a). The community of interests that draws people to a field and that provides the focal point for research and teaching has been weaker in industrial relations than in many other fields because of the vastness and diversity of the subject matter and the lack of an integrating theoretical framework. Industrial relations, therefore, has had to rely to a greater degree than other fields on ideology and values to provide the bonds of association and the sense of shared purpose.[19]

The ideology of industrial relations in its early, pre–World War II years was reformist and progressive. Both the institutional labor economists and the personnel practitioners who founded the field were drawn to it by the conviction that the prevalent methods of organizing work and managing the work force resulted in a deplorable amount of waste, inefficiency, human suffering, and enmity between workers and employers. They also agreed that these evils could be, and should be, eradicated through a combination of improved management methods, the introduction of industrial democracy into the workplace, and the enactment of protective labor legislation and social insurance programs.

This reform agenda was broad enough to accommodate a diversity of viewpoints. Thus, the members of both the PM and the ILE schools were committed to the idea that some system of shared governance was an essential part of the reform of the employment relationship but they diverged on the best method to achieve it. As discussed in chapter 2, the PM wing of the field was generally hostile to trade unions and collective bargaining and favored a nonunion form of employee representation, while the ILE wing was far more supportive of trade unions and skeptical of the effectiveness of company unions. The important point is that the ideology and value system of industrial relations was framed broadly enough during this period that people as diverse as John R. Commons, Clarence J. Hicks, and Elton Mayo could all find common ground for collaboration.

This situation began to change in the 1950s. On the one hand, the field continued to include people with a diversity of viewpoints concerning employer-employee relations, as evidenced in the vigorous debate surrounding human relations. On the other hand, it is also clear that a gradual process of disenfranchisement took place in the 1950s as the members of the PM wing were given less than an equal opportunity to participate by the labor economists and their allies who controlled the journals and professional meetings of the field.[20]

In the pre–World War II period, IR's atomized, largely noninstitutionalized state made it impossible for the ILE or the PM contingent to gain political control of the field. This situation changed dramatically after 1945 with the creation of the IR institutes, the IRRA, and the *ILR Review*.[21] These new organizations had the power to define the scope and ideological perspective of industrial relations through their control over the subjects taught in IR curricula, the articles published in IR research journals and proceedings, and the faculty invited to participate in professional meetings. This power, as we have seen, passed into the hands of the ILE wing of the field. The inevitable result was that the institutions of the field were used to promote the ILE version of industrial relations over the PM version, a fact that contributed significantly to the eventual divorce of the two in the 1960s.[22]

With the ILE school in control, the value system of industrial relations became synonymous with the value system of the leading thinkers of that school. Somers (1975:1) describes the components of this value system as "the uniqueness and value of the free collective bargaining system, voluntarism, liberal pluralism, [and] consent." Barbash (1979:453) says of it: "As I see it, two leading principles govern the American ideology of American industrial relations: the adversarial principle and the principle of voluntarism." Finally, Franke (1987:479) states, "It is probably fair to say that the distinctive character of many [IR] programs has been the study of trade unionism and collective bargaining and the value system that supported these institutions."

These statements elicited neither debate nor controversy. They had become, in effect, the reigning orthodoxy of industrial relations. The ideological character of industrial relations had gradually but perceptibly changed from broad-based, middle-of-the road progressivism to a more narrow, liberal-leaning, pro-union perspective.[23] This change in ideological orientation, in turn, contributed to the hollowing out of the field in several ways. First, the ILE ideology effectively narrowed the community of interests that defined the field and thus made involvement in industrial relations unattractive to many potential participants. Second, it led to the falloff in student enrollments and scholarly interest in industrial relations due to the decline in the union sector of the economy and the concomitant growth of the nonunion sector and human resources as a field of study. Third, the ILE commitment to unions and the New Deal system of industrial relations caused a growing number of people to see the field as increasingly stale, reactive, and out-of-date. Fourth and finally, the field became less interesting when members of the PM school left and the debates over theory and policy, such as occurred in the 1950s over human relations, largely ceased.

7

INDUSTRIAL RELATIONS IN
DECLINE

A LTHOUGH THE LAST chapter painted a less than optimistic picture of the prospects for industrial relations as a field of study, from the vantage point of 1980 the dark clouds were less obvious and threatening. In their review of industrial relations research, for example, Strauss and Feuille (1981) concluded that the academic fortunes of the field appeared to have bottomed out in the mid-1970s and then staged a modest revival, possibly presaging a "renaissance" for the field. Likewise, the consensus at a 1982 conference entitled "The Future of Industrial Relations" was that "despite the fact that major elements of the U.S. industrial relations environment have changed or are changing, the conferees expected no fundamental shifts in the industrial relations system itself. While most participants had no clear scenario as to how continued membership declines could be avoided, most expected a new surge of organizing to occur, as it had so often in the past" (*Industrial Relations*, Winter 1983:126).

From the vantage point of the early 1990s, it is clear that just the opposite occurred. While the quality and quantity of scholarly research in industrial relations improved, this "plus" was outweighed by several "negatives" that clearly signaled an overall decline in the intellectual and organizational vitality of the field. These developments included a dramatic decade-long decline in union membership and union power, significant attrition in the number of extant IR institutes and degree programs, a marked shift in student demand from IR to HR courses, a widespread perception among both academics and practitioners that IR had lost much of its relevance as an agent for change and innovation in employment practice and policy, and a marked stagnation in membership and participation in the Industrial Relations Research Association. This turn of events, and the pessimistic mood it generated among IR scholars, is amply illustrated in another review of the field that Strauss undertook in the late 1980s (1989:241, 257): "The news is more bad than good. . . . Short of an unexpected resurgence of union victories academic IR will have to make major readjustments. Otherwise it may follow the example of the Cigarmakers and Sleeping Car Porters, both leaders of their times."

A review of developments in academic IR during the 1980s does turn up more bad news than good, at least if one's attention is restricted to the United States.[1] In analyzing these developments, the first place to start is current events.

THE NEW DEAL IR SYSTEM IN CRISIS

The legislative initiatives of the New Deal period, such as the Wagner Act, the Fair Labor Standards Act, and the Social Security Act, along with the Employment Act of 1946, implemented the major planks of the ILE program for improved industrial relations. By the mid-1950s, the New Deal system was largely institutionalized in the American economy. The pillar of this system and its major dynamic element was collective bargaining. Unions had succeeded in organizing one-third of the total work force and more than half of the blue-collar workers in the goods-producing industries. Collective bargaining was without question the pacesetter in the economy in both the determination of wages and working conditions and innovations in employment practices. Union-management bargainers pioneered, for example, cost-of-living adjustment (COLA) clauses, multiple-year contracts, supplemental unemployment plans, and binding arbitration of employee grievances.

From the mid-1950s until the late 1960s, the New Deal system performed remarkably well. Unions achieved considerable success: collective bargaining led to substantially improved wages, benefits, and working conditions, making a middle-class lifestyle available to a large cross-section of blue-collar families; unions (or the threat of unions) induced companies to systematize and formalize their personnel policies and to improve their training of supervisors and foremen; and unions created a fundamentally new and more equitable system of workplace governance featuring formal grievance procedures, protection from arbitrary discipline and discharge, and joint consultation over the terms and conditions of work.

All of these changes increased labor costs for firms, as did the various protective labor laws and social insurance programs through periodic increases in standards, coverage, and benefits. Nevertheless, the system was compatible with low inflation and relatively strong output growth as a result of the low strike rates, stable fiscal and monetary policies, and, most important, strong increases in productivity. This increase in productivity was itself partially a result of the IR system in that collective bargaining demands forced firms to improve management methods, streamline the production process, and adopt new technologies and capital equipment.

From the vantage point of the early 1970s, it appeared that the unionized sector of the economy would remain the dominant influence in employment relations, particularly given the rapid spread of collective bargaining in the public sector. In hindsight, it is clear that the traditional IR system was, in fact, already slipping in power and influence while an alternative, nonunion system was rapidly gaining momentum (Kochan, Katz, and McKersie 1986). The extent of the decline of the former and the growth of the latter would not come into stark relief, however, until the 1980s.

The fundamental problem facing the union sector in the 1970s was the gradual loss of economic competitiveness as a result of developments both at the bargaining table and on the shop floor. During the decade union bargainers were able to win wage and benefit increases that far outpaced those obtained by nonunion workers. The result was a substantial increase in the union-nonunion labor cost differential (G. Johnson 1984; Kaufman and Stephan 1987). Unionized firms could still compete effectively if they could offset the growth in payroll costs with concomitantly greater gains in productivity (thus holding unit labor costs constant). Unfortunately, as the percentage increase in compensation costs began to escalate into the double-digit range, the growth rate of productivity plummeted. There are many reasons for this slowdown, but the increasingly outmoded, bureaucratized, and restrictive system of managing work in unionized firms was certainly a factor, as was the increase in government regulation of the workplace (Denison 1985; Gray 1987).

The result of this divergent trend in compensation costs and productivity gains was that unionized firms experienced significant pressure on their profit margins. To protect their profits, firms raised their prices, restricted new capital investment and/or product development, disinvested in unionized facilities and built new, nonunion plants, further automated production, and used other such methods (Hirsch 1991). During the 1970s economic growth was sufficiently strong, and barriers to lower cost competition sufficiently high, that the resulting decline in union density (membership as a percentage of nonagricultural employment) was modest (27 to 23 percent). It was clear, however, that the New Deal IR system was under stress and showing signs of atrophy.

Stress turned to crisis in the 1980s. The crisis had intellectual, political, economic and organizational origins.

The central tenet of the ILE policy program—the use of collective bargaining, government regulation, and activist management of fiscal and monetary policies to ensure competitive economic outcomes and industrial democracy—suffered a significant decline in intellectual support. In many ways the attack on the ILE program was a counterrevolution by the modern-day adherents of classical economics and the PM school. In economics, the institutional and neoinstitutional theories of labor markets, with their emphasis on labor market imperfections and inequality of bargaining power, were largely supplanted by the Chicago-based neoclassical theory with its emphasis on the virtues of free markets and competition. Viewed from a neoclassical perspective, unions, government regulation, and activist monetary and fiscal policies were undesirable institutional interventions that caused economic inefficiency and the redistribution of income to various interest groups.[2] Economists were also increasingly skeptical whether full-employment fiscal and monetary policies and extensive collective bargaining coverage were compatible with low inflation. ILE economists advocated a resolution of this contradiction through further government intervention in the form of "incomes policies" (e.g., wage-price controls), an idea that was rapidly losing support during the 1970s among both economists and policymakers.

Many management and behavioral science scholars also lost faith in the ILE policy program. In this case the theoretical inspiration for revisionism came from the related fields of organizational behavior, organizational development, and human resource management (Beer and

Spector 1984; Walton and Lawrence 1985; Lawler 1986). These fields, often lumped together under the label human resources, were the 1980s version of the PM school that had originated in the 1920s.[3] Like their forebears of the 1920s, HR scholars were unenthusiastic about labor unions and most forms of government regulation of the workplace. As they saw it, unions and government regulation were antithetical to economic efficiency and job satisfaction because they institutionalized adversarialism, stifled work effort and creativity, and promoted a rigid, bureaucratized, and litigious system of workplace organization. Harking back to the basic ideas developed by the personnel practitioners of the 1920s and the human relations academics of the 1930–50s, these scholars sought to eliminate adversarialism and promote a "win-win" outcome. The result, they thought, would be higher economic performance for the organization and greater economic and psychological rewards for the individual, achieved through the development and implementation of a "commitment model" of workplace organization in which a congruence of interests would be established between workers and the organization through the use of a consensual leadership style, participative methods of management, group production methods, pay-for-performance compensation systems, and a formalized method of dispute resolution.

The political environment in the 1980s also turned hostile to the New Deal IR system. The election of Ronald Reagan to the presidency in 1980 precipitated a significant turn toward political conservatism with respect to government labor policy. Reagan was an outspoken champion of free markets and of minimalist role for government, a philosophical belief that was at direct odds with the ILE policy program erected over the previous half-century. Over the next decade the Reagan administration, and to a lesser degree that of George Bush, implemented several policy initiatives that struck at the heart of the New Deal system. The organizing ability and bargaining power of labor unions, for example, were heavily circumscribed by adverse changes in the interpretation of law and precedent by the National Labor Relations Board (Weiler 1990). Similarly, Reagan's decision to fire the air traffic controllers when they went on strike in 1981 was widely interpreted as sending a signal to private sector employers that it was alright to play hardball with unions. Reagan and Bush also sought to eliminate or soften numerous workplace regulations or protections, such as the minimum wage and occupational safety and health laws. As a final insult, the Reagan administration seldom consulted union leaders on matters of national economic and social policy, effectively abrogating the tripartite labor-management-government system of social bargaining.

The adverse economic environment in the 1980s also contributed to the decline of the New Deal IR system. Although the cost and pricing structure of unionized firms became increasingly uncompetitive during the 1970s, their survival was protected by both modestly strong growth in the domestic economy and various barriers to entry in the product market that largely shielded them from the competitive threat posed by lower-cost rivals. Four economic events occurred in the 1980s, however, that exposed these firms to far greater competitive pressures: the back-to-back recessions of 1980 and 1981–82; the deregulation of such key industries as transportation and communication (a policy initiated by the Carter administration); the emergence of a significant nonunion segment in several hitherto heavily unionized industries as a result of the building of new plants in the South or new "double-breasted" operating divisions; and the considerably heightened level of international competition, precipitated in part by the sharp appreciation of the dollar in the first half of the 1980s. The results of these events were large-scale layoffs, plant closings, and bankruptcies among unionized firms, reflected in a plunge in both employment and union membership in the heavily organized goods-producing sector of the economy.

Finally, organizational developments, particularly with respect to management practices and strategies, played an important role in the decline of the New Deal IR system. By most accounts, American management became far more determined to operate nonunion (D. Mills 1981; Kochan, Katz, and McKersie 1986; Barbash 1986). This strategy was pursued along two tracks (Cappelli and Chalykoff 1985). One track was "union substitution," whereby companies practiced progressive employment relations in an attempt to eliminate workers' desire for a union. The epitome of this approach was the implementation of the HR-inspired commitment model of work organization. The second track was "union suppression," whereby companies tried to discourage or frustrate workers in pursuit of unionization by the use of threats of reprisal and job loss, illegal firings, and extended litigation. Permanently replacing strikers, a move that undercut the fundamental source of union power, was another key part of the management strategy.

The net effect of these events and developments was that they plunged the New Deal IR system into crisis, the brunt of which was borne by the union movement. Between 1979 and 1989, unions lost almost 5 million members and saw the proportion of the organized work force shrink from 23 to 17 percent. More ominously, by the late 1980s, unions were able to win fewer than 100,000 new members through the NLRB representation election process, while many times that number were lost through decertifications, plant closing, layoffs, and striker replacement (Freeman 1988). In effect, the organized labor movement was slowly being bled to death and its dwindling band of intellectual and political supporters were powerless to reverse the process. Not since the 1920s had the prospects for organized labor looked so bleak (Dubofsky 1985). Meanwhile, the American economy generated more than 19 million new jobs over the decade, almost all in nonunion firms. The message was clear: the New Deal IR system, and the collective bargaining process at its core, was rapidly shrinking in size and importance, while the nonunion sector of the economy was increasingly becoming the dynamic source of both new jobs and new ideas. Not unexpectedly, these trends reverberated strongly through academia, with doleful consequences for the field of industrial relations.

ACADEMIC PROGRAMS IN THE 1980s

Viewed broadly, the 1980s was a period of significant growth for academic programs specializing in employment-related subjects. For example, Georgianna Herman (1984:A-5) found that the number of master of arts and master of science degree programs in personnel, industrial relations, and human resource management grew from twenty-six in 1974 to sixty-six in 1984.[4] The number of Ph.D. degree programs in these areas more than doubled, from six to fourteen. Similarly, Joseph Krislov and John Mead (1987) conducted a survey of IR and HR programs in the mid-1980s and found that of the seventy-seven units in their sample, twenty-three had been established in the 1970s and nine in the 1980s. Finally, a directory published in June 1988 by *Personnel Journal* of universities in the United States with HR and IR programs or majors lists more than 150 entries.[5]

These trends are both good and bad news for academic IR. The good news is that a rising tide raises all boats, and one benefactor of increased student demand for employment-related subjects was the major IR academic programs. The foundation of academic IR is the multidisciplinary, degree-granting IR units, such as those at Cornell, Minnesota, Illinois, Wisconsin, Rutgers, and Michigan State. (Other important IR units, such as the ones at Berkeley and UCLA, sponsor only research.) These programs have large and distinguished faculties and good to excellent reputations in the academic marketplace. Thus, even as employment in the unionized sector of the economy plummeted in the 1980s, the top-tier IR programs not only survived the decade intact but actually experienced a modest increase in graduate enrollments. Unpublished data collected by the University Council of Industrial Relations and Human Resource Programs (the former IR center directors' group) also indicates that IR doctoral students continued to fare well in the academic job market.

The bad news for academic IR is that even in an expanding market the best the top-tier programs could do was hold their own, while smaller or lesser-known programs suffered considerable slippage. A major problem was that student demand for employment-related courses shifted sharply toward the HR end of the spectrum and away from the IR topics (narrowly defined) that had traditionally dominated IR curricula. Walter Franke (1987:476) documents, for example, that in the 1950s more than half the elective courses chosen by graduate students of the Illinois IR program were in the labor-management relations area, while only slightly more than one-third of such courses were in personnel and OB. Thirty years later, the proportions were almost reversed.

In a similar vein, Charles Rehmus (1985:592), the former dean of the program at Cornell, observed that "demand for courses and faculty in the fields of personnel, human resources administration, and organizational behavior has roughly doubled in the last decade." Reasons for this demand shift include student perceptions that better job opportunities await graduates with concentrations or majors in HRM and OB; the negative stigma carried by the IR label in the job market because of its association with unionism and a pro–collective bargaining ideology; the sizable growth of enrollment in business schools, which tend to give more emphasis to HR-related courses; and the accreditation requirements of the American Association of Collegiate Schools of Business, which mandate that master of business administration curricula require at least one organizational behavior course, but have no such requirement concerning IR (Begin 1987; Franke 1987, Fossum 1987; Lewin 1988a).[6]

The impact of this shift in demand toward HRM and OB courses and majors varied across programs and universities. The top-tier IR programs experienced the least disruption of their basic structures and identities. Several circumstances worked in their favor. First, these programs already offered concentrations and extensive coursework in HR, so it was relatively simple (internal politics aside) to augment the HR end of the curriculum and faculty. Second, they already had excellent reputations and thus employers continued to seek out their graduates despite the negative stigma of the IR label, and students continued to apply to these programs given their good record of job placement. Third, nearly all of the top-tier IR programs were in states with a relatively high level of union density, providing both greater job opportunities for students with an IR degree and greater political clout from organized labor to protect funding for the programs.

Programs that were smaller, less well known, or located in states with low union densities often had to make bigger adjustments. One common practice was to drop the IR label from the name of the program, in favor of some HR-related alternative, such as Personnel and Employment Relations (Georgia State) or Human Resources Institute (Alabama).[7] Other programs kept the IR label but added an HR-related term. Loyola University (Chicago), for example, changed the name of its institute from Industrial Relations to Human Resources and Industrial Relations. In either case, the basic multidisciplinary structure of the program was preserved, but at the cost of abandoning the original "all aspects of employment relations" meaning of the IR label.

Still other programs were forced to make more wrenching adjustments. The shift in student demand toward HR subjects, the decline of interdisciplinary (or even multidisciplinary) research in employment relations, and the loss of the membership and political power of labor unions all eroded the original justification for free-standing IR units. As curricula and student enrollments shifted toward HR subjects, these units increasingly came to resemble the personnel and OB wing of a traditional department of management (Begin 1987). Likewise, as faculty research became ever more specialized in focus because of the continued pressures of science-building, faculty interest and participation in cross-disciplinary activities waned and universities began to examine whether the research payoff of an interdisciplinary unit was worth the administrative complexities and costs.

Finally, the sharp drop in the size of the union sector and in the number of job opportunities in labor-management relations called into question both the need for and the viability of IR programs, while the erosion of organized labor's political power made it far easier for university administrators to consider the once unthinkable—shuttering or significantly restructuring the programs.

The result was that free-standing IR units were merged or absorbed into business programs or departments. The experience of the IR unit at Purdue University is typical.

In 1957, an interdisciplinary body of faculty from across the Purdue campus was organized to administer M.S. and Ph.D. programs in industrial relations. According to James Dworkin (1988:462–63), the program originally had a heavy labor relations orientation, although some coursework in personnel management was offered. Over the years several changes were made to the program. In 1962, it was transferred to the business school. Then, in 1967, the interdisciplinary Ph.D. program was eliminated because of a lack of participation by faculty. Next, the program was restructured so that more general business courses were required (partly in response to accreditation pressures). Concurrently, the number of traditional IR courses offered was reduced. Finally, in 1986, the title of the M.S. program was changed from industrial relations to human resources management. Currently, this program, as well as the Ph.D. program in organizational behavior and human resources management, is taught by faculty from the business school's Department of Organizational Behavior and Human Resources Management. Students in the M.S. program are required to take sixteen courses, of which five are OB and HRM courses, four are general management courses, four are research methods courses, one is a labor economics course, one is a labor law course, and one is a collective bargaining course.

The end result is that *industrial relations* has disappeared from the name of the program at Purdue and the program has been relocated to the business school and has a substantial management orientation. The proportion of coursework devoted to the ILE perspective on industrial relations, and to union-related topics in particular, has also been reduced significantly. The program continues to include coursework from both economics and the behavioral sciences, but the proportion of work in the behavioral sciences has been expanded significantly while the relative contribution of economics has been reduced (labor economics is

now only one course out of sixteen). Finally, the multidisciplinary character of the curriculum and faculty has also been significantly reduced.

During the 1980s the structure and curriculum of a number of other
IR programs were changed in much the same direction as at Purdue.[8]
Whether these changes are to be welcomed or lamented is, in large part,
a matter of personal opinion. Advocates of the ILE school generally
regard these developments as a quasi disaster in that they threaten the
survival of the IR label, the interdisciplinary approach to teaching and
research, and the intellectual and ideological emphasis on the adversarial
relationship, collective bargaining, and accommodated conflict. Most
advocates of the PM (HR) school, however, welcome these changes as
a long overdue shift from an outdated 1930s-era approach to the subject
of employer-employee relations to a modern, progressive approach that
is consistent with both the revolution in behavioral science research
and the economic realities of the marketplace. Whatever one's position,
clearly academic IR programs in the United States are undergoing a
fundamental transformation that represents a renaissance for the PM
school and an eclipse of the ILE school.

The forces discussed above that so significantly affected IR programs
in the 1980s also affected the birth of new IR units. For all intents and
purposes, the creation of free-standing, degree-granting IR units with
multidisciplinary faculties came to a halt. To the best of my knowledge,
no such unit with *industrial relations* in its title was created in the 1980s.[9]

The creation of IR degree programs and majors also slowed to a trickle.
Herman's surveys of IR and HR programs (1984) reveal that of the net
increase of forty-three master's degree programs between 1974 and 1984,
only eight included one or more of the terms *industrial relations, labor
relations, labor studies,* or *employee relations* in their titles, while the
remainder included one or more of the terms *personnel, human resource*
(or *human relations*), *organization,* or *management.* In some cases these
new programs were multidisciplinary in character, but more often they
were housed in a department of management or a graduate school of
business and provided a largely behavioral science, nonunion perspective
on employment relations.

Finally, even as the birth of new IR units was coming to a standstill,
a simultaneous increase in the "death" or downsizing of existing units
was occurring. Some universities, such as Columbia, Chicago, and Pace,
chose to eliminate their programs altogether. Other schools, such as

Michigan, Berkeley, and Massachusetts, reduced the operating budgets and/or the number of faculty positions of their IR units significantly. In both cases, the IR units had become vulnerable to the budget ax because they served a subject area and constituency that university administrators increasingly regarded as of marginal importance.

IR RESEARCH

The bright spot for industrial relations in the 1980s was research. By most accounts (e.g., Strauss and Feuille 1981), IR research suffered through a period of the doldrums in the 1960s and early 1970s and reached an intellectual and creative nadir sometime in the middle of the decade. As I perceive it, IR research then staged a modest rebound that persisted through the 1980s.

The clearest case of a rebound is in IR-related research monographs. The "big book" of the 1960s was Richard Walton and Robert McKersie's *A Behavioral Theory of Labor Negotiations* (1965). It is not clear what book would be selected for the 1970s, for although several are certainly high-quality works of scholarship (e.g., Getman, Goldberg, and Herman 1976), none is recognized as an IR "classic."

In the 1980s, however, several monographs significantly influenced industrial relations teaching and research and are likely to be cited by IR scholars for many years to come. They are (in chronological order) *The Elements of Industrial Relations* (1984), by Jack Barbash; *What Do Unions Do?* (1984), by Richard Freeman and James Medoff; and *The Transformation of American Industrial Relations* (1986), by Thomas Kochan, Harry Katz, and Robert McKersie.

A common characteristic of these three books, and of IR research in general during the 1980s, was the renewed interest in theory-building.[10] This must rank as one of the most heartening developments of the decade. Before the 1980s, there was much decrying the lack of IR theory but few attempts to remedy the deficiency. The most notable attempt at theorizing was Dunlop's *Industrial Relations Systems* (1958). A second effort worth mention was by Gerald Somers (1969). Somers argued that the process of exchange is the common denominator that underlies all behavior in the employment relationship and that the analysis of exchange can provide the integrating framework needed by the field. His ideas never caught on, however.

After the appearance of Somers's work, the subject of theory was rarely addressed in the United States for the next decade (but see Hills 1975).[11] As the field headed into the 1980s, however, theory-building again moved to the fore, partly as a response, no doubt, to the field's sagging intellectual fortunes. The first contribution in this regard was Thomas Kochan's book *Collective Bargaining and Industrial Relations* (1980). Although ostensibly written as a textbook, Kochan used it as a vehicle to address larger issues, particularly the integration of viewpoints and research findings from labor economics, industrial relations (institutionalism), and the behavioral sciences.[12]

Kochan's next effort, co-authored with Harry Katz and Robert McKersie, was *The Transformation of American Industrial Relations*. The book's major intellectual contribution is its development of a three-tier strategic choice framework to analyze the evolution and interaction of the union and nonunion sectors of the economy. This framework overlaps with Dunlop's in that it emphasizes the importance of the external economic and political structure in which the industrial relations system is imbedded, but it also elaborates on the different levels of decision-making in the system, the role of business strategy, and the interdependency of the union and nonunion sectors.[13] As a result of these two books, plus numerous other research contributions, Kochan came to be widely regarded as the leading research figure of the younger generation in industrial relations.

Another person who made significant contributions to IR research in the 1980s is labor economist Richard Freeman. Freeman is an indefatigable writer whose articles and books on various aspects of unions and collective bargaining are often cited. Of these, the most important is *What Do Unions Do,* co-authored with James Medoff. The book's major conceptual contribution is the exit/voice model of trade unionism. The basic idea is that unions, by providing workers with a formalized channel for making grievances, complaints, and suggestions, can contribute to increased economic efficiency through lower quit rates, higher productivity, and improved management practices. All of these factors are often ignored or underestimated in the standard neoclassical "union as a monopoly" analysis.[14] The book is also notable for its use of an impressive array of data sets and advanced econometric methods to analyze the impact of unions on a wide range of economic outcomes, such as wages, fringe benefits, quit rates, productivity, and income inequality.[15]

Jack Barbash, an institutional labor economist and emeritus professor

at the University of Wisconsin, also made important theoretical contributions to IR research in the 1980s. Barbash has been the major
chronicler of the ILE theory of industrial relations and the expositor of
the contributions of Commons to the development of the field. His most
important scholarly work is *The Elements of Industrial Relations* (1984).
The book identifies the origins of labor problems in the employment
relationship and then analyzes the response of management, workers,
and government to these problems. According to Barbash, labor problems originate in the clash between management's drive for efficiency
and workers' deep-felt needs for security. These needs lead workers to
seek various restrictive or protective work rules and regulations, which
are enforced through either the social sanctions of informal work groups
or the economic power of a union. The book represents the most historically accurate and intellectually insightful conceptualization of the
IR paradigm as conceived by the field's founding fathers, albeit with an
overemphasis on the ILE perspective.

Other significant contributions to the development of a theoretical
base for industrial relations include the integrative model of industrial
conflict by Hoyt Wheeler (1985), the employment relations systems
model by James P. Begin (1990), and the models of workplace control
by William Cooke (1985) and Steven Hills (1992). Neither these authors nor the ones cited above discovered the holy grail of industrial
relations (i.e., the integrative theoretical framework that would transform industrial relations into a bona fide academic discipline), but each
added conceptual substance to a field that desperately needed it.[16]

A modest positive trend in the direction of IR research was also
discernible during the 1980s in the field's various journals. Several new
journals were established as forums for IR research, including the *Journal
of Labor Research* and the *Employee Responsibilities and Rights Journal*, as
well as a new annual research volume, *Advances in Industrial and Labor
Relations*. Further, the *Industrial and Labor Relations Review* made a perceptible effort to broaden its mix of articles (an effort unfortunately not
apparent in the editorial policy of the field's other major journal,
Industrial Relations). There was a greater proportion of articles on personnel and HRM subjects, historical case studies and behavioral-based
research, as well as symposiums on behavioral research, labor history,
and compensation that attempted to revive the multidisciplinary coalition that had once been IR.[17] Finally, it is my impression that the

theoretical and statistical sophistication as well as the intellectual substance of the articles in the journals increased over the decade.

Another positive trend was the increased interest among IR scholars in the impact of management practices and policies on the structure, performance, and long-term evolution of the industrial relations system. During the 1960s and 1970s the management side of the employment relationship largely dropped from sight as an industrial relations research topic. This relatively one-sided perspective became increasingly untenable in the 1980s as it became obvious that companies, not unions, were the dynamic agents of change in industrial relations (Strauss 1984). The response was a boomlet of interesting, high-quality research on management strategy (Kochan, McKersie, and Cappelli 1984; Verma 1985; Kochan, Katz, and McKersie 1986; Lewin 1987) and the impact of firm IR and HR policies on profits and productivity (Clark 1984; Voos and Mishel 1986; Kleiner et al. 1987; Ehrenberg 1990). This literature had four salutary effects: it brought the subject of management back into industrial relations; it imparted a more dynamic, long-term perspective to theorizing in the field; it promoted a cross-fertilization of research between IR and OB and HRM scholars; and it motivated labor economists to become interested in such personnel and HRM topics as compensation, the structure of employment contracts, and the promotion of work effort.

Counterbalanced against these positive developments are several negative trends. First, there is an ever greater obsession among younger IR scholars with methodological and data issues, a trend that too often comes at the cost of relevance and insight. Second, multidisciplinary and interdisciplinary research remains a rarity in industrial relations, perpetuating academic parochialism. Third, much academic IR research is narrowly focused on explaining the minutiae of past or current behavior, while little examines such big questions as the appropriateness of the nation's labor law, the competitiveness of American IR practices, and the alternatives (if any) to the present system of employee representation (but see Heckscher 1988; Hirsch 1991; Voos and Mishel 1991; Weiler 1990). Fourth, American IR scholars tend to neglect work published overseas, especially in Great Britian. Finally, one has to wonder about the long-term prospects for IR research (narrowly defined) if the decline of the union sector continues through the 1990s. The burst of influential research in the 1980s most likely reflected, in part, a short-term phenomenon as scholars rushed to understand both the causes and the consequences of the dramatic decline in the fortunes of organized labor. The dramatic growth of the IR system in the 1930s and 1940s stimulated a similar burst of research. Once this vein of research is mined, and assuming the union sector continues to shrink in size and influence, it is reasonable to assume that academic researchers will abandon traditional IR topics and journals for other, more fertile fields of inquiry.

IRRA

The events of the 1980s significantly eroded the organizational vitality of the Industrial Relations Research Association. Many of the underlying causes originated in earlier years, as discussed in the previous chapter, but their effect was intensified in the adverse climate of the 1980s.

On the surface, the health of the IRRA appeared relatively good. The most explicit statement of this viewpoint is in the final report of the IRRA's Comprehensive Review Committee (IRRA 1988a). The committee was appointed in 1986 by the association's executive board to take stock of and make recommendations concerning the organization's structure, membership, finances, programs, and publishing activities.[18] The committee was codirected by Clark Kerr and John Dunlop, two of the early presidents of the organization. The final report states (pp. 2–3):

> In at least four fundamental respects, the IRRA has proved to be a viable and effective association: First, its membership has grown steadily throughout the years. . . . Second, its finances are in sound and satisfactory condition. . . . Third, IRRA has benefited greatly from a lean and professionally sophisticated administration. . . . Fourth, IRRA has indeed attracted into its membership (a) academics from a variety of disciplines, and also (b) practitioners from the ranks of the unions, management, government at all levels, and neutrals. . . . These findings and developments lend support to the view that the IRRA's founding objectives remain valid and that an Association designed to implement these objectives retains relevance and vitality.

A critical review of the four areas mentioned above, as well as of other indicators of organizational health, suggest a far less sanguine assessment. Consider IRRA membership, for example.

As the report claimed, IRRA membership has grown steadily since the organization's founding. Membership in the national IRRA increased from almost 1,000 in 1948 to 4,780 in 1990 and, significantly, this upward trend continued, albeit quite modestly, through the 1980s (from 4,589 in 1979 to 4,780 in 1990, or about a 4 percent increase). Membership growth at the local chapter level was substantially greater, from 6,619 in 1979 to 8,900 in 1990 (a 34 percent increase) (see IRRA 1990:405).

The report largely omits discussion of three other less favorable developments. The first is that although national membership increased in the 1980s, membership among academics declined (from 1,590 to 1,499, or 6 percent). The drop-off occurred in all disciplines (except the "other" category). Second, as academic membership in the IRRA was falling, the number of academic members of the Academy of Management, the IRRA's major academic rival, was expanding rapidly. The number of persons belonging to the organizational behavior and personnel and human resource management sections of the Academy grew 42 percent during the 1980s, from 3,580 to 5,078. Third, the growth area for IRRA membership was among nonacademics, but even here the IRRA lagged behind other professional organizations that catered to IR and HR practitioners. Membership in the Society for Human Resource Management (SHRM, formerly the American Society for Personnel Administration), for example, grew from 27,501 in 1980 to 44,299 in 1990, a 61 percent increase. Among nonacademics in the IRRA, the two occupational groups that registered the largest increase in membership in the 1980s were unionists and arbitrators, two of the occupations in the economy that are *least* likely to grow in the future.

The second and third indicators of the organization's vitality listed in the report are its "sound finances" and "lean and professionally sophisticated administration." Certainly, sound finances are a prerequisite for a viable and effective organization, and a high-quality professional staff is a big plus, but do these indicators really tell us whether the IRRA is a robust organization or one headed for stagnation? The link is quite weak, I think, and suggests a certain groping for good news.

Finally, the fourth indicator listed is the association's ability to attract academics from a variety of disciplines and practitioners from management, unions, and government. The IRRA does draw academic members from a wide variety of disciplines, including most of those with relevance to the employment relationship. What the report does not say, however, is that the proportion of members from the behavioral sciences (the growth area in employment relations) is small and probably decreasing. In 1990, for example, only about 15 percent of the academics affiliated with the organization listed their major specialty as human resources, organizational behavior, sociology, or psychology.

The IRRA changed the occupational classification system in the mid–1980s, which prevents a reliable comparison of membership growth rates over the 1980s for individual behavioral science disciplines except organizational behavior. In the case of OB, membership registered a net decline between 1979 and 1990. Further, membership in sociology, psychology, and political science apparently became so small that in 1987 these categories were lumped under the "other" designation.

The IRRA does have a diverse and fairly well-balanced membership among nonacademics. In 1990, the following groups were represented at the national level: business (18 percent), union (10 percent), government (9 percent), and arbitration, legal, and consulting (22 percent). The only question I would raise is what proportion of the management members come from nonunion companies. Data are unavailable, but I conjecture that the proportion is small. If this is so, the IRRA has once again allied itself with a segment of the employment relations community that has a dim prospect for future growth.

For the reasons cited above, I do not think that the data support the claim of the IRRA Comprehensive Review Committee that the association has retained its vitality and effectiveness. Rather, the data support the opposite conclusion; namely, that the IRRA has experienced a significant hollowing-out of membership and participation. A look beyond the four criteria listed above strengthens this conclusion.

The most disturbing sign of organizational decline is the substantial diminution in the number of nationally prominent scholars who are active members of the group. While national prominence is admittedly difficult to measure, there is some evidence to back up this claim. Specifically, many labor economists consider the labor studies group of the National Bureau of Economic Research (NBER) to be the leading forum for economics research on labor unions and collective bargaining. Only 28 percent of the members belong to the IRRA. Another piece of evidence pertains to the percentage of IRRA members who are researchers in human resource management. Only nine of the thirty people (30 percent) on the editorial board of *Human Resource Management Review* are IRRA members.

The underrepresentation of intellectual talent in the IRRA reflects both developments in the broader field of industrial relations and organizational problems specific to the association. The first such problem is that most academics do not regard the association's publications as comparable in intellectual and analytical quality to leading academic journals or the proceedings of other professional associations.[19] The second problem is that the IRRA's winter meetings (the more research-oriented of the two annual meetings) are held at the same time and place as the meetings of the American Economic Association, an arrangement management and behavioral science scholars do not find attractive. The third problem is that the IRRA's meeting arrangements have discouraged participation by academics who are not already part of the organization or who lack connections with active members. The principal barrier is the small number of competitive paper sessions and the large number of by-invitation sessions at both of the annual meetings, an arrangement that fosters the operation of a strong "old-boys' network."[20] The fourth problem is the association's close intellectual and ideological ties to trade unionism and collective bargaining. On a research level, the decline of the trade union movement has reduced the number of scholars interested in labor-management relations, yet it remains the central focal point for IRRA program sessions and publications, while others object to the pro-union value system that permeates the organization.[21] The fifth and final problem is that the political process in the IRRA has tended to concentrate effective control of the organization among ILE-oriented labor economists and their allies, as revealed by who has been selected to serve as the organization's president over the last two decades.[22] This narrow political base, and the feelings of disenfranchisement that it fosters, has likewise discouraged participation by faculty from other disciplinary and ideological perspectives.[23]

8

INDUSTRIAL RELATIONS IN THE 1990s AND BEYOND

THE EVIDENCE INDICATES that industrial relations suffered a significant decline in intellectual and organizational vitality in the 1980s. Assuming this assessment is correct, the question then is whether the decline was a cyclical phenomenon, and thus to be followed by a revival of the field, or whether it was part of a long-term trend that will lead to the field's marginalization if not its eventual disappearance.

After analyzing alternative scenarios, I conclude that the experience of the 1980s is a harbinger of continued decline for the ILE version of industrial relations that now defines the field. If this bleak forecast is correct, the major challenge facing IR scholars is the development and implementation of a strategy for change that will ensure that industrial relations as a field, if not its name, not only survives but prospers in the years ahead. This chapter endeavors to provide such a strategy.

ALTERNATIVE SCENARIOS OF THE FUTURE

Predicting the future of academic IR, like the stock market, is inherently risky because of the significant influence played by external economic and political events that are largely impossible to anticipate. One must also be leery of making linear extrapolations based on the recent past, for the history of the field has unfolded in a decidedly nonlinear manner. Considering the remarkable number of parallels between the economic and political events of the 1920s and those of the 1980s, one should be doubly cautious in making predictions about the

1990s in light of the tremendous upheaval in employment relations that occurred in the 1930s (Dubofsky 1985).[1]

IR AS A FIELD OF STUDY

The future of industrial relations as a field of study depends crucially on how the intellectual boundaries of the field are defined and on what the field is called. Two definitions of the field co-exist today. The first is a broad, all-inclusive definition that equates the field with the study of all aspects of the employment relationship. According to this definition, the intellectual domain of industrial relations includes both the ILE and the PM schools and their principal subfields of study, labor economics, labor history, labor law, organizational behavior and human resource management, industrial and organizational psychology, and industrial sociology. This is the original pre-1960s definition of industrial relations.

The second definition is more recent in origin and more narrow in scope. According to this definition, the field is divided into two wings, HR and IR, where HR is the modern-day equivalent of the PM school and IR is the modern-day equivalent of the ILE school. Industrial relations is thus defined as one particular approach to the study of labor problems and employer-employee relations. This approach is based on certain assumptions and values (e.g., the irreducible level of adversarialism in the employment relationship; labor's inequality of bargaining power; the necessity of independent employee representation; the importance of accommodating rather than eliminating conflict; and the efficacy of economic, social, and political pluralism) and on the value of certain methods or policies for resolving or ameliorating labor problems, such as collective bargaining, protective labor legislation, social insurance programs, macroeconomic full-employment policies, and tripartite (management, union, government) policy formulation and problem-solving at the national level. In practice, this definition tends to equate the field with the study of trade unionism and collective bargaining, although the intellectual boundaries are actually wider.

The label attached to the field will also influence its future. One approach is to define the field generically in terms of its subject matter, while the other is to define it in terms of a particular label. Thus, from the perspective of the second approach, the field is "industrial relations" only as long as the IR label is attached to it and loss of the label is tantamount to demise of the field. From the perspective of the first approach, industrial relations can be called employment relations, human resources and labor relations, or any other name and it will still be industrial relations in content and spirit as long as the basic intellectual approach to the subject does not fundamentally change.

The future of the field depends crucially on which combination of perspectives is adopted. For example, if industrial relations is broadly defined to include all aspects of the employment relationship and a generic title is acceptable, then the future of the field is bright. The outcomes of the employment relationship, and the organizations and administrative practices that condition them, are arguably among the most important topics studied in all of the social sciences. Rates of pay, conditions of work, levels of productivity, the amount of conflict between workers and managers, and the degree of job satisfaction among employees are at the nexus of two fundamental social concerns: the performance of the economic system and the remuneration and well-being of the work force. These concerns can only increase in importance as a higher proportion of the population works at a paying job; competitive pressures on the American economy from overseas rivals intensify further; and the nation attempts to overcome the productivity slowdown and stagnation in real incomes of the last two decades. Add to these trends the growing movement in the United States to view employees and the organization and administration of work as strategic sources of competitive advantage and the outlook for industrial relations has to be judged as quite promising. This would presumably be reflected in strong growth in new IR academic programs and student enrollments, in the emergence of industrial relations as a major area of study in business school curricula on a par with marketing and finance, and in a major increase in the membership of the various IR-related professional associations.

A different conceptualization of the field leads to a diametrically opposite conclusion, however. For example, if the field is narrowly defined as the study of unions and collective bargaining and is labeled industrial relations, then the future is relatively gloomy. The best prognosis is that the unionized sector of the economy will continue to shrink in size and importance until it represents less than 10 percent of the work force (Freeman 1988). An academic field built on the study of unions will perforce have to shrink in tandem. For example, with the decline of the union sector and job opportunities therein, and the negative stigma carried by the IR label because of its association with unionism, students will increasingly shun IR-labeled programs and union-related courses, forcing first the weaker programs and then the stronger ones to transform themselves into HR units. As the number of IR courses and IR units shrink, so too will the number of graduates of doctoral programs who are trained in industrial relations, leading to a gradual withering of academic talent in the field and a concomitant decline in IR research, journals, and professional associations. As long as there are labor unions, there will be a field of industrial relations, but it will become a niche field with a presence at only a few universities.

Somewhere between these two extremes lies the actual future of industrial relations. My guess is that, absent significant changes, the latter scenario more closely represents the future than does the former. The reasons are several.

First, industrial relations sacrificed its claim to intellectual sovereignty over the employment relationship some thirty years ago and too much has happened for the field to reassert its rights of ownership. The field does not have the intellectual manpower, integrative theory, or flexibility in its values to accomplish the task. For better or worse, therefore, industrial relations will continue to be seen as one approach to the study of employment problems—an approach currently identified with the ILE policy program of support for collective bargaining and various forms of government regulation of labor markets.

Second, given the ILE orientation of industrial relations, its future depends critically on the course of employer-employee relations and, in particular, on the fortunes of the organized labor movement. If union membership and political power continue to decline and no major economic or political upheavals disrupt the employment relationship, academic and popular interest in industrial relations will slide further. Alternatively, if the trade union movement becomes revitalized or the nation's labor law is changed in a way that makes it substantially easier for unions to win new members, or a new form of employee representation (e.g., works councils) becomes widely established, or some national crisis precipitates significant conflict and unrest in the workplace, industrial relations will be well positioned to experience a renaissance. Although either outcome is possible, the odds favor the former.

Third, the future of industrial relations also depends on its ability to generate new, intellectually exciting ideas in the world of science and for these ideas to serve as catalysts for the development of new, progressive business practices and public policies pertaining to the workplace.[2] As currently practiced, ILE-style industrial relations falls significantly short of this goal. A serious problem in this regard is that academic research, in response to the culture and incentives spawned by science-building, has become ever narrower, more obsessed with methodology, and more detached from the world of practice and policy. This is reflected, in turn, in the research reported in the IR journals, most of which makes a contribution to knowledge but at the same time is too narrowly academic and backward-looking to serve as a significant source of the "new thinking" that the field requires.

Another problem militating against such "new thinking" is the strong intellectual and philosophical commitment of many scholars to the New Deal industrial relations system and their corresponding fear that a critical examination of this system and/or advocacy of some alternative will place them in a position that is perceived as anti-union.[3] This commitment to past practices and policies may well result in industrial relations playing a largely reactive role in what will surely be two of the major IR policy issues of the 1990s—the overhaul of the Wagner Act and the search for new and improved models of workplace governance and employee representation.

Finally, there is a part of industrial relations that clearly faces a bleak future. That is the name of the field. The term *industrial relations* is perceived by most people as associated with unionism and collective bargaining and with a blue-collar, factory economy. This liability most affects academic programs since they must actively compete for students who increasingly regard an industrial relations–labeled degree as a handicap in the job market. The label is also a liability, though to a lesser degree, as a title for an area of academic research, and the journals and professional associations therein, since in this arena industrial relations stands for a set of ideas rather than a credential in the job market. Some scholars have attempted to preserve the term's lease on life by arguing that *industrial* applies to the study of all employment relationships, not just those in manufacturing and/or in unionized firms.[4] I predict that this effort will be unsuccessful, however, and that the term *industrial relations* will gradually fade (not always quietly) from the academic scene, particularly as a label for academic programs.

IR INSTITUTES AND ACADEMIC PROGRAMS

The future of IR institutes and academic programs will closely mirror that of IR as a field of study. Several events can be anticipated. First, no new IR-labeled academic programs will be established in the United States. Second, several existing IR-labeled programs will abandon the IR label altogether or will modify it significantly by including an HR-related term. This process will initially affect smaller, less prominent IR programs and those in lightly unionized states, but eventually it will also affect most, if not all, of the programs in the top tier. Third, nearly all IR programs will reduce the ILE focus of their programs by means of freezes or outright cuts in faculty positions and courses devoted to trade union and collective bargaining subjects and/or by hiring new faculty and creating courses in the HR area. Fourth, some free-standing IR units will be merged into business schools, resulting in a significant dilution of their interdisciplinary and ILE orientation, while others will be abolished altogether. The units most susceptible to outright elimination are those with the strongest collective bargaining and labor studies orientation and those that exist primarily to sponsor research (closing them provides a relatively easy way for universities to save overhead costs and generally does not threaten faculty positions and academic programs, and faculty today are much less interested in interdisciplinary research).

On the other hand, the next decade may well be a boom period for HR academic programs. Fueled by the tremendous increase in business school enrollments, the transformation of HR from a tactical area of business practice to a strategic one, and the growth in the complexity and cost of human resource activities and programs in business firms, personnel and human resource management, once academic backwaters, have become newly emergent areas of growth. We can thus expect universities to expand significantly their courses, faculty, and academic programs in the HR area. These programs will be substantially different from those established in the immediate post–World War II period, however. For example, nearly all new HR programs will be in business schools. Further, universities will generally forgo a formerly constituted institute or center with faculty positions attached to it in favor of other approaches. The least ambitious will be to create a separate concentration or major in personnel and HRM in the undergraduate or graduate business curriculum, wherein the staffing of the courses and the administration of the major will generally be the responsibility of the management faculty.

The more ambitious will be to create a separate, multidisciplinary HR degree program within the business school, typically at the graduate level, with a coordinator and jointly appointed faculty.

The curricula of the new programs will be heavily oriented toward business subjects, will emphasize the management perspective in employment relations, and will draw most of their intellectual and research content from the behavioral sciences. The students and faculty in them will not identify their field of study as "industrial relations" but, rather, will think of it in terms of some HR-related title. If the term *industrial relations* is used at all, it will be to connote the labor-management relations part of the curriculum.

RESEARCH

The pattern of research in industrial relations in the 1990s, and the associated strengths and weaknesses, will closely match those of the 1980s. Since the record for IR research in the 1980s was relatively good by my reckoning, the outlook for the 1990s is also optimistic, albeit modestly so.

I expect to see the publication of several influential, highly regarded IR books and articles. The current crisis affecting the New Deal industrial relations system, and the concomitant intellectual crisis afflicting industrial relations, open up a host of important research issues that scholars are just beginning to investigate. In this respect the research performance of the 1990s is likely to resemble that of the 1950s, in that both periods followed a dramatic sea change in the level of union density. Among the most important topics demanding attention are national labor policy, particularly the continued appropriateness of the Wagner Act; new forms of employee representation, such as works councils and associational unionism; international dimensions of unionism, such as divergent growth rates, organizational and legal structures, and economic effects; innovations in union practices and contracts as unions attempt to broaden their appeal to the unorganized and deal with the competitive problems of unionized employers; and the impact of IR practices in the workplace on economic competitiveness.

In addition to collective bargaining–related topics, fertile areas for research exist on the causes of and solutions to the many serious economic problems facing the American work force, including the heightened insecurity of employment, the stagnation in real income, the growing racial divisiveness, and the shortfalls in education and training. IR researchers also need to subject to critical analysis the intellectual premises and workplace performance of the HR-inspired models of work organization and management.

Another development that bodes well for IR research is the increasing number of scholars who are marrying modern statistical techniques with the case study "go and see" approach pioneered by the early institutionalists. Part of the reason for the sterility of IR research in the 1970s and early 1980s was that it resulted from a combination of obsessiveness with methodology and use of secondary data sources. The net result was that the research was remote, esoteric, and of little relevance to policy makers or practitioners. Fortunately, a growing number of IR scholars are getting out in the field and conducting investigative case studies of employee involvement programs, dispute resolution procedures, and NLRB representation election campaigns and, at the same time, are grounding the research in as much of a theoretical framework as is available and applying multivariate techniques to analysis of the data. The result is research that combines the strengths of both the traditional case study approach and the modern analytic approach. I expect (and hope) that this trend will continue.

I also detect a modest increase in the amount of multidisciplinary research being conducted. For example, greater efforts have been made in recent years to bring to the analysis of unions and collective bargaining various concepts and ideas from the management and behavioral science literature. This is evident in the discussion of management strategy and industrial relations (Kochan, Katz, and McKersie 1986; Lewin 1987) and in the application of psychological and sociological concepts to models of strikes (Wheeler 1985), union joining (Fiorito 1987), and union participation (Gallagher and Strauss 1991). In addition, there appears to be a recent boomlet in interest in the study of comparative and international industrial relations, a vein of research that promises to bring a greater number of political scientists, sociologists, and historians into contact with mainstream IR.

Set against these positive developments are several negatives. Industrial relations research will continue to focus disproportionately on union and labor-management issues. If the organized sector of the economy continues to shrink in size, the long-term prospects for the vitality of IR research are slim. And, although a somewhat greater amount of multidisciplinary research will be produced in the 1990s, the amount of *inter*disciplinary research is likely to remain minuscule because of the trend toward research specialization and the desire of researchers to avoid being caught in a crossfire of criticism from journal referees of different disciplinary backgrounds. Finally, I believe IR as a field would benefit if greater emphasis were placed on applied, problem-solving research. Such research has greater relevance to practitioners and policy makers and stimulates a more holistic, interdisciplinary perspective. I suspect, however, that the bulk of IR scholars (particularly younger scholars subject to the pressures of promotion and tenure) will continue to emphasize academic issues of theory and research methodology.

IRRA

One source of the IRRA's problems is that its academic membership base has become increasingly narrow and hollowed out. Although the organization is nominally committed to representing all disciplines and ideological factors interested in employer-employee relations, in practice it has become the de facto intellectual home for advocates of the ILE wing of industrial relations and the major academic interest group representing trade unions and their economic and political allies (e.g., arbitrators). Over time, the organization's alliance with these two constituencies has resulted in a significant reduction in the number of academics who wish to participate in the organization, for those who are most welcome and who will be nominated for high office are increasingly rare birds—scholars who not only are interested in labor-management relations but also can pass the organization's ideological litmus test (i.e., they have a philosophical belief in the desirability of pluralism in general and unions and collective bargaining in particular). Given that even fewer academics will possess these attributes in the future, I expect that the academic membership of the IRRA will continue to decline in the 1990s.

The IRRA's troubles go beyond a decline in the number of dues-paying academic members, however. A significant problem, for example, is that the organization faces the prospect of losing to retirement the postwar neoinstitutional economists who in effect have run the organization for the last several decades. Given the declining appeal of the IRRA to younger scholars, there will be a dearth of "rising stars" waiting in the wings to take over leadership positions.[5]

Likewise, the IRRA no longer attracts to its meetings many of the most talented researchers in the field, and, indeed, an increasing number of these people are not even members of the organization. One of the problems is the ideological litmus test, but another is that the organization's published proceedings and monographs are viewed as relatively "lightweight" and thus unattractive to scholars who are trying to gain tenure or a big name in the field. I see this trend intensifying, absent a major effort to increase the rigor of at least some of the association's publications.

The IRRA has also traditionally neglected behavioral science, non-union, management-oriented research, yet it is this segment of the field that is growing the most rapidly. The ability of the organization to accommodate to this shift is limited, however, by both intellectual and political constraints. The theoretical and conceptual core of present-day industrial relations is largely incompatible with that used by most HR researchers. Giving greater organizational access to HR researchers may therefore result in an equal or larger defection of traditional IR researchers. As noted in the last chapter, the IRRA's ability to shift its research focus significantly is also limited by internal political factors. In particular, for both philosophical and economic reasons, a sizable faction of the IRRA membership would probably strongly resist any attempt to refocus the organization's research thrust toward the nonunion sector and/or the practice of management.[6]

Another potential problem is the possibility that at some point in the future the University Council of Industrial Relations and Human Resource Programs (UCIRHRP, the former IR center directors' group) may reschedule the date of its annual meeting to coincide with the meetings of some other professional association such as the Academy of Management (or rotate the meeting between the IRRA and this other group). To date, most of the directors of the various IR institutes and centers have come from the ILE wing of the field and have thus had a natural affinity for the IRRA. As the behavioral science, HR side of the field grows, however, it is likely that the HR faculty will outnumber the IR faculty in the institutes and centers. We can expect, then, a greater push to abandon the IR label for the academic programs, a greater likelihood that future generations of institute directors will be behavioral scientists with research interests in OB and HRM, and a concomitant push to have the center directors' meeting at a different time and place than the IRRA meetings (e.g., at the meetings of the Academy of Management). Since the center directors' meeting brings to the annual winter IRRA meetings some of the key players in the field, the loss of this group would deal the IRRA a serious blow.

Finally, the IRRA is hampered by a growing gap and lack of interaction between the academic and practitioner wings of the organization. One of the fundamental goals of the founders of the IRRA was to promote the interchange of ideas and perspectives between academics and practitioners, so as to enrich both the study and practice of industrial relations. Over time, however, the two sides have grown apart until they inhabit largely separate worlds. The domain of the academics is the winter meetings of the IRRA, an event that mainly attracts professors and graduate students. The domain of the practitioners is the local IRRA chapter meetings, which are sparsely attended by academics and to which they contribute little.

A Strategy for Survival and Growth

If the assessment offered above is anywhere close to correct, the field and its major institutions are in trouble. What can be done to turn around the situation? The next section provides one strategy for change.[7]

IR AS A FIELD OF STUDY

The first requirement for a resuscitation of industrial relations is a name change. Although the term *industrial relations* has a long and honored history, in recent years it has acquired an overly narrow and out-of-date meaning that is an increasing handicap for the field. The most attractive replacement is *employment relations.* The virtues of this term are that it continues to emphasize the field's emphasis on relations between employers and employees but at the same time broadens the focus of the field from the industrial sector of the economy to the totality of employment relationships.[8]

The second requirement is to broaden and reposition the boundaries of the field and redefine its core subject matter. The intellectual domain of present-day IR is largely the product of the historical development of science-building and problem-solving in the ILE wing of the field. A broadening and repositioning of the field requires, therefore, a fundamental reexamination of the subject matter included within both science-building and problem-solving. It is the combination of topics and concepts subsumed within these two perspectives that represents the essence of what I propose as the "new IR."

From a science-building perspective, a field of study such as industrial relations needs to be organized around a specific phenomenon or form of behavior so that theory construction and the deduction of hypotheses can take place. The phenomenon focused on in the pre–1960s version of industrial relations was the employment relationship, as indicated by the definition of IR then widely in use—"the study of all aspects of the employment relationship." The problem with this conceptualization of the field was that it subsumed such a disparate range of activities and behaviors that theory construction and hypothesis-testing became quite difficult. As described in chapter 6, industrial relations largely abandoned the employment relationship as an organizing concept for research after 1960 and narrowed its attention to trade unions and collective bargaining. While these topics afford much greater opportunities for theory construction and hypothesis-testing (and thus the creation of a community of interests among research scholars), the drawback is that the phenomena chosen for investigation are now found among only a small minority of U.S. employers.

I propose an intermediate position. The focus of IR research should be squarely centered on the employment relationship and, most particularly, on the outcomes of the employment relationship that affect efficiency, equity, and individual growth and well-being. The place to start the study of industrial relations is thus at the organization level, for it is within the organization (shop, plant, firm, and so on) that outcomes such as rates of pay, decisions to join a union, productivity growth, strikes, and promotion opportunities are determined. Consideration of these topics is not the sole province of industrial relations, however, but is divided between it and the field of human resources. The division runs along what I perceive to be a fundamental intellectual fault line in research on the employment relationship. This fault line has the "internalists" of the HR wing on one side and the "externalists" of the IR wing on the other.[9]

The internalists seek explanations for employment outcomes in factors internal to the organization, such as the nature of management practices, the structure of the organization, the psychological determinants of worker and manager behaviors, and the tenor of social relations between managers and workers. Scholars in this camp come primarily from management-related fields, such as organizational behavior and human resource management and the behavioral science disciplines of anthropology, psychology, and the micro side of sociology.

In contrast, the externalists seek explanations for employment outcomes in factors external to the organization, such as economic conditions in product and labor markets; sociological characteristics pertaining to the demographic, occupational, class, and urban versus rural structure of the local community or nation; the legal structure surrounding the conduct of employer-employee relations; and prevailing cultural, political, and social norms in the society. Scholars in this group come primarily from economics, law, political science, history, and the macro side of sociology.[10]

This conceptual dichotomy has several virtues. First, it highlights the common intellectual roots of both HR and IR in the study of the employment relationship, thus facilitating greater interaction and dialogue between the two. Currently many scholars regard HR and IR as separate subjects, the former dealing with human resource management issues and the latter with labor relations. The perspective advocated here suggests instead that they are concerned with the same broad subject but represent different approaches and points of view.[11]

Second, IR is broadened and repositioned so that it covers a wider set of subjects and appeals to a wider audience of scholars. As framed above, IR is transformed from the study of unions and collective bargaining to the study of all the practices, behaviors, and institutions relevant to the employment relationship. Thus, not only the traditional union and labor economics topics fall within the domain of IR research (or what might be thought of as dependent variables) but also subjects often considered outside the purview of the field, such as the determinants of employee work effort, methods of employee recruitment and selection, and the structure of business organizations.[12]

Third, although IR research spans the gamut of subjects related to the employment relationship, because of the concentration on the external environment to the organization, and how this environment affects the structure of the organization, its human resource policies and practices, and the behaviors of its workers and managers, the field has an intellectual foundation that can be used as the basis for the development of conceptual models around which scholars from disciplines as diverse as economics, law, and sociology can build a community of interest. Dunlop's industrial relations systems model (1958) provides one example; the strategic choice model developed by Kochan, Katz, and McKersie (1986) provides another.[13] What makes the external environment a viable organizing device for the field is that it brings together disciplines with enough complementarity in their theoretical and methodological approaches to research that scholars will find associating with one another to be an intellectually rewarding experience. These complementarities include a mutual concern with conditions affecting the employment relationship that arise outside of the firm, are the result of aggregative forms of behavior (e.g., the operation of markets, social groups, and political institutions), and are more easily measured for use in large-scale cross-section and time-series empirical studies. Because of these commonalities, researchers from these disciplines are more likely to have an interest in many of the same independent variables and research designs, an interest not likely to be shared to the same degree by HR researchers.[14] The externally oriented disciplines are also united by their far greater concern with and relevance to issues of national employment policy.

Science-building defines one of the "faces" of industrial relations as a field of study; problem-solving defines the other. Here too repositioning is required.

The focus of current-day industrial relations on unions and collective bargaining reflects not only intellectual considerations but also the commitment of the ILE wing to a set of assumptions and values concerning the employment relationship. From a problem-solving point of view, whether this preoccupation with unions and collective bargaining is desirable depends on whether they (and the rest of the ILE policy program) remain the most effective method to promote the goals of industrial relations—increased efficiency, equity, and personal growth and well-being. Clearly, there is a range of opinion on this matter. Social and economic conservatives (e.g., Heldman, Bennett, and Johnson 1981; Reynolds 1984), for example, typically advocate less government intervention in labor markets, and in particular a reduction in legal protections and encouragement of the right to organize and bargain collectively, while persons on the opposite end of the philosophical spectrum maintain that the nation's well-being would be promoted by further unionization and a strengthening of the protective net of labor legislation (Freeman and Medoff 1984; Weiler 1990). Where should industrial relations position itself? I believe the field is again best served by an intermediate position.

My reading of the evidence is that economic and social conditions both inside and outside the workplace have evolved in the post–World War II period in ways that have seriously undercut the net contribution of the New Deal industrial relations system to the achievement of the three aforementioned goals. Unlike some of the critics, I do not believe that this evolution has made the current IR system obsolete or that it should be dismantled in favor of a deregulated, union-free environment. The system does need a substantial overhaul, however. The case becomes obvious when one examines the reasons advanced for the establishment of the current system.

As described in chapter 2, the ILE view of the employment relationship provided a number of rationales for the enactment of the Wagner Act and other pieces of protective labor legislation in the 1930s. One major pillar was the assumption that restrictions on labor mobility, collusive practices by employers, and the frequent existence of substantial involuntary unemployment tilt the plane of competition against individual workers in a nonunion situation, leading to substandard wages, working conditions, and treatment by management. Another fundamental pillar of ILE support for trade unions and collective bargaining was that they replace the autocratic master-servant relationship in the workplace with a system of industrial democracy, thereby ensuring due process and opportunities for employee involvement in both the management of the enterprise and the determination of wages and working conditions.

Do these rationales make sense in the economic and social context of the 1990s? The answer, I think, is a qualified yes; yes because at the most elemental level the major ILE premises retain validity but with a strong note of qualification because they require significant modification and adaptation if they are to be relevant in today's economy and workplace.

A prime example concerns one of the principal justifications for the Wagner Act—labor's inequality of bargaining power. A good case can be made that the labor market was not a level playing field for many workers in the 1930s and that the development of industrial unions and companywide and industrywide collective bargaining helped restore balance into the wage determination process (see Kaufman 1989a, 1991a).

Over the last half-century, however, most of the causes of labor's disadvantageous position have been significantly reduced through full-employment macroeconomic policies, labor's increased geographical mobility, antidiscrimination legislation, and so on. Thus, in the 1930s, union bargaining power could justifiably be regarded as a countervailing force that tended to offset the market power of employers. In the 1990s, however, fewer workers suffer from a disadvantage in bargaining power and the extent of this disadvantage is likewise smaller. As a result, the playing field is more level, thereby reducing the demand for collective bargaining by unorganized workers and making it far more likely that once a union is recognized its exercise of bargaining power will lead over time to monopolistic wage premiums and attendant forms of resource misallocation. The implication, then, is that a set of public policies that made sense in the 1930s may no longer be appropriate.

Similar considerations apply to the voice function of unions. One of the strongest arguments for unions is that, by providing workers with an independent form of representation (or voice), they not only ensure greater workplace equity through the bargaining and grievance processes but also lead to increased efficiency by leading to lower turnover rates, higher productivity, and so on. Even granting the correctness of these assertions (a strongly debated issue, particularly with regard to the latter point), one must still wonder whether traditional collective bargaining as practiced under the Wagner Act is as successful in achieving these ends as it was several decades earlier. Evidence indicates, for example, that unionized workers continue to value formalized grievance systems but that the effectiveness of these systems is coming under increasing scrutiny because of their high cost, significant time delays in resolving disputes, and the residue of adversarialism left after a settlement is reached (Dalton and Todor 1981).

Likewise, while research studies from forty years ago found that the process of union voice had a positive impact on productivity and corporate personnel practices (e.g., Slichter, Healy, and Livernash 1960), the evidence from today is more mixed (Freeman and Medoff 1984; Hirsch 1991). A particularly salient issue in judging the continued efficacy of collective bargaining is whether the adversarial principle on which the system is built is still compatible with the attainment of world-class standards in product quality and productivity.[15] The newest generation of best-practice plants, for example, rely heavily on trust-building, employee involvement, and flexible work rules, attributes that seem to be considerably more difficult to initiate and maintain successfully in unionized situations (Kochan, Katz, and McKersie 1986).

While the evidence is suggestive at best, it nevertheless is indicative of a trend; namely, that the ILE policy program—and its cornerstone, trade unions and collective bargaining—has lost a considerable degree of effectiveness as a solution to the employment problems of both workers and employers. If I am correct in my assessment, industrial relations as a field needs to become far more active in its efforts to develop new laws, institutions, and practices that can do a better job at solving these problems, whether through a modification of the existing New Deal IR system or the development of a new (possibly imported) system. In any case, these new laws, institutions, and practices will come to define the second "face" of industrial relations as a field of study. What will this face look like? The answer will not be known until IR scholars undertake a reevaluation and reformulation of the basic assumptions that underlie the field and devise the institutional solutions to the problems at hand— a process that has already been initiated (see Kochan, Katz, and McKersie 1986; Weiler 1990; Katz 1991) but that has made only modest progress. My guess is that at the end of this reevaluation process the problem-solving face of IR will be dominated by several issues.

The first defining feature of this face of industrial relations (or employment relations) will be the continued emphasis on the term *relations*, as opposed to the HR side, where the term *management* will be at center stage. The emphasis on the term *relations* communicates two messages about the field that will not change: first, that labor is embodied in a human being whose interests and concerns as both a person and factor of production must be given equal weight with those of management and consumers and, second, that the inherent conflict of interest embodied in the employment relationship is of sufficient importance to warrant there being a separate field of study devoted to the consideration of these relations.

The second notable feature of the problem-solving face of industrial relations in the years ahead will be its association with systems of workplace governance. Trade unions and collective bargaining will remain an important subject in industrial relations, but they will no longer define it. Rather, collective bargaining will increasingly be seen as only one of many systems of control, rule-making, and employee representation, or what are generically referred to as systems of workplace governance. The impetus behind consideration of other forms of governance is the search for some institutional means that provides effective justice and voice in the workplace and at the same time does a better job than collective bargaining at both promoting productive efficiency and appealing to the currently unorganized segments of the work force.

While the HR wing will also have an interest in workplace governance, this topic will be perceived as an intellectual pillar of industrial relations, given the field's historic and continuing commitment to the promotion and protection of workers' rights and equity interests. The emphasis on workplace governance will also perpetuate IR's historic focus on the study of workplace institutions and the role of institutions in supplementing both the market and management as control mechanisms in the employment relationship.

The third feature of industrial relations will be the continued attention given to labor-management conflict and dispute resolution. The field was born out of public concern over the mounting scale and intensity of strikes and labor violence in the 1910s, and the principal purpose of early research in the field (as exemplified by the activities of the Commission on Industrial Relations) was to discover the underlying causes of this unrest and methods to promote reconciliation and compromise. It is not coincidental that the field's high points in years since have largely coincided with similar outbursts of labor-management conflict and attendant concerns with dispute resolution. Given the field's continuing emphasis on the *relations* between employers and employees, I would expect that labor-management conflict and the resolution of disputes will remain a central part of the problem-solving agenda of industrial relations in the years ahead. Consistent with the shift from a narrow focus on collective bargaining to a broader concern with alternative forms of workplace governance, however, there must be a concomitant broadening of the field's approach to the subject of conflict in the workplace, including alternative forms of conflict (e.g., various forms of individual withdrawal behavior, such as shirking and quitting), and systems of conflict resolution (e.g., peer review).

The fourth notable feature of the problem-solving face of industrial relations will be an increased emphasis on topics such as competitiveness, productivity, and product quality. In the past, industrial relations largely took for granted the management side of the employment relationship and the impact of IR policies on the economic performance of the firm. The rise of powerful international competitors such as Germany and Japan, and the lackluster performance of the American economy in productivity growth, will make this neglect untenable in the future. Even a field that has workers' rights as a major focal point cannot ignore the adverse impact that a loss of international competitiveness has on job opportunities, employment security, rates of pay, and living standards. In addressing such concerns, IR will have to be willing to examine current labor market institutions and practices critically to ensure that they are part of the solution, not the problem.

In short, industrial relations will not have a unitary focus or theoretical model, such as economics does with the operation of markets and the model of supply and demand, but it will have a series of connected intellectual themes defined by the field's interest in both science-building and problem-solving. The core of the field will be at the intersection of these two dimensions; that is, the study of the impact of external environmental forces on the organization and performance of work and the resulting relations between employers and employees, and the development of a system of workplace governance that is congruent with these external forces, promotes efficiency in the internal operation of the enterprise, protects workers' equity interests, and contributes to the development and growth of the nation's human resources.

I see the intellectual themes described above as being of sufficient generality as to demarcate a distinct intellectual boundary for the field within the social sciences. This field would be of interest to a large group of scholars across numerous disciplines yet intellectually cohesive enough to provide for the development of broad-based conceptual frameworks and a well-defined community of research interests. These themes must be sufficiently elastic that the field remains identified with reform and progressivism with respect to policy and practice yet avoids being wedded to any particular set of institutions or practices. I believe the themes suggested above meet these criteria and could provide the basis for a new, reconstituted field of industrial relations that is consistent with much of its past yet is broadened and updated to make it more competitive in the years to come.[16]

IR UNITS AND ACADEMIC PROGRAMS

The next part of the strategy concerns the preservation of existing IR units and academic programs and the creation of new ones. These programs are essential in fostering integrative, interdisciplinary research and teaching on the employment relationship and in providing both ILE and PM perspectives on that relationship.

The most important step in this direction is successful marketing of an intellectual idea; namely, that it is *the employment relationship* that defines the field and is the concept around which teaching and research in the field is organized. Once this proposition is accepted, it then follows as a matter of course that a well-rounded program will have a multi-disciplinary faculty and curriculum and will provide coverage of *both* the employer's and the worker's side of the relationship and both the internal (HR) and the external (IR) perspective on research. The advantage of this construct is that it allows enough flexibility for academic programs to vary the proportion of the faculty and curriculum devoted to HR versus IR as suits their strategic goals and student demand conditions, but at the same time it contains intellectual constraints that prevent programs from adopting one extreme position or the other (all IR or all HR). If the organization of the field is defined in terms of IR versus HR, however, the battle will be lost, for most schools will choose a relatively pure HR approach that will be far more one-sided in disci-plinary coverage, topical focus, and ideological perspective.

If the employment relationship defines the program focus of IR units, then the titles of the programs must reflect this focus. I have already proposed using the term *employment relations* to replace *industrial relations* as the label for the ILE (or external) wing of the field, a suggestion that if adopted makes *employment relations* too restrictive to serve as a stand-alone label for academic programs that span both IR and HR. What is needed is an entirely new label that conveys that the intellectual territory under consideration covers the entire employment relationship and, most particularly, both the IR and HR wings. No such label exists that I can identify, a situation that illustrates both the tremendously expan-sive nature of the intellectual territory associated with the subject of employment and the futility of past attempts to discover the conceptual thread that binds these intellectual remnants into a single discipline. Given this lacuna, the next best solution is for programs to use a combination of labels in the title, such as "Human Resources and Industrial Relations" (the new title for the IR program at Loyola University in Chicago).[17]

The survival of traditional IR units also depends on their maintaining a strong market demand for their doctoral graduates. Changing the name of the field and broadening it to encompass a macro-level, employment governance perspective of the employment relationship would certainly help make IR students, particularly those in business schools, more marketable.

Another important step is to increase the job market value of a cross-disciplinary degree. The route has been outlined earlier; namely, emphasize that high-quality teaching and research on the employment relationship requires training in both the behavioral and nonbehavioral sciences. This is a message that the University Council of Industrial Relations and Human Resource Programs should vigorously promote.

Finally, IR doctoral programs may need to further scale back the multidisciplinary nature of their programs so that students can acquire a greater degree of specialization in business-related subjects. Several IR units, have already done this, with the result that the social science and liberal arts component of the curriculum has been significantly reduced relative to what it was twenty and thirty years ago.

Universities should also be encouraged, when they create HR programs, to give them multidisciplinary faculty and curriculum and to provide courses on both PM and ILE subjects. The UCIRHRP, for example, should actively foster the creation of independent HR majors and degree programs in business schools that are separate from the course offerings and degree programs in management. The stand-alone status of these programs would facilitate the development of a more comprehensive, integrated curriculum, a part of which would involve courses not generally offered as part of a degree in management (e.g., labor economics, employment relations theory). The UCIRHRP might also establish an accreditation program that would have as one of its requirements a multidisciplinary curriculum with some balancing of ILE and PM perspectives. Finally, the UCIRHRP should aggressively recruit multidisciplinary HR programs to join the association and encourage the directors of these programs, when their programs are not housed in some autonomous unit, to work toward the creation of such.

RESEARCH

IR research must also be repositioned if industrial relations is to survive and prosper in the future. The first step is to widen the scope of the research. The approach to be taken follows directly from the discussion in the previous sections. Suggestions similar in spirit if not in detail have also been made by Strauss (1990), Cappelli (1990), Cutcher-Gershenfeld (1991), and Sherer (1991). As I conceive it, the aim of IR research is to explain how conditions in the economic, legal, technological, social, and political environment external to unions and firms affect the structure, practices, and policies of these organizations, and the behavioral outcomes that emerge out of the employment relationship. So conceived, industrial relations research encompasses a wide variety of topics. Certainly among these is the traditional forte of industrial relations, trade unions and labor-management relations. Other topics also qualify, however, even though by the conventional definition of the field their relationship to the study of industrial relations is unclear. Two examples illustrate the point.

A subject popularized by Kochan, Katz, and McKersie (1986), for example, is the relationship between business strategy and corporate capital investment decisions and human resource practices. This subject is squarely within the domain of IR research because it focuses on a macro-level explanation for an organization-level employment outcome—the effect of heightened international competition on corporate business strategy and the consequent decision to close unionized plants, open new plants in the South, introduce self-managed work teams, and so on.

Employment systems are another example (see Osterman 1987; Begin 1990). Employment systems are alternative technical and social systems for organizing production and the performance of work. Each employment system carries with it a particular set of human resource policies concerning recruitment, selection, compensation, and retention. A wide diversity of such systems and associated human resource policies exist across firms (e.g., compare a fast-food restaurant, a bank, and an auto-assembly plant). Why do firms choose a particular employment system? Why are firms abandoning the traditional "control" model of work organization for a "high-involvement" model? Industrial relations is well positioned to answer these questions, for much of the variation in employment systems and individual human resource practices (the dependent variables) both in a cross-section and over time are linked to variations in economic, technological, and demographic conditions (the independent variables) that are external or exogenous to the firm (Dunlop 1993).

Improving the quality or social "value-added" of IR research is the second step of the strategy. The particular strengths of IR research are its integrative character and its relevance to issues of practice and policy. The integrative feature comes from the field's location at the crossroads of several disciplines, a conjunction that has led to the development of distinctive "middle-range" theories—theories that synthesize concepts across disciplines at an intermediate level of generality (Kochan 1992). The relevance of IR research springs from the field's concern with applied problem-solving issues. The 1950s was a golden age for industrial relations precisely because the research of the period was extremely rich in both middle-level theory and practical relevance. There is no reason IR research could not attain the same level of prestige in the 1990s, particularly given the plethora of serious employment problems facing the nation. But will it?

I suspect the answer is no. The IR scholars of the 1950s brought to the research process a combination of excellent training in the theory and research methods of their home disciplines, a receptivity to a multidisciplinary approach, and extensive practical experience gained from personal involvement in the activities of business, unions, and government. While only the first characteristic is essential for research success within individual disciplines (as exemplified by articles in the *Journal of Labor Economics* and *Journal of Applied Psychology*), all three are required to conduct high-quality research in a multidisciplinary, problem-oriented field such as industrial relations. Unfortunately, present-day IR scholars (particularly younger scholars still subject to the publish or perish pressures of tenure and promotion) all too often have excellent theoretical and methodological skills (certainly dwarfing anything possessed by the researchers of the 1950s) but lack both practical experience and interest in cross-disciplinary research. The result is that a significant share of IR research, and particularly that published in research journals, exhibits a narrowness and sterility that is the product of a unidisciplinary focus, an obsession with methodological considerations, and an author who has had relatively little personal contact with the subject under investigation. The blame lies not with the individual researchers but with the reward system and culture in academe that overemphasizes science-building.

The solution is to devise mechanisms that facilitate and encourage cross-disciplinary research, the collection of primary data, interviews with company and union officials, and immersion in the nitty-gritty of institutional details and daily practice. (Some researchers are already doing it, but more are needed.) This unglamorous process must take place if scholars are to discover the true nature of the labor problems confronting employers and workers and develop the theories and practices needed to resolve them. Accomplishment of this goal is difficult, however, in the current environment of science-building in American universities. Nonetheless, several actions could make a difference.

To help broaden and strengthen the field, the mainstream IR journals need to reposition the mix of articles accepted for publication. For example, the number of "pure" labor economics articles accepted for publication should be reduced, since these often have only a tangential link to the employment relationship and offer little, if any, cross-disciplinary perspective. Articles on economic aspects of human resources management should be encouraged, however, for they are directly relevant to the field and are more likely to span disciplinary boundaries with respect to content. Another step is to increase the number of papers published by authors from other "external" disciplines, such as sociology and political science. At the same time, research that is clearly of an "internal" nature (e.g., organizational commitment studies) should be published elsewhere if IR is to develop a coherent image vis-à-vis HR. Mainstream IR journals should also give preference to articles that involve primary data, interviews with company and union officials, and participant-observer techniques so as to encourage the development of more relevant, problem-solving research. Each of these steps will probably require an "affirmative action"–type editorial policy. Simply requesting more such articles, the journal editors tell me, will yield little change.

Another useful action would be to create additional outlets for case study and applied policy-oriented research. Such research promotes the goal of developing informed, relevant theory and empirical work that tends to be excluded from mainline IR journals. The field could benefit, therefore, from the creation of a new journal, monograph series, or annual volume that would feature more applied, case study research.

IRRA

The future of industrial relations as a field of study also depends significantly on the strategic choices made by the Industrial Relations Research Association. The declining fortunes of the association in many respects mirror those of the field in general, with the cause-and-effect relationship going both ways.

The IRRA is caught up in the same intellectual contradiction as are the IR academic programs and journals; namely, it professes allegiance to the broad definition of industrial relations but practices the narrow version. The IRRA needs to resolve this contradiction one way or the other. Two approaches are possible: to maintain the current ILE orientation of the organization and abandon the stated claim to represent all segments of the IR and HR community or to retain the stated commitment to represent all segments of the IR and HR community and implement a series of wide-reaching changes to broaden the organization's programs and membership.

The latter option would require that the association take at least five actions: change its title to signify that it includes both the IR and HR wings; establish an annual meeting date and place independent of the Allied Social Science Association (an umbrella group of associations that includes the American Economic Association) or rotate the annual meeting so that one year it is with the economics group, another year with the sociologists, and so on; expand significantly the number of program sessions and annual research volumes devoted to HR topics; give balanced weight and perspective at all association meetings and in all publications to the practice of nonunion employment relations; and provide equal political representation and access to high office to academics from the HR wing and executives and practitioners from nonunion companies.

I suspect that this package of revisions could not command sufficient support in the IRRA to gain ratification. Nor could it be implemented without significantly damaging and quite possibly destroying the viability of the organization. I therefore advocate an alternative, second-best strategy. It has three parts.

The first part requires people to accept that the IRRA will serve as the professional association for only half the field—IR, not HR. At the same time, the association should work to reposition its programs and activities to make them consistent with the broader definition of industrial relations advanced earlier in this chapter. In practical terms, this means structuring the program of the winter meeting so that less emphasis is given to collective bargaining topics and more to topics related to the external environment and employment governance. This also means making concerted efforts to encourage more active participation by scholars from externally oriented disciplines that are now underrepresented (e.g., sociology, political science). A greater interface between IR and HR scholars should also be encouraged, although the focus needs to be on the themes that define the field (as opposed to an open-ended session on organizational behavior research). Finally, the association's name should be changed so that the term *industrial relations* is dropped in favor of *employment relations* or some other more inclusive label.[18]

The second part of the strategy is for the IRRA to promote a wide-ranging review of the underlying assumptions and policy program of current-day industrial relations (i.e., to reexamine the problem-solving face of the field). If the field is to enjoy a renaissance, the IRRA must play a central role through its meetings and publications in developing a new way of looking at the employment relationship that is consistent with modern realities and that yields new practices and policies that promote efficiency and equity. In particular, it must sponsor a variety of paper sessions at meetings and dedicate annual research volumes to a balanced, critical examination of the current system of collective bargaining and labor law, proposals for change in the IR system, and innovative employment practices and institutions in both the union and nonunion sectors.

The third part of the strategy entails both reversing the decline in membership of the national organization and increasing participation by academics from outside the ILE school. This can be done by addressing some serious structural issues. The first such issue concerns the academic-practitioner interface. While the goal of encouraging a cross-fertilization of ideas between academics and practitioners is excellent in intent, it largely fails to accomplish its purpose and, worse, creates significant disincentives for participation in the national association by academic researchers. Academics are attracted to the association (and to the winter meeting in particular) primarily for science-building reasons, most notably the opportunity to discuss and publish scholarly research. In an attempt to keep the discourse at a level that is accessible to practitioners, however, the IRRA has imposed a variety of strictures that together significantly weaken the incentive for academics to attend (e.g., short page limits on published articles, practitioner discussants for academic papers, the low level of rigor of accepted papers). The result is that neither group is happy—the practitioners still find the meetings and publications largely irrelevant to their concerns, while the academics find them too watered down to be of real value.

One suggestion is to devote the winter meeting to science-building and the spring meeting to problem-solving. Thus, the winter meeting becomes a strictly academic affair, and the sessions, paper selection process, and published proceedings are structured with the goal of science-building in mind. The spring meeting then becomes the forum for problem-solving research. Thus, preference might be given in the paper selection process to studies that use primary data sources, interviews with company and union officials, and other methods of "hands-on" research.

The second structural problem confronting the IRRA is the timing and location of the winter meeting. It is currently held at the same time as the meetings of the other associations affiliated with the Allied Social Science Association (ASSA), the most important being the American Economic Association. This arrangement has both benefits and costs. A major benefit is that more labor economists are able to attend the IRRA meetings than would be the case if they were held separately from the ASSA. This was a significant consideration in years past, when economists represented the largest academic group in the association. Now that economists represent less than one-fifth of the association's academic membership, the synergies are less obvious. Another important benefit is the substantial financial savings the IRRA obtains by piggybacking the winter meeting with that of the ASSA. On the cost side, the current arrangement discourages participation by academics from disciplines outside economics, either because they cannot afford to travel to a separate set of meetings from those in their home discipline or because they find the economics-dominated environment of the ASSA meetings unattractive. It also perpetuates the perception that industrial relations is an intellectual offshoot of labor economics.

No clear-cut resolution of this problem exists. The 1991 president of the IRRA, James Stern, suggested in his presidential address (Stern 1992) that the winter meeting be rotated among the professional meetings of all of IR's affiliated disciplines (i.e., one year it would be held in conjunction with the American Sociological Association, the next year with the American Political Science Association, and so on). He also proposed moving the spring meeting to early summer, holding it independently of any other association meeting, orienting it around problem-solving, and making it, rather than the winter meeting, the "showcase" meeting of the association. His suggested revisions regarding the spring meeting seem to have considerable merit, but I fear that his proposal to rotate the winter meeting among other professional associations would result in substantially reduced attendance and a further weakening of the core group of committed members. If forced to choose, I would advocate holding the winter meeting at an independent time and place from meetings of the ASSA or any other association. Although this would reduce the attendance of economists in the short run, it would materially benefit the association in the long run: participation by academics from other disciplines would increase; it would provide the association with an opportunity to redefine its mission and image and, in the process, facilitate the repositioning of the field advocated earlier; and it would allow the association considerably more freedom to structure the meeting (e.g., number, length, and format of sessions) in a way that participants would find most rewarding.[19]

If the IRRA is to reverse the decline in membership and participation, another structural change is necessary. This involves opening up the organization in both a political and ideological sense to a wider range of people and beliefs. Thus, the IRRA needs to take steps, in addition to those already implemented as a result of the reports of the Lester review committee (1977) and the Kerr-Dunlop review committee (1988a), to ensure that all groups feel welcome and equally represented.

For example, a commonly voiced complaint of the academic membership is that there are too few competitive paper sessions on the program. Having more such sessions would promote not only equal opportunity but also higher-quality research. Ideological neutrality is also important in the selection of sessions and papers, a goal that would be advanced by delegating authority for the planning of the winter meeting to academics only (a change that dovetails with the suggestion made earlier to devote the winter meeting strictly to science-building academic research). Finally, adopting a system of research "tracks" (e.g., labor economics, collective bargaining, labor law, human resource management, organizational behavior, and so on), much as in the Academy of Management, is worth considering. Each track would have an elected president who teaches and conducts research in that area and is responsible for planning one or more sessions and selecting papers. Such a system would encourage participation in the IRRA by a wider range of academics, help expand the topical and disciplinary base of the field, and provide a broader political base for governance of the organization and training ground for future leaders. Given the disenchantment of a number of the members of the personnel and human resources track of the Academy with the domination of that group by industrial and organizational psychologists, many from this group might participate more actively in the IRRA if it provided them with an explicit home base and had its winter meeting separate from that of the ASSA.

SUMMARY AND CONCLUSION

SEVERAL KEY POINTS have emerged from the analysis in this book. The following section summarizes them.

SUMMARY

• The field of industrial relations was born in approximately 1920. Two events marked its birth: the establishment at the University of Wisconsin of the first academic program in industrial relations, a concentration in industrial relations in the economics major; and the creation of the first professional association dedicated to the study and practice of industrial relations, the Industrial Relations Association of America. The IRAA was a forerunner of the American Management Association.

• The establishment of the field was motivated by both science-building and problem-solving considerations. The scientific motive was a desire to advance the state of knowledge on the employment relationship and, in particular, to understand better the causes of the frictions between employers and workers. The problem-solving motive was a desire to discover the means to resolve labor problems through improved methods of organization and practice in industry and the promulgation of progressive public policy. The end product of these new practices and policies was to be increased efficiency in production, equity in the distribution of economic rewards and authority in the plant, and opportunities for personal growth and well-being.

187

♦ For the first two decades of IR's existence, the problem-solving motive significantly outweighed the science-building motive in drawing researchers to the field. The predominance of the problem-solving motive imparted to IR research a heavy emphasis on fact-gathering, the descriptive analysis of institutions and practices, a multidisciplinary approach to the study of labor problems, and a strong normative, policy-oriented perspective. In the decade and a half after the end of World War II, the problem-solving motive remained strong but greater emphasis was given to science-building. The result was research characterized by its continued emphasis on relevance, its multidisciplinary approach, and its use of case study methods of empirical investigation combined with greater attention to the development of theory and the use of scientific research methods. After 1960, the major motive behind IR research became science-building. This shift was associated with a decline in multidisciplinary research and case study methods of empirical fact-gathering and in the relevance of the research to policy and practice, coupled with a significant increase in the use of deductive model-building, hypothesis-generating and testing, and the use of secondary data sources and advanced statistical techniques.

♦ From its earliest days, industrial relations was divided into two major schools of thought regarding the best means to resolve labor problems. The personnel management (PM) school maintained that labor problems were caused primarily by defective management in the form of poor business organization, workplace practices, leadership styles, and communication. The methods advocated to resolve these problems were the introduction of scientific methods into personnel administration (e.g., formal selection tests and incentive pay systems), the use of human relations practices in dealing with employees, and the establishment of nonunion forms of employee representation. The goal was a congruence of interests between workers and the business organization, an end to industrial conflict, and a joint commitment to the efficient operation of the enterprise.

By contrast, the institutional labor economics (ILE) school maintained that labor problems were caused primarily by two factors: imperfections in the market system external to the business organization that tilted the plane of competition against employees and the autocratic nature of the master-servant relationship, in which employees were denied democratic rights and the protection of due process. The solution of labor problems involved various institutional interventions, such as trade unions, protective labor legislation, social insurance programs, and full-employment monetary policies by the Federal Reserve Bank. The goal was a system of economic and political pluralism (competition among socioeconomic groups of roughly equal power) that ensured an equality of bargaining power between labor and management, industrial democracy through the independent representation of workers by trade unions, and a moderation of the adversarial relationship between managers and workers through institutionalized methods of conflict resolution.

♦ The PM school is built on two complementary fields of knowledge: the organizational and administrative science part of the field of management and the behavioral science disciplines of anthropology, psychology, and sociology. The early (1920s) writers of the PM school were primarily management practitioners and consultants. The PM school entered academe largely through two routes: the industrial relations sections established during the 1920s and 1930s at five American universities, principally through the efforts of Clarence Hicks; and the research spawned by the Hawthorne experiments at the Western Electric Company, as originally described in the writings of Elton Mayo and later Fritz Roethlisberger and William Dickson. The Hawthorne experiments, coupled with other research efforts at the time (e.g., research on group dynamics by Kurt Lewin), led to the emergence of the human relations movement, which became the most important branch of the PM school in the 1940s and 1950s.

In the late 1950s, human relations merged with the heretofore separate branch of management research on the study of organizations and administration to form the new field of organizational behavior. Organizational behavior and its applied offshoot, human resource management (formerly personnel management), represent the core of the modern-day version of the PM school.

♦ The intellectual foundation of the ILE school is primarily the discipline of economics but with significant contributions from law, history, political science, and the macro wing of industrial sociology. The founder of the ILE school, and of industrial relations as a field of study in the United States, was the institutional economist John R. Commons. During the 1920s and 1930s, the ILE school was represented in academe mainly by labor economists, but after World War II scholars from the other fields cited above also participated. In the 1940s and 1950s, labor economics gradually split into two branches, with one branch composed of ILE-oriented economists (persons such as John Dunlop, Clark Kerr, and Richard Lester) and the second branch composed of neoclassical-oriented economists.

The ILE group gradually drifted apart from their mother discipline because of both their divergent research interests and disagreements over theory and policy, with the result that by the late 1950s industrial relations had become their de facto home, leaving labor economics proper under the control of the neoclassical group (e.g., H. Gregg Lewis, Gary Becker, Jacob Mincer). The ILE school continues to have its primary base of representation in the present-day field of industrial relations, although both its membership and its intellectual status have weakened significantly with the decline of institutionalism as a scientific approach to the study of labor problems and the concomitant decline in the trade union movement.

◆ The golden age of industrial relations as a field of study occurred during the fifteen years following the end of World War II. Public interest in the subject reached a high point because of the rapid spread of trade unionism and collective bargaining, the unprecedented level of strikes, and concerns over the balance of power between labor and management and the impact of collective bargaining on inflation and productivity. Numerous universities established free-standing, multidisciplinary IR programs, and a new professional association, the Industrial Relations Research Association, and a new academic journal, the *Industrial and Labor Relations Review*, were founded. Industrial relations was thus transformed from a small-scale, relatively uninstitutionalized field of study in academe to a major growth area of teaching and research with all the institutional trappings of a bona fide scientific field of inquiry.

◆ The period from 1945 to 1960 was also the high watermark with respect to the disciplinary breadth and intellectual quality of research in industrial relations. Scholars from fields as diverse as anthropology, psychology, history, law, economics, and political science became active in industrial relations and contributed to a great outpouring of articles and books on the organization and practice of management, the structure and internal political process of unions, and the process and outcomes of collective bargaining.

Another hallmark of the period was the heavy emphasis given to interdisciplinary research as scholars made a concerted effort to bridge disciplinary boundaries and meld theories and concepts into a more holistic view of industrial relations. The outcome of this effort was the production of a number of pathbreaking studies that remain influential today.

◆ From the 1920s through the early part of the 1950s, the proponents of both the PM and the ILE schools perceived themselves to be members of the field of industrial relations. Beginning in the decade after the end of World War II, however, the bonds that had held the various disciplines together weakened noticeably, resulting in the 1960s in the dissolution of the confederation between the PM and ILE schools. The causes of the divorce were, first, incompatibilities in their theoretical frameworks, research methods, policy perspectives, and value systems (particularly regarding unions) and, second, the incentives for disciplinary specialization in research engendered by the growing emphasis in academe on science-building.

After the late 1950s, the PM school largely dropped its association with industrial relations and became a rival school of thought under the HR (human resources) label, leaving the ILE school as the major claimant of the field of industrial relations. What was once a confederation thus evolved into separate, competing fields of HR and IR.

◆ Before the divorce of the PM and ILE schools, industrial relations could legitimately claim that all aspects of the employment relationship were in its intellectual domain. By the late 1960s, however, the perceived domain of industrial relations had narrowed to the study of unions and collective bargaining and, of secondary importance, the employment problems of special groups in the work force (e.g., minority workers, the aged). This narrowing of focus was a consequence of the departure of the PM school, and the resulting dominance of industrial relations by the ILE school, and the pressures in academe for disciplinary specialization in research engendered by science-building and the consequent spin-off of non–collective bargaining related topics to other fields of study that had better developed, more relevant bodies of theory.

Membership and active participation in the field also experienced a distinct hollowing-out as faculty from the various disciplines elected to remain apart from industrial relations because of the lack of emphasis on the organization and practice of management, their lack of interest in labor-management relations, their antipathy to the pro-union value system predominant in industrial relations, or their belief that the most fertile research opportunities were in intradisciplinary work rather than in cross-disciplinary projects.

◆ The association of industrial relations with the study of unions and collective bargaining, coupled with the decline in union density and power in the United States, precipitated a corresponding decline in the organizational and intellectual vitality of the field that began in the early 1970s and accelerated in the 1980s. One casualty was IR academic programs. Student demand shifted away from such traditional IR courses as collective bargaining, IR theory, and union government and administration toward HR subjects, such as compensation and employee selection. Although most IR academic units were able to accommodate this shift in demand in the short run by augmenting the HR part of their faculty and curricula, their continued existence was clouded by the decline in the intellectual and job market appeal of the IR label; the loss of a rationale for having free-standing, multidisciplinary IR units; and the loss of political support in local and state communities for the maintenance of academic programs serving the organized labor movement. Although the top-tier IR programs weathered the 1980s intact, other programs were abolished, merged into a business school or management program, or given a more HR-like title.

◆ The close association between the field of industrial relations and the study of union-management relations also worked to the detriment of IR research. Starting in the 1960s, IR research gradually became more narrow in scope as scholars concentrated on labor-management relations and the employment problems of special labor force groups, most often from the perspective of labor economics (both institutional and neoclassical). A corresponding decline in behavioral science research occurred, particularly on the organization and practice of management. A degree of intellectual mediocrity and staidness also afflicted IR research as labor-management relations became institutionalized and the nonunion sector of the economy became the locus of new innovations in employment practice and policy.

Paradoxically, the 1980s witnessed a modest increase in both participation by behavioral science scholars in IR research and the quality and policy relevance of the research produced by traditional ILE-oriented scholars. These events were fueled at least in part by the quest to understand both the causes and consequences of the process of deunionization. It is reasonable to assume, however, that if the union sector of the economy continues to decline, research talent and resources in academia will gradually flow from IR (as currently defined) to other more promising areas of study.

◆ The close link between industrial relations and the study of labor-management relations also worked to the detriment of the field's major professional association, the Industrial Relations Research Association. The IRRA was intended to represent all the disciplines and topical areas related to the subject of employment relations. From the beginning, however, the organization has been controlled by, and served the interests of, scholars affiliated with the ILE school. The result has been that labor economists and other institutionally oriented scholars interested in collective bargaining have dominated the activities and research program of the association, the mix of subjects in IRRA publications has been heavily weighted toward labor-management relations, and the prevailing ideology has been supportive of the New Deal system of collective bargaining and protective labor legislation. As the organized labor movement in the United States has declined in membership and influence, the IRRA's continued focus on, and support of, the traditional system of labor-management relations has tended to isolate it in the academic community. The appeal of the IRRA to new, research-oriented scholars is also hurt by its attempt to keep its meetings and publications "practitioner-friendly," a goal that promotes a much-desired cross-fertilization of ideas between academics and practitioners but at the cost of reduced scientific rigor and, thus, opportunities for science-building.

♦ The final chapter of the book examined the future of industrial relations as a field of study. The conclusion was that if the organized labor movement continues to decline in membership and political power over the 1990s, as seems likely, and absent major changes in the current structure and intellectual orientation of academic IR, the number of academic programs, students, researchers, and teachers will most likely contract further. It is argued, therefore, that maintenance of the status quo is not a viable option for the field and its major institutions. Fundamental change is necessary.

♦ One suggestion for change is to replace the term *industrial relations* with a new label for the field, such as *employment relations*, that is both more inclusive and contemporary-sounding. Another suggestion is to reposition the intellectual boundaries and core subject matter of the field. Industrial relations should be defined along the two dimensions that have guided teaching and research in the field: science-building and problem-solving.

With regard to science-building, the focus of industrial relations should be on the employment relationship and all the institutions, practices, and outcomes associated with the world of work. An intellectual fault line runs down the middle of teaching and research on the employment relationship, however, and it is this fault line that divides the subject into human resources and industrial relations. The field of HR includes the internalists; that is, those scholars who seek explanations for the outcomes of the employment relationship within individuals and organizations. Thus, HR scholars typically come from academic areas such as organizational behavior, human resource management, industrial and organizational psychology and the micro end of sociology and focus on internal management and union practices, the social structure of organizations, and psychological and social determinants of human behavior (e.g., trust, feelings of inequity, group cohesion).

The externalists, by contrast, typically come from academic areas such as economics, law, history, political science, and the macro end of sociology and focus on factors external to the organization to explain employment-related outcomes, such as economic conditions in product and labor markets, the body of law and judicial opinion, the demographic, occupational, and rural versus urban structure of the local community or industry, and the prevailing ideology, culture, and social norms of the nation.

These are several virtues to this division between IR and HR. It implies that the two fields are different approaches to consideration of the same subject (the employment relationship), rather than separate fields of inquiry as is often assumed (labor relations versus human resource management). It broadens the subject of IR from unions and collective bargaining to a consideration of all aspects of the employment relationship, and, by broadening the subject area, it also increases the cross-disciplinary representation of researchers active in IR. Yet, despite the widening of the topical and disciplinary focus of the field, the external perspective still creates the basis for a community of research interests among scholars (because of complementarities in theory and methods across the externally oriented disciplines) that will make participation in the field an intellectually rewarding experience.

From a problem-solving perspective, the focus of industrial relations should be on those methods, practices, and policies that resolve labor problems and contribute to increased efficiency, equity, and individual well-being in the workplace. The preoccupation of present-day industrial relations with trade unionism and collective bargaining reflects the long-held conviction of the ILE school that these institutions (along with the other parts of the New Deal IR system) are central to the attainment of these three objectives. Long-term social and economic trends have undermined the effectiveness of, and a portion of the rationale for, this approach to the resolution of labor problems and, hence, a revised approach to problem-solving is required. It is this revised approach that defines, in turn, the problem-solving boundaries of the field of industrial relations. I conjecture that this revised approach will emphasize several themes. Some are quite similar to themes of the past, and others represent a significant shift in emphasis. Among these themes are a continued focus on the relations between workers and managers and a concern for the protection of workers' rights and interests; a broadened emphasis on systems of workplace governance that subsume not only traditional-style collective bargaining but also other forms of employee representation such as enterprise unions, works councils and self-managed work teams; continued concern with the causes of worker-management conflict and its resolution; and a greater emphasis on promoting efficiency, competitiveness, and quality in the production process through IR and HR policies.

Industrial relations as conceptualized above does not have a unitary topical focus or conceptual model but, rather, represents a series of connected themes defined by the field's interests in both science-building and problem-solving. The heart of the field lies at the intersection of these two dimensions; that is, the impact of external environmental forces on the organization and performance of work and the resulting relations between employers and employees, and the development of a system of workplace governance that is congruent with these external forces, promotes efficiency in the internal operation of the organization, protects workers' equity interests, and contributes to the development and growth of the nation's human resources.

CONCLUSION

The events of the last decade have been hard on U.S. industrial relations and have raised the question of whether the field will survive into the twenty-first century as anything more than a marginal area of teaching and research. The prognosis for the field as it is currently structured is relatively gloomy. I do not foresee IR going the way of home economics, but, absent significant change, the future surely entails a further shrinkage in the number of IR academic programs and faculty with IR training and interests and in the organizational vitality and membership of the IRRA.

These events are not foreordained, however. It is possible that my assessment is overly pessimistic and academic IR will ride out the current period of turbulence relatively intact. It is also possible that economic and political events in the remainder of the 1990s will become favorable for the field. Although I do not wish a crisis to befall the nation, the history of the field clearly reveals that major disruptions to the employment relationship, be they in the form of war or depression, benefit industrial relations by drawing public attention to the subject of employer-employee relations and bringing academic researchers into greater contact with the real world of employment practice and policy.

The odds do not favor either event, however. The evidence is overwhelming, I think, that the status quo position for the field is not viable in the long run. Nor do I think industrial relations can count on an economic or political crisis to save the day. A crisis of some sort may well be brewing, judged by the growing perception among the populace that the nation is embarked on a road of economic and social decline, but the New Deal–era policy program associated with the field of industrial relations is more likely to be seen as part of the problem, not the solution. The only path with real promise for industrial relations, therefore, is change, both intellectual and institutional in nature.

Two aspects of this change process are crucial to the long-term fortunes of the field. The first is a reconceptualization of the intellectual boundaries and core subject matter of industrial relations. Industrial relations will secure its future only if it carves out a distinct intellectual area of inquiry that is independent of specific institutions and practices (e.g., trade unions and collective bargaining). The approach I advocate defines industrial relations as the study of the employment relationship from the perspective of the environment external to the organization. This definition would not only provide the field with a distinct place in the social sciences but is consistent with the intellectual approach to the subject taken by the ILE school from the early 1920s to the present.

The second equally important aspect of the change process is the development of a problem-solving program for change in employment practices and policy that promotes the objectives of increased efficiency, equity, and individual well-being. Industrial relations scholars have for too long accepted the verities of the past, with the consequence that industrial relations is now seen as a reactive, out-of-date field that has little relevance for resolving the employment problems of the 1990s. The challenge facing IR scholars is to reexamine the assumptions and values that underlie the field, keep what remains valid and graft on new material where necessary, and then develop and advocate a set of practices and policies that are both congruent with the intellectual foundations of the field and responsive to the needs of employers, workers, and the larger society.

Like all challenges to the status quo, this process carries the risk of failure and the potential for conflict. If IR scholars can successfully meet the challenge, however, the future of industrial relations will be bright indeed.

197

NOTES

INTRODUCTION
1. Industrial relations as both a concept and a field of study is largely Anglo-
    American in origin, although interest in the field spread across the world
    in the post–World War II period. In the chapters that follow, attention is
    focused primarily on developments in the United States, although reference
    is occasionally made to events and research in Canada and Great Britain.
    Limiting the discussion to the United States, besides being a matter of
    practicality, is justified to the extent that industrial relations first emerged
    as a formal concept and field of study in the United States and many of
    the field's most influential institutional and scholarly developments oc-
    curred here. The downside is that the development of the field in the
    United States, and consequently the conceptual and ideological perspec-
    tives of U.S. researchers, are unique in certain respects to this country,
    thus limiting the generalizability of the findings of this study.

    For a survey of industrial relations thought and practice in Canada, see
    Hebert, Jain, and Meltz (1988); a survey of IR academic programs in Canada
    is provided by Boivin (1991). For Great Britain, see Roberts (1972), Ber-
    ridge and Goodman (1988), and P. Beaumont (1990). A summary of
    developments in international IR is provided by R. Adams (1992).

1. THE ORIGINS OF INDUSTRIAL RELATIONS
1. The origins of the term *industrial relations* are obscure. Richard Morris
    (1987) claims that the term first appeared in Great Britain as early as 1885,
    while Thomas Spates (1944:6) states that in America the term "was born
    of strife, unrest, and economic hardship among factory workers back in
    1894." Although Spates is probably referring to the Pullman strike, he
    does not give a specific reference. The Commission on Industrial Relations
    got its name from a petition presented to President Taft on December 30,
    1911, entitled "Petition to the President for a Federal Commission on

Industrial Relations" signed by twenty-eight people prominent in social reform circles. The petition was also published concurrently in the *Survey* (27 [December 30, 1911]: 1430–31). According to Morris (p. 535), the first official usage of the term *industrial relations* did not occur in Britain until 1924 with the creation of an Industrial Relations Department in the Ministry of Labour.

2. The commission had an important impact not only in spawning the name industrial relations but also in stimulating early academic research in the field. John R. Commons, who would later be described by many (e.g., Kochan 1980; Barbash 1991b) as the father of industrial relations, was one of the commission's nine committee persons. According to LaFayette G. Harter, Jr. (1962:131–59), Common's field investigations and interviews with company officials and workers during the hearings of the commission were a rich source of inspiration and material for his subsequent writings on labor issues. Robert Hoxie, another important figure in industrial relations, was appointed to a research staff position and from his field work later published an authoritative book on the subject of scientific management (Hoxie 1915). Finally, a number of graduate students who later went on to publish significant scholarly works in industrial relations, such as Selig Perlman, William Leiserson, Sumner Slichter, Leo Wolman, David McCabe, and Edwin Witte, were introduced to real-world labor problems through their role as research assistants to the staff of the commission.

3. On this subject Leiserson (1929:127–28) states: "A generation ago it was common to speak of *The* Labor Problem. . . . The most usual way of referring to employers and their employees was in the abstract terms, Capital and Labor; and the relations between the two were conceived as presenting a more or less mechanical problem of removing the friction between these opposing forces. . . . Then the idea of a single labor problem . . . gave way to the conception of a multiplicity of problems or evils, for each of which separate, practical remedies were to be devised. But further study revealed that what were evils from one point of view appeared as remedies from another. Thus strikes, boycotts, and trade unions might be evils to the employer; but to the wage earner they are remedies."

4. The transition from labor problems to personnel problems is indicated by the interchangeable use of the two terms by Meyer Bloomfield (1923:3–4): "All new countries are confronted with two typical personnel problems. First, the scarcity of labor; second, the instability of labor. These are the two most ancient of so-called labor problems." Although the term *labor problems* gradually faded from the personnel literature, some authors continued to use the term through the late 1940s (see Jucius 1948).

5. The relationship between social Darwinism and classical economics is alluded to by Joseph Dorfman (1963:15–16): "Spencer [Herbert Spencer, the leading English proponent of social Darwinism] asserted, in *Social Statics* (1872 edition), 'that the poverty of the incapable, the distresses that come upon the imprudent, the starvation of the idle, and those shouldering aside

of the weak by the strong . . . are the decrees of a large far-seeing benev-
olence.' This conclusion was seized upon by the staunchest advocates of
dominant extreme laissez-faire economics as reinforcing their position."

6. The distaste of early American socialists and Marxists for industrial
relations is reflected in modern times by the paucity of academics of a
radical or Marxist bent who are active in the field. By contrast, a relatively
strong contingent of British academics approach the subject from a radical
or Marxist perspective (e.g., Hyman 1975). To some degree this reflects
the fact that economists have dominated academic IR research in the
United States, while sociologists and historians have played a larger role
in Britain.

7. Taylor's (1895) first paper on the subject of scientific management was
entitled "A Piece Rate System, Being a Step Toward a Partial Solution of
the Labor Problem."

8. Symptomatic of the growing use of the term was the publication in 1919
of *Industrial Relations: A Selected Bibliography* by the Russell Sage Foundation
Library. The bibliography was divided into two subtopics, employment
management and participation in management.

9. As far as I can determine, the first academic article containing the term
industrial relations in the title was chapter 1, "Industrial Relations," by John
R. Commons in the 1921 edition of *Trade Unionism and Labor Problems* (a
book of collected readings on labor). The first doctoral dissertation to have
the term in the title, "Industrial Relations in the West Coast Lumber
Industry," was written in 1923 by Cloice Howd (University of California,
Berkeley).

10. A fairly complete list of the local chapters still in existence as of 1940 is
in "Among the Local Industrial Relations Associations," *Personnel* 17 (August 1940): 79–83. The article states (p. 79), "Nearly every major city of
the United States and all important industrial regions have their local
industrial relations associations, whose membership is comprised of personnel executives from neighboring plants." Several of these local associations, including the ones in Chicago and Philadelphia, remain active.
(The Chicago chapter changed its name several years ago to the Human
Resource Management Association, while the Philadelphia chapter continues to call itself an industrial relations association.)

11. Dale Yoder (1931:123) states in this regard, "The most widely accepted
approach to the study of industrial relations is one which involves an
examination of phenomena that are usually described as labor problems."

12. J. Douglas Brown, director of the IR section at Princeton from 1926 to
1954, states (1976:5): "It was the intention of the founders [of the section]
to broaden the scope of the field studied to include *all* factors, conditions,
problems and policies involved in the employment of human resources in
organized production or service. It was not to be limited to any single
academic discipline. Nor was the term 'industrial relations' limited to activities within *private* enterprise but was assumed to cover the relations of

governments and all other institutions with those people who constituted the working forces of the country" (emphasis in original). For a similar view see Watkins (1922:5).

13. The map was reproduced in 1929 in *Personnel Journal* 7 (5):391. A brief discussion of the work of the committee that prepared the map is given on pp. 390–93.

14. Slichter (1928:287–88) states in this regard: "There are two ways of looking at labor problems. One is from a scientific point of view. . . . It is aspired to by the scientist who studies trade unions, child labor, unemployment, in order to find out what *is* or what *might be,* without speculating about what *should be.* . . . To the vast majority of people, however, even to the economists and sociologists, the labor problem is more than this. It is also a problem of ethics, a matter not simply of what is or what might be, but of what should be. . . . From the ethical point of view, therefore, the labor problem is concerned with two principal things: with the effect of the prevailing economic institutions . . . upon the conflict between life and work, and with the institutional changes needed to harmonize men's activities as laborers with their interests as men." The terms *science-building* and *problem-solving* are from Barbash (1991a).

15. As detailed in the next chapter, the early literature on industrial relations was written largely by two groups, academic economists and management practitioners (with a modest contribution by industrial psychologists). Although references to the goals of efficiency, equity, and enhanced individual well-being can be found in the writings of both groups, the economists tended to emphasize efficiency and equity while the management practitioners and psychologists tended to emphasize efficiency and enhanced individual well-being or happiness. This difference probably reflects a difference in disciplinary perspectives: the economists were trained to think in terms of markets and the processes of production and distribution, while the management practitioners and psychologists generally focused on the interaction of managers and workers inside the firm, most often from an individualistic, psychological frame of reference. The difference in emphasis also reflected the greater weight the economists gave to the adversarial nature of the employment relationship, a point of view that focused attention on distributional or equity issues, while the emphasis among the management practitioners and psychologists was on the congruence of interests that exists in the employment relationship, a perspective that tended to downgrade the saliency of equity issues. This difference in perspectives persists to the present day in the IR and human resources literatures. Noah Meltz (1989:109), for example, states that "industrial relations is concerned with balancing efficiency and equity," while Richard Walton (1985:36) states that "the theory [the new human resource management model] is that the policies of mutuality will elicit commitment which in turn will yield both better economic performance and greater human development."

2. THE SCHISM IN INDUSTRIAL RELATIONS

1. In his autobiography, Commons (1934a:170) explains the motivation for his involvement in industrial relations: "What I was always trying to do, in my academic way, was to save Wisconsin and the nation from politics, socialism, or anarchism, in dealing with the momentous conflict of capital and labor." He states in another place (p. 143), "I was trying to save capitalism by making it good." In a similar vein, J. Michael Eisner (1967:5) says of William Leiserson, a student of Commons who went on to a highly influential career in industrial relations: "Although Leiserson was rooted in the new economics and institutionalism, he was not an "institutionalist" or a member of any formal school of thought. He was a pragmatic reform economist who was concerned with individuals and their problems and not with economic theory."

   Two of the most prominent writers among management-oriented practitioners of industrial relations in the pre–World War II period were Clarence J. Hicks and Thomas Spates, both of whom wrote autobiographies. Hicks had intended to become a lawyer but instead chose a life in industrial relations because "the law was too far removed from people and their everyday problems to satisfy an urge the good Lord had given me. The next step brought me close to my goal, a life spent in working with people, helping them in the job of earning a living and making it worthwhile" (Hicks 1941:15). Spates (1960:50) says: "Up to the time of my going into the army in World War I, most of my employment experiences followed a pattern of mistrust, goldbricking, sabotage, petty theft, and a severe economic waste, as expressions of resentment against inconsiderate leadership. . . . It was about then, while reflecting upon my employment experiences, that I resolved to devote my remaining time to trying to improve the lot of my fellow man on the job."

2. This division of opinion was revealed clearly in the two industrial conferences convened by President Wilson in the fall of 1919. The conferences included distinguished representatives of employers, employees, and the community who were brought together for the purpose of reaching joint agreement on methods to be adopted in industry to eliminate the most egregious sources of waste, inefficiency, and conflict in the employment relationship. Both conferences ended in stalemate over the insistence of the employers' group on the open shop and the insistence of the labor group on the union shop and the replacement of nonunion employee representation plans with bona fide collective bargaining. The divisiveness posed by the issue of unionism also was manifested at the 1920 national meeting of the IRAA in the speeches given by John McConc (1920), a newspaper publisher and ardent promoter of the open shop, and the reply by John R. Commons (1920).

3. Roy Adams (1983) distinguishes between four competing paradigms in industrial relations: the labor market school, the political school (Marxism), the management school, and the institutional school. The PM and

the ILE schools distinguished here correspond to the latter two. At least in America, the former two are not, in my opinion, bona fide parts of industrial relations since the systems of employment relations envisioned (laissez-faire capitalism and socialism/syndicalism) were exactly what the founders of the field were trying to avoid. If one thinks of alternative systems of employment relations as ordered along a political and economic continuum, the righthand end point would be the labor market school and the lefthand end point would be the political school, with the management and institutional schools in the middle (the institutional school would be to the left of the management school). As discussed in chapter 1, the founders of industrial relations desired to steer a middle course between these two extremes, thereby promoting reform rather than reaction or revolution. It is also apparent that early participants in industrial relations regarded the field as divided into two competing schools of thought, not four. Paul Brissenden (1926:444), for example, mentions two "lines of thought" in industrial relations: the "academic line" of the economists and the "labor-management line" of the personnel practitioners. A similar division of thought is suggested by William M. Leiserson (1929:126), by James Bossard and J. Frederic Dewhurst (1931:430), and by Martin Estey (1960:93).

4. It is worth reiterating that the PM and ILE labels represent alternative schools of thought or approaches to *problem-solving* in industrial relations, not specific intellectual fields of study associated with science-building. Thus, the label "PM" does *not* designate the field of personnel management per se but rather represents the basic point of view held by personnel professionals concerning the cause and resolution of labor problems. As described in later chapters, the PM school grew to include academics from a variety of fields, including human relations, organizational behavior, and human resource management. While these academics differ significantly with respect to the theoretical constructs and research methodologies used in science-building, they nevertheless share a core set of beliefs about how best to promote improved industrial relations in the workplace. This is what the PM label is meant to connote. The same consideration applies equally well to the ILE label, which is meant to be an umbrella term for people who share a common set of beliefs about the source and solution of labor problems, even though they may differ substantially in their approach to the study of labor markets. From a problem-solving perspective, it is thus appropriate to combine the institutionalists of the Wisconsin school and the "neoclassical revisionists" (Kerr 1983) of the 1950s, even though from a science-building perspective the two groups had much less in common.

5. The employment management movement started in Boston in early 1913 with the founding of the Boston Employment Managers' Association, a group in which Meyer Bloomfield and Daniel Bloomfield played important roles (Lange 1928). Other local associations were soon founded, followed

by the founding of the National Association of Employment Managers in 1919. This group then changed its name to the Industrial Relations Association of America in 1920 and, in turn, the National Personnel Association in 1922 and the American Management Association in 1923. The first university course in employment management was offered at Dartmouth in 1915. The term *employment management* was largely replaced by *personnel management* by the early 1920s.

6. Clarence Hicks, the leading exponent of the PM school among practitioners, defined industrial relations for Scribner's *Dictionary of American History*: "The term 'industrial relations'... has grown to include all contacts between labor and all grades of management, connected with or growing out of employment. Specifically, it covers items usually classified as personnel work" (Hicks 1941:x).

In a similar vein, William Leiserson (1929:126) states: "Personnel Management, being concerned with the management of employees in the interest of business enterprises, must be clearly distinguished from the scientific study of industrial relations, just as Labor Economics [the study of the principles, methods, and policies wage earners and trade unions have developed for managing their employers] is so distinguished. Unless this distinction is made, hopeless confusion results."

Another piece of evidence on this matter is provided by the labor problems texts of the period (e.g., Watkins 1922; Furniss 1925). These texts contained a survey of industrial relations theory and practice as it existed in the 1920s. The surveys included extensive coverage of both the subjects of personnel management and labor-management relations.

Finally, evidence comes from industry, where the typical company organizational chart placed both the staff functions of personnel management and labor relations under the direction of the vice-president of industrial relations (Roethlisberger and Dickson 1939; Aspley and Whitmore 1943).

7. An example of the conventional wisdom is provided by Keith Davis (1957:5): "The term 'human relations' was used in business very little before 1940." Dozens of examples of its use can, in fact, be found.

8. The constitution of the National Personnel Association, created in 1923, stated that the organization's purpose was "to advance the understanding of the principles, policies and methods of creating and maintaining satisfactory human relations within commerce and industry." A monograph written by Whiting Williams in 1918, entitled *Human Relations in Industry*, also used the term.

9. One of the most important findings of the Hawthorne experiments was that informal work groups can either encourage or restrict individual work effort and production. On this subject J. David Houser (1927:140) says: "Like their employer, workers exercise control, though it is quite different from his in extent and kind. . . . Whatever type of supervisors they may have, individual employees can 'soldier' on the job, can practice sabotage in a variety of ways, and can limit executive accomplishment. By group

action, they can multiply these gestures of protest many times over. . . .
But on the other hand, there are vast and comparatively untapped reservoirs
of energy and interest which they can put at the service of industry. . . . "
On the next several pages Houser discusses two other themes later advanced
by Mayo and his colleagues, namely, the concept of equilibrium in the
social system of the plant and the overemphasis given to the role of financial
incentives in motivating work effort.

10. Although most of the influential writers in the PM school of the 1920s
were businessmen or consultants, many nevertheless had close ties to universities and actively participated in scholarly research. Sam Lewisohn, for
example, was vice-president of the Miami Copper Company, co-author
with John R. Commons and others of *Can Business Prevent Unemployment?*
(1925) and author of *The New Leadership in Industry* (1926), president of
the American Management Association, and chairman of the Industrial
Relations Research Committee of the Academy of Political Science. Other
members of the PM school who had close ties to universities or who
published research of a scholarly nature were Ordway Tead, Henry Metcalf,
Mary Parker Follett, Henry Dennison, Clarence Hicks, Chester Barnard,
and Arthur Young. Biographical sketches of these people, and of other
prominent PM writers of the 1920s, is provided in Spates 1960.

11. On this subject Lewisohn states (pp. 48–49): "To approach labor unrest
as if it were mainly due to peculiar defects of capitalism is thus a profound
error. . . . We should, therefore, focus our attention for a while on the
individual plant where the daily contact between employer and employee
takes place. Here is the starting point of any endeavor to improve industrial relations." He goes on to say (p. 202), "There is no escaping the conclusion that the most important factor in sound industrial relations is
management."

12. Pyschology affected the development of personnel management in two
ways, first, through the development of theories of motivation, group dynamics, leadership, and other such factors associated with human relations
and, second, through its impact on particular personnel practices and techniques, such as applicant interviewing, hiring tests, job analysis, and training. A major catalyst in this regard was the set of psychological experiments
conducted by the army during World War I involving aptitude tests and
rating systems. The practical applications of these experiments were soon
transferred to personnel practice in private industry after the war (Ling
1965). The psychological work associated with human relations had a major
influence on the field of industrial relations and is thus discussed at length;
the psychological work on specific personnel practices, while of major
significance to the development of personnel management per se, had only
a secondary impact on the broader issues associated with industrial relations
and thus is not discussed further. Much of the discussion of the PM school
in this chapter is derived from the writings of business practitioners and
consultants, not academic industrial psychologists. The reason is that the

industrial psychologists tended to focus on the narrow issues associated with specific personnel practices, while the human relations themes were, at least in the 1920s, more often the province of the practitioners and consultants.

13. Mary Parker Follett (1925:82) states the idea thus: "When you have made your employees feel that they are in some sense partners in the business, they do not improve the quality of their work, save waste in time and material, because of the Golden Rule, but because their interests are the same as yours."

14. The term *economic man* as used in the 1920s referred to the assumption that only pecuniary considerations motivate human behavior. Economists have long since abandoned this conception of human behavior (if, indeed, most ever believed it in the first place). The term is now used to connote a model in which it is presumed that human behavior is guided by the desire to maximize individual satisfaction, be it from pecuniary or non-pecuniary sources, and that preference relations over items of choice satisfy conditions such as transitivity, completeness, and nonsatiation (see Kaufman 1989b).

15. As indicated, the PM literature tended to have a "micro" focus on the management of labor inside the plant and the relationships therein between workers and managers. More "macro" issues concerning the structure of organizations and the functions of management were addressed in a largely independent stream of management thought by people such as Henri Fayol, Max Weber, Chester Barnard, James Mooney, and Ralph Davis. These two perspectives were integrated in the late 1950s when human relations and organization theory were fused together to form the new field of organizational behavior (Wren 1987).

16. In 1886, Ely, Clark, Seligman, and several other economists trained in Germany established the American Economic Association. According to Ely (1938:132–64), the association was established to provide a forum for the "young rebels" in the profession who opposed laissez-faire and favored inductive, historical, and statistical research methods.

17. For purposes of this discussion, the institutional school includes any labor economist who subscribed to these themes. Economists such as George Barnett, Summer Slichter, Paul Douglas, and Harry A. Millis are thus included, even though they were not "institutionalists" per se. The field of labor economics was, in fact, segmented into several groups in the pre–World War II years (Dorfman 1959; McNulty 1980). The earliest split was between the labor economists, such as Barnett and Jacob Hollander at Johns Hopkins University, and Ely and Commons at the University of Wisconsin. Both groups were distinguished by their research on trade unions, but Ely and Commons took a more normative, less analytic approach. Commons's approach was propagated in the 1930s by the "Wisconsin school" of Selig Perlman, Don D. Lescohier, Edwin Witte, Elizabeth Brandeis, David Saposs, and others, while the more analytic approach was

carried on by Summer Slichter, Paul Douglas, and Harry Millis. A perusal of the three-volume set of labor texts by Millis and Royal E. Montgomery (vol. I: *Labor's Progress and Some Basic Labor Problems,* 1938; vol. II: *Labor's Risks and Social Insurance,* 1938; and vol. III: *Organized Labor,* 1945) clearly reveals, nonetheless, that even these more "middle-of-the-road" labor economists subscribed to the basic institutional point of view regarding labor markets and labor unions.

18. The following passage from the Webbs (1897:658) gives the flavor of the argument: "When the unemployed are crowding around the factory gates every morning, it is plain to each man that, unless he can induce the foreman to select him rather than another, his chance of subsistence for weeks to come may be irretrievably lost. Under these circumstances bargaining, in the case of the isolated individual workman, becomes absolutely impossible. The foreman has only to pick his man, and tell him the terms. Once inside the gates, the lucky workman knows that if he grumbles at any of the surroundings, however intolerable; if he demurs to any speeding-up, lengthening of the hours, or deductions; or if he hesitates to obey any order, however unreasonable, he condemns himself once more to the semi-starvation and misery of unemployment. For the alternative to the foreman is merely to pick another man from the eager crowd, whilst the difference to the employer becomes incalculably infinitesimal."

19. Commons was a tireless advocate of protective labor legislation, such as workmen's compensation and unemployment insurance, and played an important role in their eventual adoption in Wisconsin. His rationale for these laws provides a classic illustration of the institutional perspective on labor problems. Commons argued that the rates of both unemployment and industrial accidents were far higher than was socially justified because the market mechanism imposed little if any penalty on employers for high numbers of layoffs or injuries and deaths. (In a competitive labor market, firms that provide unstable employment or unsafe working conditions must pay a correspondingly higher wage to attract a work force, thus motivating them to stabilize employment and reduce accidents. Market defects, such as externalities and public goods, however, reduce or eliminate these wage premiums and thereby the incentive to reduce layoffs and accidents.) Commons advocated using an institutional device (in this case a social insurance program) to create a nonmarket incentive scheme to supplement the forces of supply and demand. In particular, employers' contributions to the insurance funds are made a positive function of the number of their layoffs and accidents. The net effect is that the tax rate in the insurance programs provides an additional incentive for employment stability and increased safety, thus leading to an increase in *both* efficiency and individual well-being.

20. This divergence in perspectives is evident in the remarks of Frank Stockton, dean of the business school at the University of Kansas (1932:224): "Labor economics men who have the social point of view, coupled perhaps with

an anti-management complex, look with suspicion upon personnel management as a means of driving labor and eliminating trade unionism. They disdain personnel further because of its apparent lack of theory. The personnel instructor, on the other hand, thinks that he at least is working in terms of reality, and may be inclined to dislike the fault-finding tone of labor economists and to belittle the socioeconomic approach to industrial questions."

21. In this vein Commons (1911:466) states: "The employer's business is to attend to the increase in efficiency; the wage earner's business is to sell himself to do the employer's bidding. The two interests are necessarily conflicting. Open conflict can be avoided in three ways: by the domination of the employer; by the domination of the union; by the equal domination of the two interests. The first and second methods do not solve the problem, they suppress it. The third meets it in the same way that similar conflicts are met in the region of politics; namely, a constitutional form of organization representing the interests affected, with mutual veto, and therefore with progressive compromises as conflicts arise."

22. C. Canby Balderston was one of the few members of the PM school who stressed the contingent relationship between economic conditions and personnel practices. He (1935:2) stated, for example: "To discuss industrial relations apart from the economic forces that affect them is one of our pet follies. . . . John Jones is not entirely his own master in dealing with his employees. He too has a 'boss'—competition, usually harsh enough, but at times an inexorable tyrant demanding that he choose between his announced personnel policies and the survival of his business."

The approach of most other proponents of PM to this issue took two forms. One was to minimize the importance of the economic environment. For example, Lewisohn (1926:226–27) states: "The real difficulty of labor relations has been one of neglect. Executives have treated the question of human organization as a minor matter not a major problem. . . . In some countries other parts of the industrial fabric are so weak that the strengthening of this particular strand of labor relations could not make up for these other weaknesses. . . . In this country we are suffering from no such economic maladjustments. With our foundation of economic well-being, the adoption of effective methods of human organization should have a maximum effectiveness, both in securing production and in promoting an identity of social interests."

Another approach was to counsel employers to focus on the long-term goal of good labor relations, even if this meant sacrificing profits in the short run. Thus, Catchings (1923:492–93) argued that wages and working conditions should be based on fairness and fact, not economic conditions: "The employer shall not, at any time, force upon the employee wages, hours, and working conditions, merely because he has at the time the economic power to do so. . . . At any time, for any company, there is a fair wage that can be paid. . . . What this wage is, what these hours are, what these conditions of employment are—these are questions of fact, to be determined as such."

23. Commons (1921:4) says: "The fluctuation of the currency is the greatest of all the labor problems. . . . If we could find a system of currency in which the great price movements which have been occurring in all these years could be stabilized, we would do more to stabilize industry, to bring about industrial peace, than any other one thing."

   Commons's emphasis on the macroeconomic origin of labor problems was born out of the depression of 1920–22, an event that quickly led to the liquidation of the new personnel programs and progressive employment practices established during and shortly after World War I (Harter 1962:75–76; Douglas 1922). In 1920, Commons, Wesley Mitchell, and Malcolm Rorty founded the National Bureau of Economic Research, an organization that pioneered the study of business cycles. Commons also became president of the National Monetary Union, authored several scholarly articles on monetary policy, and drafted legislation to require the Federal Reserve Bank to stabilize the price level. Thus, although it is seldom recognized, an important plank of Commons's institutional program was the use of collective action in the form of Federal Reserve monetary policy to ensure a stable, full-employment economy. On this subject, see Whalen 1991.

24. Proponents of the PM perspective recognized that some firms had substandard labor conditions but maintained (as noted in the text) that the best remedy was a positive one of education. In reaction to this argument, Commons (1920:130) stated in an address to the IRAA convention of 1920: "I have listened here to what seemed to me to be the most marvelous and keen discussion of what employers could do, of what foremen could do, of what management could do, and I am firmly convinced that if these most informing discussions we have heard could be carried out . . . the capitalist system could be saved, that there will be no need of either unionism or of revolution. But we know that will not be done; we know that you are but a small number. . . . There is, therefore, a need for unionism to supplement management."

25. The position of the institutionalists on this issue also conflicts with that of neoclassical economists. The latter hold that the production of goods and services should be so arranged that it maximizes the welfare of individuals in their roles as consumers, a goal promoted by production at minimum cost. This fact, coupled with the penchant of neoclassical economists to view labor as an inanimate factor in production (such as is generally the case in the production function literature), leads them to oppose in principle union work rules, such as restrictions on the speed of the line or promotion on the basis of seniority. Institutionalists, however, hold that restrictive practices by unions can promote the social welfare and thus are not to be rejected out of hand. Their position is based on the idea that labor is embodied in human beings and human beings have an interest not only in low prices for consumption goods in the marketplace

but also in safe and humane working conditions at the work site and that some balancing of these interests is appropriate. A recent statement of this position is provided by Lester Thurow (1988).

26. A belief in the social efficacy of pluralism is one of the strongest philosophical threads running through the ILE school from Commons's time to the present. See, for example, Kerr (1954b) and the winter 1983 issue of *Industrial Relations*. The latter contains a report (pp. 125–31) on a two-day conference attended by twenty-nine leading IR scholars on "The Future of Industrial Relations." The last paragraph of the report states: "The conference closed with what came close to a consensus: our economic and social problems can best be resolved through tripartite union-management-government discussion and collaboration. No better model was presented." Also see Dunlop (1984b) and Schatz (1993).

3. INDUSTRIAL RELATIONS IN THE INTERWAR YEARS

1. A fifteen-month strike at the company was finally broken in 1914 when National Guardsmen stormed a miners' village and killed twenty people, an event that became known as the Ludlow massacre. Rockefeller was widely excoriated for his alleged culpability in the disaster, a public reaction that motivated him to take a strong personal interest in industrial relations and progressive personnel practices (see Rockefeller 1923).
2. The unbalanced view of industrial relations contained in many of the texts used in introductory labor courses was attested to by Dale Yoder (1931:125): "It [the labor problems text] is apt to portray modern industry as though it were in the agonizing throes of a host of diseases. It probably misrepresents the feelings of both workers and employers, and, at best, it presents a distinctly one-sided picture."
3. Hicks (1941:150) mentions in his memoirs that the University of Wisconsin had agreed to create a sixth industrial relations section. Although the Department of Economics approved the creation of the section in 1939 (stated in unpublished departmental minutes, as told to me by Robert Lampman), for unknown reasons the section never came into existence. Given that Wisconsin was the home of the ILE school of industrial relations, the section, had it materialized, would have been something of a coup for Hicks in his efforts to provide "balance" in the teaching of industrial relations.
4. A businessman also played a key role in introducing industrial relations into British universities. According to Benjamin C. Roberts (1972), in the early 1930s Montague Burton, a clothing manufacturer, donated funds for the establishment of three chairs in industrial relations at Cambridge, Cardiff, and Leeds. His expressed reason for doing so was to promote peace between labor and capital. These chairs were apparently the first time that industrial relations was formally represented in British academe.
5. Of the five IR units Hicks created in the United States, the two most successful have been the ones at Princeton and at MIT. They remain in

existence and continue to produce noteworthy research. In contrast, the units at Stanford and at the California Institute of Technology never established a perceptible presence in the field. The Stanford unit was discontinued in the late 1960s upon the retirement of Dale Yoder. The unit at the California Institute of Technology remains in existence but does little work in industrial relations. Its primary mission is to sponsor extension classes and research on the management of technology. The situation at Michigan is in some respects the most interesting. Upon Hicks's instigation, a bureau of industrial relations was established in the school of business in 1935. Its primary function was noncredit management education. In 1960, in conjunction with Wayne State University, the university established another IR unit outside the business school, called the Institute of Labor and Industrial Relations. The focus of the institute was on labor-management relations, and it offered on-campus courses and sponsored research. Thus, until the late 1960s, when the bureau was phased out, Michigan had *two* IR units that existed side by side, one representing the PM school and the other the ILE school.

6. The first IR department in the United States was established in 1944 at Rockhurst College, a Jesuit school in Kansas City (Bradley 1945). Although no stand-alone industrial relations program existed in the interwar years, industrial relations was nevertheless recognized as a distinct area of study in academe, albeit of small size. In their survey of the forty-two member schools of the American Association of Collegiate Schools of Business (AACSB), for example, Bossard and Dewhurst (1931:314) found that 14 of the 1,398 faculty at these schools claimed industrial relations as one of their areas of specialization (compared to 31 for personnel management and 48 for labor).

7. As an example, in the introductory chapter of his labor text *Labor Economics and Labor Problems* (1933:1–22), Yoder provides an extensive discussion of the subject matter of labor economics and the origins of labor problems without once mentioning the terms *labor market* and *supply and demand*.

8. Several aspects of the figure are questionable. First, the institutional economics branch and the industrial and labor economics branches contain numerous names that have a dubious connection to those fields; one could argue that people such as Commons, Witte, and Perlman belong on the institutional branch, not the labor economics branch. Second, the sociometry and sociatry and group dynamics branches would appear to have had a sufficiently modest impact on industrial relations that they should not be identified separately. Third, a good case could be made that the public administration and industrial management branches should be merged together. Fourth, the fields of labor history and labor law are omitted altogether. These quibbles aside, the figure provides compelling evidence that into the 1950s industrial relations included in both theory and fact a wide range of disciplines from both the behavioral and nonbehavioral sciences and that behavioral science

scholars such as Miller and Form saw themselves as participating members of the field of industrial relations.

9. Commons deserves the title "father of American industrial relations" on several counts: he was the foremost academic expert of his day on labor issues, a fact revealed by his selection to serve on the Commission on Industrial Relations; more than any one person he was responsible for the establishment of industrial relations as a field of study in academe in this country; although he was an advocate of the ILE perspective, he wrote influential scholarly works that pertained to both the management and the labor sides of industrial relations. A thorough discussion of Commons's contributions to the development of industrial relations is provided in Barbash 1991b.

   In Britain, the "fathers" (perhaps more accurately the father and the mother) of industrial relations were Sidney and Beatrice Webb. Their two works on labor, *A History of Trade Unionism* (1894) and *Industrial Democracy* (1897), were landmark studies. The latter, in particular, represents in my view the bible of the ILE perspective on industrial relations. Unlike Commons, however, despite their profound intellectual impact on industrial relations, the Webbs did little to institutionalize the subject in British universities. As detailed by Roberts (1972), the Webbs founded the London School of Economics (LSE) but made no efforts to introduce the study of labor into the curriculum. This reflected, according to Roberts, the Webbs's belief that the study of labor problems was not sufficiently "scientific" for LSE, the fact that their research interests shifted from labor to issues of local government and social administration, and their growing estrangement from the trade union movement.

10. One indicator of the expansive nature of economics during this period was the publication of various management-related articles in the leading journals of the field. Examples include Slichter's article "Industrial Morale" (1920), in the *Quarterly Journal of Economics,* and Tead's article "The Problem of Graduate Training in Personnel Administration" (1921), in the *Journal of Political Economy.* Another indicator is the diverse range of courses offered by the typical economics department. At Wisconsin, for example, courses in employment management, general sociology, and social psychology were all listed under the department's course offerings in the 1920s. A similar situation existed at MIT through the late 1940s, where the Department of Economics and Social Sciences offered courses ranging from Paul Samuelson's doctoral seminar in microeconomic theory to Douglas McGregor's seminar on human relations.

11. Edwin Witte, a student of Commons, states (1954:131–32): "In the last quarter century of his life, Commons tried to pull together into a comprehensive, systematic body of economic thought the theoretical ideas he developed out of the work he did on practical public policy issues. . . . They were lost on me. I confess I have had the same difficulty following Commons' terminology and some of his reasoning which so many students of-

his later theoretical writings have experienced." He goes on to say (p. 133): "Institutional economics, as I conceive it, is not so much a connected body of economic thought as a method of approaching economic problems. ... In seeking solutions of practical problems, they [the institutionalists] try to give consideration to all aspects of these problems: economic (in the orthodox use of that term), social, psychological, historical, legal, political, administrative, and even technical."

The association of institutionalism with a particular methodological approach to research, rather than a theoretical point of view, is not unique to Witte. In a "Notice to Potential Contributors" in the October 1989 issue of *Industrial and Labor Relations Review,* the editors (p. 4) say: "We wish to receive more 'institutional' papers. Scholars and practitioners in our field ... have long debated the implication of the trend among researchers toward model building and quantitative analysis. ... Some readers may have concluded that because the proportion of *Review* articles containing quantitative analysis has escalated so rapidly in recent years, we have taken sides in the debate on methodology and have abandoned the institutionalists. That is decidely not the case."

I maintain that both Witte and the editors of the *Review* have fundamentally misinterpreted the essence of institutional economics, which was an attempt to construct an alternative theoretical paradigm based on a behavioral model of man, models of imperfect competition in markets, and the important role played by institutional (organizational and sociological) factors in resource allocation. Although Commons was unable to articulate such a paradigm successfully (hence the confusion by Witte and the editors of the *Review*), it is nevertheless clear that this was his goal.

The editors of the *Review* also err in associating institutional research with a nonquantitative approach. The institutionalists' fundamental critique of neoclassical economics is that the theory is derived from assumptions that in some cases diverge widely from reality. The solution to this problem is not so much an inductive style of research as an *adductive* style, where adductive means using detailed historical and empirical investigations to determine the facts of a situation from which correct theoretical assumptions can be adduced. The point, then, is that institutional research, far from being nonquantitative as alleged by the editors of the *Review,* is by its very nature heavily empirical and quantitative both in the formulation of theories and in the testing of the hypotheses of these theories, as evidenced in the 1920s by the central role played by Wesley Mitchell and John Commons in the founding of the National Bureau of Economic Research.

12. In 1931, R. M. Berg published a bibliography of management literature. The section entitled "industrial relations" contained more than 150 citations, most to nonacademic periodicals such as the *Bulletin of the Taylor Society* and *Industrial Management.* Also see Milton 1960 for more such references.

13. The opinion of Richard Lester and Maurice Neufeld as stated in telephone conversations.

14. Mention should also be made of the Personnel Research Federation, a nonprofit group founded in 1921 to promote "the cooperation of research activities pertaining to personnel in industry, commerce, education, and government" (U.S. Department of Labor 1921:111). Interestingly, one of the charter members of the group was the American Federation of Labor. The Personnel Research Federation sponsored numerous conferences and publications on industrial relations–related topics, including Stanley Mathewson's (1931) well-known monograph on restriction of output among unorganized workers and the monthly periodical *Personnel Journal*. Although *Personnel Journal* became largely practitioner-oriented after 1935 (because of a change in editors), before then many of its articles had a significant research element. It is noteworthy, for example, that seven of the ten members of the editorial board in the early 1930s were academics (including Wesley Mitchell from economics and Morris Viteles from industrial psychology), but not one was a business person.

4. THE INSTITUTIONALIZATION OF INDUSTRIAL RELATIONS

1. Keynes's book *The General Theory of Employment, Interest, and Money* was not published until 1936, three years after Franklin Roosevelt's election to office, and the ideas in it (activist use of monetary and fiscal policies to keep aggregate demand at a full-employment level) were not fully incorporated into government economic policy until the early 1960s (Stein 1990). Although there was relatively little interaction between Keynesian macroeconomists and institutional labor economists, the two schools of thought were nevertheless highly complementary in that both stressed the imperfect nature of markets, particularly the labor market, and both provided a rationale for government intervention in the economy. The link between modern-day Keynesian economics and institutional economics is discussed in Appelbaum 1979 and Whalen 1991.

2. The preamble of the Wagner Act states, "The inequality of bargaining power between employees who do not possess full freedom of association or actual liberty of contract, and employers who are organized in the corporate or other forms of ownership association . . . tend to aggravate recurrent business depressions, by depressing wage rates and the purchasing power of wage earners in industry and by preventing the stabilization of competitive wage rates and working conditions within and between industries."

3. The strong impetus given to the creation of new IR programs by public concern over the breadth and depth of labor-management conflict after the war is evident in the events surrounding the founding of the Industrial Relations Research Institute at the University of Wisconsin. In 1947, the board of regents directed the university "to study ways and means to protect the public interest in labor-management disputes"; and in 1949, the *Wis-*

consin State Journal said of the newly created institute that it provided "a giant microscope into which to peer into America's number one domestic problem, Big Business versus Big Labor" (quoted in Fried 1987:2–3).

4. A brief description of these programs (with the exception of the one at the University of Hawaii) is given in Industrial Relations Counselors 1949. Detailed histories of the IR programs at Illinois and Wisconsin are provided in Derber 1987 and Fried 1987. The establishment of IR units and developments at existing units are also chronicled in the "News and Notes" section of each issue of the *Industrial and Labor Relations Review.*

5. While the immediate post–World War II period saw a tremendous expansion in industrial relations programs in America, the same was not nearly so true in Canada and Great Britain. Canada saw the establishment of an IR institute at Laval University in the mid-1940s and the subsequent publication of an IR journal, *Industrial Relations—Quarterly Review* (R. Adams 1992). The major expansion of IR programs, and the establishment of the Canadian Industrial Relations Association, did not occur until two decades later, however. Speaking of the situation in Britain in the postwar period, John Berridge and John Goodman (1988:156) state, "Prior to the 1960s, the process of acceptance of industrial relations in the academic world was slow and problematic." Although the British Universities Industrial Relations Association was founded in 1950, the major period of growth took place from the mid-1960s to the late 1970s. The most important British IR programs in the 1960s were at Oxford University, Cambridge University, and the London School of Economics. In the 1970s, the IR program at Warwick University became the leading center for industrial relations research in Great Britain. This disparate pattern of growth in the three countries in IR largely reflects different cycles of union growth and accompanying public concern over issues such as strikes and inflation.

6. According to Derber (1987) and Fried (1987), the creation of the IR institutes at Illinois and Wisconsin was actively opposed by the schools of commerce at each university. The frosty relations between the IR institute and the school of commerce at Illinois is illustrated by the fact that as many as six faculty members from economics and one to three from sociology and psychology but only one from the business school held joint appointments with the institute in the 1950s (Derber 1987:28). While the situations at Illinois and Wisconsin were the norm in this regard, there were exceptions. At Berkeley, for example, a majority of the IR faculty held joint appointments with the business school, and the two units maintained a relatively amicable relationship (George Strauss, personal correspondence).

7. The compromise worked out at Illinois was that the IR institute was to specialize in labor relations and the school of commerce was to specialize in management. Both units shared responsibility for subjects dealing with the interaction of labor and management (Derber 1987:16).

8. The low interest in personnel management among students can be inferred from data presented by Robert A. Gordon and James E. Howell (1959:260). They surveyed thirty-three schools of business accredited by the American Association of Collegiate Schools of Business and found in 1955–56 that only 25 percent required a human relations or personnel course as part of their graduate course requirements. Of these schools, only one (3 percent) required a course in industrial relations.

9. Julius Rezler (1968a) reports the results of a 1967 survey of forty-seven IR units. Only six (Cornell, Illinois, Loyola–Los Angeles, Massachusetts, Michigan State, and Utah) qualified as "full-service" programs. Fifteen units offered degree programs, thirty were involved in nondegree labor-management education, and seven limited their activities to research (e.g., Chicago, New York).

10. The Ph.D. degree at Wisconsin was established in 1956 and, according to Amy E. Fried (1987:15–17), was the subject of some controversy among the university faculty. The principal arguments advanced in its favor were that it promoted a cross-disciplinary perspective on employment relations, facilitated students' ability to take courses in different academic departments, and enabled students to acquire the blend of theory, methodology, and concepts most relevant to their precise research interests. L. Reed Tripp, director of the institute at the time (then called a center), explained the motivation for the program this way (quoted in Fried 1987:16): "A labor economics student would have to meet a lot of rigid requirements to get a degree. What we really would prefer is proficiency in labor economics combined with a little bit of psychology, business, and law." Arguments against the program were that it lacked a conceptual foundation, fostered undesirable competition for students between the IR center and traditional departments, and was likely to produce weak researchers since students would have considerable breadth but little depth in the theory and methods of any one discipline.

  In hindsight, the decision by Cornell, Wisconsin, Illinois (in 1966), and other universities to offer doctoral programs in industrial relations was clearly a mixed blessing. On the one hand, the programs conferred legitimacy to the field, helped institutionalize it in the academic community, and provided a source of new faculty who were trained specifically for careers in research and teaching in industrial relations. On the other hand, the programs intensified the pressure to develop a unique theoretical core for the field in order to promote model-building and hypothesis-testing (the primary skills one learns in a Ph.D. program). This pressure was reflected in the creation of IR theory courses in graduate curricula and in the publication of various research works (such as John T. Dunlop's *Industrial Relations Systems* in 1958) that attempted to elucidate a general theory of industrial relations.

  The problem set off by the quest for IR theory was that it conflicted

217

with the field's multidisciplinary structure, given that rigorous, formalized theory is extremely difficult to construct across disciplinary lines. The result was that the imperatives of science-building inherent in IR doctoral programs contributed significantly to the pronounced narrowing of the intellectual boundaries of the field that took place after 1960. This subject is discussed at length in chapter 6.

11. Many of the IR units with jointly appointed faculty have encountered increasing difficulty in recent years in obtaining new faculty with the desired research and teaching interests. In the 1950s, for example, a labor economist who was hired by an economics department was generally similar in orientation to the economist an IR unit might hire, given the institutional orientation of most labor economists of that period. In recent years, however, the Chicago-style neoclassical labor economist that most economics departments seek to hire is of limited appeal to IR units, while the institutionally based labor economist desired by IR units faces great difficulty in getting hired by economics departments. This situation led the IR unit at Wisconsin to petition the university (unsuccessfully) in the late 1970s for departmental status (Fried 1987:36–43).

12. The virtues of the interdisciplinary approach were cogently expressed in the first bulletin issued by the newly founded IR section at the California Institute of Technology (IRS Cal Tech 1939:9): "In many fields, furthermore, it is being discovered that various branches of the social sciences (economics, political science, history and social ethics), *if used in conjunction with one another,* offer clearer insight into the causes of social phenomena, as well as a more realistic measurement of effects and greater promises of 'solutions' than does any alternative approach" (emphasis in original). The considerable emphasis placed on the interdisciplinary approach in the new IR units created after World War II arose in part from the involvement of many IR academics in the activities of the War Labor Board and other such government agencies. These experiences impressed upon them the multifaceted nature of wage determination, collective bargaining, and industrial conflict.

13. The ILE orientation of the Cornell program is suggested by the disproportionate share of the faculty who taught and conducted research in the areas of labor economics, collective bargaining, and labor law. Two other pieces of circumstantial evidence support this claim. One is from a report ("Report of the Board of Temporary Trustees of the New York State School of Industrial and Labor Relations, State of New York Legislative Document no. 20, 1945) submitted to the state legislature which contained the justification for the establishment of the school and an explanation of its intended structure and mission. The report contained an appendix prepared by Phillips Bradley that presented the results of a survey of all academic and nonacademic educational programs offered in the United States pertaining to the relations between labor and management (thirty-seven programs altogether). A notable feature of the survey was that it included

labor education programs but excluded any mention of personnel programs, suggesting that the emphasis of the school was intended to be on the study of unions and labor-management relations.

The second piece of circumstantial evidence comes from the name chosen for the school. The term *industrial relations,* as originally conceived, suggested that the program would cover all aspects of the employment relationship, while the inclusion of the modifier *and labor relations* was presumably included to indicate that particular emphasis was to be given to labor-management relations (thus giving the program, on net, an ILE emphasis).

While a substantial majority of the school's faculty were from the ILE wing of industrial relations, a significant minority represented the PM wing. For example, in the early 1950s, the faculty in the personnel, human relations, and industrial education (training) areas included Charles Beach, Earl Brooks, John Brophy, Temple Burling, Alexander Leighton, and William Foote Whyte.

14. The ILE orientation of the Wisconsin IR unit is suggested by the following remarks of Gerald Somers (1967:740): "It is not surprising, then, that much of the early research and activities of the Institute centered on the University of Wisconsin's long-standing interest in the problems of collective bargaining and the law of labor-management relations. Under the direction of Professors Witte, the late Selig Perlman, Elizabeth Brandeis, and others in the Department of Economics, and of Professors Nathan Feinsinger, Robben Fleming, and Abner Brodie of the Law School, large numbers of graduate students, in keeping with the John R. Commons tradition, engaged in the study of the organization, history, and legal-economic problems of particular national unions and of union-management relations as a whole." The ILE interests of the Illinois faculty is suggested by Melvin Rothbaum (1967:733–35): "The faculty agreed that the interdisciplinary approach to the study of labor-management problems would be the most meaningful and defined three broad areas for the first phase of a long-range research program: labor-management relations in the community setting, labor legislation and its administration, and wage employment and related trends." William A. Faunce (1967:737–38) listed four major areas of research interest among the faculty of the Michigan State IR unit: automation and manpower retraining, international aspects of labor and industrial relations, collective bargaining, and labor history and trade union administration. It should be noted that no PM-related topic was mentioned as a major area of interest at any of these three IR units.

15. In their comprehensive review of business education, Gordon and Howell (1959:189) state: "Next to the course in production, perhaps more educational sins have been committed in the name of personnel management than in any other required course in the business curriculum. Personnel management is a field which has had a particularly small base of significant

generalization with which to work (beyond what is important in the area of human relations), and, partly for this reason, it is an area which has not been held in high regard in the better schools." Also see Drucker (1954) and Dunnette and Bass (1963).

Few members of what I have labeled the PM school engaged in personnel research per se, and several criticized the field for its intellectual shallowness (see Whyte 1944). It may be questioned, therefore, whether it makes sense to include these people in something labeled the PM school when they lacked significant intellectual interest in or sympathies for the subject. To resolve this paradox, it must be remembered that the PM school is defined as an approach to problem-solving. This approach, first articulated in the personnel management literature of the 1920s, is one the human relations and management academics of the 1950s (such as Whyte) also subscribed to in broad outline. Thus, it is quite consistent for these people to have criticized personnel management in its science-building mode yet to be classified as members in good standing of the PM school of problem-solving.

16. Derber (1987:14–15) describes the experience at Illinois as follows: "Perhaps the high point of business distrust and hostility came in the spring of 1949, when several legislators . . . accused the Institute of pro-labor and Socialist sentiments, attacked the Institute director for once being a member of the Society for Cultural Relations with Russia, and castigated a faculty member for allegedly telling the campus Socialist Club that there was 'more incentive for workers under Socialism than under capitalism.' They called for disciplinary action against the faculty member and a reduction in the university appropriation for the Institute." Clark Kerr, the first director of the Institute of Industrial Relations at Berkeley, related in a telephone conversation that he was visited by a group of businessmen who threatened to have the governor eliminate funding for the institute if it did not cease its "pro-union" activities (e.g., labor education).

17. A brief history of the founding of the IRRA is provided in the front of the first proceedings of the association (published in 1948). I have also benefited from extensive discussions on this subject with Richard Lester and Clark Kerr.

An important antecedent of the IRRA that has gone largely unnoticed in the literature is the Labor Market Research Committee of the Social Science Research Council, which was organized in the late 1930s to promote social science (i.e., multidisciplinary) research on labor market phenomena. Directed by Paul Webbink, it included as members many of the labor economists who would later be leaders of the IRRA. The activities of the committee were an important influence on the birth of the IRRA in three respects. First, the committee sponsored conferences on IR research (the first such meeting was the "Conference on Research on Industrial Relations," held at Harvard University in April 1939) that helped generate academic interest among economists on the subject of industrial relations.

Second, it held periodic meetings where labor economists interested in industrial relations could get to know one another and discuss and develop research projects of mutual interest. Third, starting in 1945, the committee sponsored an annual labor-management conference at the University of Minnesota that served as an important role model for the programs of the future IRRA.

5. THE GOLDEN AGE OF INDUSTRIAL RELATIONS

1. The term *golden age* comes from Strauss and Feuille (1981), although they use it to refer to the period 1935–59.
2. The high degree of interest in the study of industrial relations during this period was attested to by Witte (1947:7), who noted that "there are more members of the American Economic Association who list labor as their major field of interest than any other." Witte also noted that a 1944 survey of the postwar plans of armed service members concluded that "industrial relations ranked only below engineering and accounting in the choices of service men and women who were thinking of a college education."
3. The factual validity of these conclusions, as opposed to their implications for policy and practice, were not seriously challenged until forty years later, when the original data were reanalyzed using modern multivariate statistical techniques. The first study to do so by Richard H. Franke and James D. Kaul (1978), found that human relations practices played only a minor role in explaining the variations in output of the relay assembly workers. The more important variables were variations in the external economic environment, managerial control of the work process, and the number of rest periods. Franke and Kaul's conclusions were subsequently called into question by Schlaifer (1980), leaving the verdict on this matter in doubt.
4. Mayo's perspective was heavily influenced by his work in medicine and psychopathology and by the theories of several important psychologists, sociologists, and businessmen. Inspired by the writings of Pierre Janet, a leading thinker in psychopathology, Mayo concluded that people's work performance was blocked by various mental obsessions having to do with problems or maladjustments in their personal or work lives. These obsessions, Mayo said, led to "pessimistic reveries" in the workplace and undesirable behaviors, such as disobedience, low work effort, and hostility. Another important influence on Mayo was the French sociologist Emile Durkheim and his concept of anomie. Mayo thought many workplace problems were caused by this condition of rootlessness and disorientation because it destroyed the worker's sense of self and place in society and thereby the basis for effective cooperation. The Italian sociologist Vilfredo Pareto was influential in the development of Mayo's idea of the factory as a social system and of the managerial elite as the guiding force for the promotion of social order and integration in the plant. Finally, business executive Chester Barnard, author of *The Functions of the Executive* (1938),

impressed Mayo with his ideas about business leadership, particularly the idea of leadership through consent rather than command.

Mayo was particularly critical of economists and their promotion of individualism and competition, for, in his view, these forces destroyed the sense of community and social order necessary for effective collaboration and thereby reduced society to a "rabble." Mayo (1945:59) states: "Economic theory in its human aspect is woefully insufficient; indeed it is absurd. Humanity is not adequately described as a horde of individuals, each actuated by self-interest, each fighting his neighbor for the scarce material of survival. Realization that such theories completely falsify the normal human scene drives us back to the study of particular human situations [e.g., internal plant studies such as at Hawthorne]."

5. Of all the implications derived from the Hawthorne experiments with regard to successful management, Mayo considered the most important to be the use of human relations techniques to foster cooperation and teamwork among workers and supervisors (1945:73): "Here then are the two topics which deserve the closest attention of all those engaged in administrative work—the organization of working teams and the free participation of such teams in the task and purpose of the organization as it directly affects them in their daily rounds." This theme was echoed twelve years later by Conrad D. Arensberg and Geoffrey Tootell (1957:312): "They [the Mayoites] retain the distinction of having demonstrated again and again the crucial role of teamwork in the creation of work morale and in the productivity of the workers. They show that morale and output depend, not on individual incentives alone or directly, but upon the 'informal organization' of interpersonal relationships and small-group sentiments within the immediate workforce."

6. Mayo himself had largely neglected the social dimension of the workplace in his early writings. In an article published in *Harper's* (1925), for example, Mayo said (pp. 229–30), "When we talk of social problems we are apt to forget that every social problem is ultimately individual." In emphasizing the individual, Mayo was following the dominant trend among industrial psychologists of the period, which was to seek explanations for differences in human behavior by searching for variations in individual mental attitudes, needs, motives, and so on. The emphasis in his later writings on the social dimension of work thus represented a significant intellectual conversion.

7. Warner's first academic research work was an anthropological field study of a primitive tribe in the South Pacific. Acting as a participant-observer, he recorded the tribe's various social relationships and the economic function of its various rites, customs, and so forth. Warner was then recruited to assist in the development of the bank wiring room experiments at Hawthorne. Thus, the decision to study the workers as an autonomous social group and to observe and record their daily routines and patterns of interaction was solidly in the anthropological tradition.

This methodological approach to research was subsequently used by other human relations scholars. But although it provided a comprehensive and detailed view of plant life, this research methodology was also the source of much criticism of human relations research for fostering an undue neglect of the external environment, particularly the impact of changing political and economic conditions (which could legitimately be ignored on a South Pacific island). In William Foote Whyte's study of labor-management conflict in a steel plant over the period 1937–50, for example, Whyte states (1951b:221) that "it has been possible to tell the story of that plant almost as if it were a completely independent unit." This statement was almost literally true since at only three points in the book did he make reference to any exogenous influences on the plant's internal social system. Likewise, in *The Human Group* (1950), Homans identifies three external environmental influences on group behavior—social, technical, and physical (p. 88)—but gives no consideration whatsoever to either economic or legal conditions.

8. Argyris (1954) conducted a thorough review of the human relations research then under way at twenty different research centers or departments (ten of which were IR institutes) in the United States. He concluded that human relations research focused on three issues: the nature of the organization, the determinants of an individual's behavior in an organization, and managing and integrating the individual's behavior so as to enhance organizational effectiveness. For each of these three topics he found there were multiple theoretical frameworks or research methodologies in use. In an earlier review of human relations research, Arensberg (1951) identified three separate subschools of human relations.

9. From a science-building perspective, personnel management and human relations were distinctly different fields of study. From a problem-solving perspective, however, they shared similar views of the causes of labor problems and of the best approach to obtain improved industrial relations (i.e., increased efficiency, equity, and personal well-being in the workplace); hence, their joint inclusion in what I have called the PM school. As evidence, compare the suggestions for improved industrial relations given in McGregor and Knickerbocker 1941 with the discussion of the PM school in chapter 2. They exhibit a high degree of similarity.

10. It is noteworthy that the experiments at the Hawthorne plant were considered within the domain of industrial relations research even though the plant was nonunion and the experiments involved no aspect of union-management relations. George Pennock, assistant plant superintendant at Hawthorne, published an article (Pennock 1930) describing the results of the relay assembly experiments. In the first sentence of the article, he states (p. 296), "If there is to be a science of industrial relations, there must be a scientific approach by individuals to the problems of industrial relations." Likewise, the *Personnel Journal* described *Management and the Worker* as

"the most outstanding study of industrial relations that has ever been published anywhere, anytime" (Miller and Form 1951:4).

11. My claim is that the majority of academics engaged in human relations research regarded their investigations as falling under the intellectual umbrella of industrial relations, just as was true of labor economists. The identification with industrial relations weakened, however, the further the person's research interests were from the subject of employer-employee interactions. Thus, researchers such as Kurt Lewin and Rensis Likert in the PM school, who were primarily interested in the psychological and administrative aspects of management, saw little intellectual kinship with industrial relations, while others such as Chris Argyris and George Homans saw a modest connection (Argyris, for example, was a member of the executive board of the IRRA), while still others such as Benjamin Selekman and William Foote Whyte saw a substantial connection. The same was true of economists, although in this case the connection with industrial relations weakened as one moved closer to the neoclassical school. Clark Kerr and Richard Lester, for example, were closely affiliated with industrial relations, while Melvin Reder and H. Gregg Lewis saw only a modest connection (as told to me by Lewis in telephone conversation) and Milton Friedman most likely saw none at all (although he did write articles in the 1950s on labor). Finally, to say that persons such as Homans and Kerr both perceived themselves to be members of the field of industrial relations suggests no more than that they possessed a common interest in employer-employee relations. Their specific research interests and disciplinary perspectives (sociology and economics) were quite distinct.

12. Blum briefly discussed the concept of a labor market and stated that (1925:128) "of all markets the labor market is the poorest [i.e., least efficient in operation]." He later states (pp. 372–73): "Under competitive conditions, the demand of the buying public for cheaper goods . . . forces a cut-throat competition and breaking down of wage rates that finally reaches an extreme, but logical conclusion in the sweatshop" and "the trade union is a group united to protect a common interest . . . [and] has been forced by the weakness of the individual bargainer. Large scale industry, concentration of capital and reduction of skill have reduced the isolated workman to an insignificant unit in the full scheme of production, but has increased enormously the power, influence and resources of the large employer."

13. Indicative of this is Witte's comment (1954:131) that "I shifted to economics from history because my major professor, Frederick Jackson Turner, . . . left Wisconsin and told me that the best historian among many good historians on our campus was John R. Commons, although he was attached to the economics department." Commons was also well versed in sociology and anthropology, in part because those fields were housed in the economics department at Wisconsin until 1929 and he was chairman of that depart-

ment. Anthropology also had a particularly marked impact on the writings of fellow-institutionalist Thorstein Veblen (Dorfman 1959).

Mayo and the other members of the human relations movement rarely acknowledged the work of the institutional economists, although the two research programs heavily overlapped. Commons, Hoxie, and Slichter, for example, had all written on the problem of restriction of output and had noted how workers used group sanctions to control production levels (see Commons 1919; Hoxie 1915; Slichter 1919b), yet Mayo (1933) and Roethlisberger and Dickson (1939) wrote about the phenomenon as if it were a new discovery. (The Harvard group also neglected an influential book on the subject of output restriction by Stanley Mathewson [1931], an engineer.) With regard to research methods, Mayo (1945) argued that researchers should first use clinical interview techniques to discover workers' perceptions and attitudes before embarking on theory development and hypothesis-testing, a position similar to that of the institutionalists, who advocated that researchers develop theories only after an intensive gathering of facts through the case study "go and see" approach. Finally, the emphasis given by the human relationists to the important effect that informal work groups, workplace custom, and social relationships have on the operation of firms and level of production was exactly the type of collective influence that Commons sought to make the core subject area of institutional economics. Landsberger (1958:89) notes this connection when he says of *Management and the Worker* that "the book contains the psychological underpinnings of an institutional analysis, whether sociological or economic."

14. Commons's *Institutional Economics* (1934b) is extremely difficult reading, as Commons acknowledges on page one, where he states that reviewers of earlier drafts of the book told him they "could not understand my theories nor what I was driving at, and that my theories were so personal to myself that perhaps nobody could understand them." A critical appraisal of Commons's theoretical works is provided by Coats (1983); for a more favorable interpretation, see Harter (1962) and Chamberlain (1963).

15. The major exception to this statement is the work of Paul Douglas, a labor economist at the University of Chicago. Douglas had a foot in both the neoclassical and the institutional camps, for, on the one hand, he was a first-rate theorist and statistician (he co-invented the Cobb-Douglas production function and co-authored the first study that estimated a labor supply function), while, on the other, he was a knowledgeable authority on management and personnel subjects, placed considerable emphasis in his writings on the imperfect nature of labor markets, and, for that reason, supported trade unions and protective labor legislation. In addition to Douglas, Sumner Slichter of Harvard and Harry Millis of Chicago also deserve mention, for although their writings in labor were more institutional in nature, they had a clear command of economic theory (see Slichter 1931).

16. Another young economist who took up the study of labor in the early 1940s was H. Gregg Lewis. Lewis did his doctoral work at Chicago in the late 1930s under Paul Douglas and, upon graduation, was appointed to a faculty position. Lewis's name is not included in the list of prominent labor economists cited here because his research had relatively little impact on the field until the publication of his book on unions and relative wages (Lewis 1963). Lewis had a significant but more indirect impact on the field in earlier years through his influence on graduate students at Chicago, such as Albert Rees and Gary Becker.

    Lewis has been called the father of "modern" or "analytical" labor economics (see Rees 1976; *American Economic Review*, September 1982, frontispiece). I believe a more correct title is father of the Chicago school of labor economics or, what is essentially the same thing, the neoclassical revival in American labor economics. As I have argued elsewhere (Kaufman 1988:197), Lewis can be considered the father of analytical or modern labor economics only if these terms are interpreted narrowly to mean the thorough application of competitive price theory to labor markets and, more particularly, the testing of hypotheses through rigorous statistical analyses. If *modern* and *analytical* are interpreted more broadly to mean the analysis of the operation of labor markets and the determinants of labor demand and supply, then Paul Douglas deserves to be listed as the progenitor of the field and economists such as Dunlop, Kerr, Lester, and Reynolds as the "fathers."

17. The clearest dividing line between the labor problems and labor markets approach to labor economics is provided by Richard Lester's text *Economics of Labor* (1941). Three features of the book distinguish it from earlier labor problems texts: its focus on labor markets rather than labor problems per se, the important role it gives to the determination of labor market outcomes by demand and supply conditions, and the use of analytical techniques such as graphical representation of demand and/or supply curves. The text also represents an interesting middle ground between the institutionalism of Commons and the neoclassical economics of Hicks. Lester clearly follows Hicks and the neoclassical approach to labor economics in that he focuses attention on the operation of labor markets and demand and supply, but he clearly follows the institutional perspective in the amount of attention given to the imperfect nature of labor markets and in the relatively favorable treatment of unions and protective labor legislation.

18. A recurrent debate concerns the appropriate label to attach to these labor economists and, in particular, whether they are an offshoot of the neoclassical or the institutional school (see Kaufman 1988). Glen Cain (1976), for example, has labeled them neoinstitutionalists on the grounds that, like the earlier institutionalists, they largely rejected competitive neoclassical theory as a useful tool to understand the behavior of labor markets; desired to incorporate into economic theory a more behavioral model of man, models of imperfect competition, and the influence of organizational

factors (rules, social relations, company policies); and were advocates of economic pluralism and, in particular, collective bargaining. Kerr (1988) argues that the neoinstitutional label is inaccurate and that "neoclassical revisionists" would be a better term. His rationale is that these economists saw themselves as the lineal descendants of Marshall, not Commons, made the focus of their research the operation of labor markets and used demand and supply theory to study these markets, and desired to reform economic theory to make it more realistic rather than replace it outright as the institutionalists allegedly did.

I have avoided using these labels given the lack of consensus as to which is appropriate. My own view is that these economists started their careers as neoclassical reformers but gradually shifted over time and by the late 1950s were for all intents and purposes neoinstitutionalists. For example, other labor economists of the 1950s regarded them as members of the institutional school (e.g., McConnell 1955; Ferguson 1965). Further, they made frequent use of theoretical concepts or ideas analogous to those developed by Commons, such as working rules (Kerr and Siegel 1955; Dunlop 1958), reasonable value (Lester 1973), pluralism (Kerr 1954b), and the imperfect nature of labor markets (Kerr 1950; Lester 1951; L. Reynolds 1951). Finally, they attempted to infuse economic analysis with insights from other disciplines. Regarding the book *Industrialism and Industrial Man* (Kerr et al. 1960), for example, James L. Cochrane (1979:141) states: "The problems of interest to Kerr, Dunlop, Harbison, Myers and their collaborators were not focused on market phenomena. The orientation of these writers was to combine economics and sociology. . . . Thus, while a body of orthodox, neoclassical theory did exist, the Inter-University Study represented a portion of the post–World War II generation which chose to ignore or at least to suppress their enthusiasm for orthodoxy. They followed in an earlier tradition, but struck out in their own direction."

Another piece of evidence comes from two recent articles by Dunlop (1984a, 1988) that critique present-day labor economics. Dunlop argues that neoclassical theory is defective because it omits consideration of the complex of rules that govern the employment relationship, the pattern of social relations in the workplace, the existence of noncompeting groups, and the various institutional forms taken by labor markets. From my point of view, these suggested reforms are clearly in the institutional tradition. Dunlop rejects this position, however, arguing instead that current-day labor economics has been subverted by a small band of imperialistic Chicago-based microtheorists and that the position he advocates is not abandonment of neoclassical theory for an institutional alternative but, rather, a return to its "mainstream" version as represented in the work of Paul Samuelson, Robert Solow, John Hicks (post-1960), and others. The issue then becomes whether mainstream economics (so identified) ever gave much weight in theoretical or empirical work to the omitted factors Dunlop identified and whether the omission of these factors in modern-day labor economics reflects the intellectual coercion of a minority or the willing acquiescence of the majority. I suspect the answer is "no" to the first part and "willing acquiescence" to the second part.

In recent telephone conversations, Richard Lester suggested that a more accurate term than those discussed above might be "social science labor economists," while Clark Kerr suggested "Keynesian labor economists." Both capture an important aspect of these economists' perspectives.

19. Lester (1952:485) expresses this point of view as follows: "An explanation of the complex phenomena of wage differentials . . . clearly involves the development of a new type of theory. It means hewing out a theoretical position somewhere between the narrowly based traditional theory and the all-inclusive confusion of the German historical school or the American institutionalists." He goes on to say that the theory should allow for multiple motivations on the part of managers and workers and include an interdisciplinary blend of economic, psychological, political, social, and institutional factors.

20. Kerr and Dunlop exemplify this dual set of interests. Kerr received his formal training in economics from teachers such as Abba Lerner and Oscar Lange, both theorists, and read Hicks's *Theory of Wages*, not Blum's *Economics of Labor*. His first research project, however, was an investigation of a cotton pickers' strike (Kerr 1988). Dunlop, in turn, had the best analytical skills of any of the new generation of labor economists of this period and published several influential articles and books on various aspects of economic theory (e.g., bargaining models, models of union wage determination, labor supply and demand functions). At the same time, he was involved at the highest levels of government and industry in the resolution of labor disputes and the administration of wage-price control programs (Dunlop 1984b). This duality in their careers reflects, I hypothesize, their interest in both the practice of science-building and problem-solving and, hence, the study of labor economics and industrial relations.

21. A review of the research of Dunlop, Kerr, Lester, and Reynolds reveals that before the mid-1950s the majority of their publications were on some aspect of the operation of labor markets or the impact of unions on the labor market, while after this period their research interests shifted toward labor-management relations, the function, structure, and evolution of unions, and the role of labor in industrialization (see Kaufman 1988:233–44). From 1954 onward, Dunlop and Kerr, for example, devoted much of their attention to the completion of their Ford Foundation project, the Inter-University Study of Labor Problems and Economic Development, out of which was published *Industrialism and Industrial Man* (Kerr et al. 1960) and *Industrial Relations Systems* (Dunlop 1958). Also of note in this regard, the professional association these economists were most actively involved in was the IRRA, not the AEA. If polled today, I suspect that most labor economists would identify industrial relations, not labor economics, as their principal field of research.

22. Another event that is suggestive of the gap between the theorists and the ILE-oriented labor economists was the publication of *The Impact of the Union* (Wright 1951). The book contained a series of articles by eight prominent economic theorists and a round-table discussion by these men on the impact of labor unions on wages, employment, inflation, and other such market outcomes. No labor economist was invited to contribute to the volume, leading Lloyd Reynolds (1953:474) to observe, "This volume seems to have developed from a feeling that—to paraphrase a famous remark about generals—that labor economics is too important to be left to the labor economists." Another piece of evidence in this regard comes from a biography of the institutional economist Edwin Witte. Theron F. Schlabach (1969:224) states that "Witte's feeling of alienation from his profession approached its peak in the late 1940s" and that Witte complained that identifying himself as an institutionalist was "equivalent to admitting that I am not an economist at all."

23. The different perspectives of the two groups of economists regarding unions is clearly revealed in the debate over the "labor monopoly" issue. See, for example, Lester 1947b and Lewis 1951.

24. The most detailed discussion of the goals and objectives of the founders of the IRRA is contained in an article by Clark Kerr (1983) commemorating the thirty-sixth anniversary of the founding of the association. That the IRRA was founded as an act of rebellion in economics and that its dominant goal was to provide an organizational home for more institutionally oriented labor economists and their soulmates from other disciplines are clearly revealed in his article (p. 14): "We [the young labor economists] started out as rebels. We first met almost like conspirators in the hallways during the annual meetings of the American Economic Association to grumble about what then seemed to us to be the neglect of labor economics at these meetings. . . . It seemed to us then almost incredible . . . that labor . . . was so ignored as compared, for example, with the role of capital; that the firm was the source of so much attention and the union hardly mentioned; that labor markets, when noticed at all, were viewed as though they were commodity markets; that collective bargaining, then in the daily headlines, had not penetrated into the domain of the interests of most traditional economists; but, most of all, that theory seemed to move along at the microeconomy level with so little contact with reality."

Kerr goes on to describe the goals of the founders of the association (p. 15): "We had several goals in mind when we founded the association. First of all, we wanted to meet together, to get to know each other better, to find out what others of us were doing, and this was not possible in the crowded mass atmosphere of the American Economic Association. Second, we wished to have an impact on the programming of the Association . . . [and to call the attention of] the theorists to our field of interest and to our own research. Third, we wanted to create a forum which would be participated in by practitioners in the unions, in industry, and in government who would never feel at home and would consequently never come to meetings of the American Economic Association. . . . We had a fourth goal which was to bring in scholars from related social sciences, particularly law, sociology, political science, and psychology, to discuss matters which clearly transcended the traditional boundaries of economics."

It seems clear from these remarks that the IRRA was born out of dual motives. The purported motive was to foster the study of the employment relationship from all disciplinary and ideological perspectives (as stated in the IRRA constitution). The second motive, and the one that clearly was the more salient to Kerr and the other founders of the organization, was to provide a forum for labor economists who wanted to pursue a more institutionally oriented, interdisciplinary mode of research than was welcomed in the American Economic Association. In hindsight, it would have been better for the founders of the IRRA to pursue one objective or the other but not both. If the IRRA was to promote industrial relations, it should have had a wider disciplinary and ideological representation and most certainly would not have been centered in economics given that economics was the disciplinary base of the ILE school. (Kerr [1983:17] suggests that sociology might have been a better disciplinary base for industrial relations, a suggestion with considerable merit, given that sociology seemed to be centered on the disciplinary fault line that separated the PM and the ILE schools.) If the IRRA was instead to be devoted to the propagation of a more institutionally oriented brand of labor economics, it would have been preferable to state this as its mission, to give the organization an appropriate name, and to pursue this objective explicitly in the organization's programs and publications. (Yoder [1958:3] states that the original name selected for the IRRA was the American Association for Labor Research, which would have better conveyed the second objective). As it is, the IRRA has been too timid in its pursuit of rebellion in labor economics, and, worse, it has corrupted the original meaning and spirit of the term *industrial relations* by its refusal to give equal representation to the members and viewpoints of the PM school.

25. The active participation of behavioral scientists in industrial relations is illustrated by the titles of several books: *The Sociology of Industrial Relations* (Knox 1955), *Industrial Relations and the Social Order* (Moore 1951), and *Psychology of Industrial Relations* (Lawshe et al. 1953).

26. In the 1940s–50s, most industrial relations research was done by academics, unlike earlier periods, when businessmen, union officials, and consultants authored a significant share of the literature. Exceptions in the latter period include works by Clinton Golden and Harold Ruttenberg (1942) and by Solomon Barkin (1950, 1957), all of whom were union officials, and by Robert Johnson (1949) and Carter Nyman (1949), who were business executives.

27. Wilensky was apparently unaware of the earlier map of industrial relations that had been prepared by the Social Science Research Council in 1928

(see fig. 1–1), for he makes no mention of it. The major differences between the maps are that Wilensky omitted some of the fringe fields of study (e.g., physiology, chemistry, education) that were included in the earlier survey and provided a much more in-depth treatment of the research literature. The maps are similar in that both define industrial relations quite expansively to include all manner of relations in the workplace (e.g., vertical "man-boss" relations within a company, horizontal relations between workers and work groups in a plant or workshop, relations between workers and labor organizations, and relations between organizations such as unions and firms) and a broad range of disciplines and fields of study across the behavioral and social sciences.

28. According to Strauss (1979:371), "The project was widely viewed as a failure; it is rarely cited . . . [and] appears to have had little influence on other research."

29. Derber (1968) found that international studies comprised 17.3 percent of the research projects conducted at fifteen IR centers during 1956–59. Of the fourteen subject areas Derber surveyed, management organization and communication was the most researched topic (18.6 percent), followed by international IR.

30. A thorough review of the origins and development of the Inter-University Study project, as well as an assessment of the strengths and weaknesses of the book *Industrialism and Industrial Man,* is given in Cochrane 1979. A retrospective look at the conclusions by the four authors is contained in Dunlop et al. 1975.

31. Empirical evidence in support of Dunlop's position was provided in a study by Kerr and Siegel (1954) on the propensity to strike across industries. They demonstrated that certain industries such as coal and longshoring are strike-prone in nearly every industrial country. They argued that this pattern reflected common environmental characteristics of these industries (e.g., the dangerous nature of the work) rather than plant-specific human relations practices.

32. The extent and degree of the anti-union bias in human relations is a matter of considerable debate (see Landsberger 1958). Mayo certainly seemed ambivalent about unions and suggested that they often played an undesirable role by interfering with the development of "spontaneous collaboration" in the plant. Later human relations writers took some pains, however, to accord unions legitimacy in the conceptual model of human relations and its normative prescriptions for practice and policy. Whyte (1951b), for example, argued that the union was an integral part of the social system in the steel plant he studied, while Homans (1954:57) allowed that "if unions did not exist, we should have to invent them. . . . We must not only accept the fact that unions are here to stay but accept the idea that they need to stay."

These concessions did not allay the fears of the critics, however (see Kerr and Fisher 1957). As they saw it, the emphasis on cooperation and enlightened management was anti-union in both theory and practice. In terms of theory, human relations seemed to deny the cardinal principles of the ILE school—the unavoidable element of adversarialism in the relations between workers and managers, management's inherent power advantage vis-à-vis workers and the limited checks posed on the opportunistic exercise of this power by economic and legal forces, the inevitability of worker-management conflict and the social utility of such conflict, and the desirability of pluralism in the nation's economy and political system. In terms of practice, many of the critics viewed collective bargaining as a net social and economic plus and favored it as the principal means of workplace governance. From their point of view, the bottom-line effect of human relations was to reduce workers' interest in union representation, a goal that was inimical to the long-term interests of workers and society at large. In effect, then, the proponents of the ILE school saw the human relations group as wolves in sheep's clothing on the subject of unionism and for that reason remained hostile to them.

George Strauss (1992) expresses his view on this subject in an autobiographical article: (p. 20): "As late as 1989, in a discussion of the role of human resources management in the Industrial Relations Research Association, John Dunlop insisted on calling HRM, 'human relations,' which, as he saw it, was just another method of union busting. These attacks still sting. As someone studying human relations in unions I felt it grossly unfair to charge human relations with being anti-union. Quite the contrary. My 1948 McGregor class notes make it clear that he viewed human relations without unions as a sham. . . . Mayo, it is true, might be viewed as paternalistic and even a bit fascistic. Roethlisberger hoped that management would work so well that unions weren't necessary. But for him unions were merely the bearer of bad news."

Finally, it is worth nothing that while a number of the academic members of the PM school were either neutral or favorable toward unions, the same was definitely not true among practitioners. Chapter 3 documented that in the 1930s a large proportion of the writers on industrial relations subjects in the PM school were practitioners and consultants. As long as trade unions were only a minor threat, as in the early part of the 1930s, these writers felt comfortable with their affiliation with industrial relations and largely soft-pedaled their antipathy to unions. Passage of the Wagner Act in 1935 and the dramatic growth in union membership in the late 1930s quickly changed the situation, however. Not only did their attacks on trade unionism and the nation's labor policy become more overt and critical, but their sympathies with, and allegiance to, the field of industrial relations also noticeably weakened (see Spates 1944). The result was that the practitioner wing of the PM school largely divorced itself from industrial relations five to ten years earlier than the academic wing.

33. The experience of Chris Argyris is illustrative. He received his Ph.D. in industrial relations in 1951 from Cornell University. His major research

interest was human relations, and his doctoral training was primarily in social psychology, clinical psychology, and sociology. He stated in a telephone interview that in the early 1950s he felt a strong sense of affiliation with industrial relations and perceived that human relations research was an integral part of the field. Participation in industrial relations was attractive, Argyris said, because it provided an opportunity to integrate the social and psychological research of human relations with the economics and institutional research of the ILE school. He discovered, however, that the majority of economists were not interested in such an integration.

In the early 1950s, the IRRA and the Social Science Research Council asked Argyris to conduct a survey of human relations research at major American universities. In 1954, he presented his findings at a meeting of the council (see Argyris 1954). He said that, while some ILE participants expressed genuine interest in human relations research, his perception was that the attitude of the majority ranged from indifference to hostility. Given such an attitude, he largely ceased active involvement in industrial relations by the late 1950s. Argyris cited several reasons the majority of economists were unreceptive to human relations research: it was perceived as a threat to unions and collective bargaining, was regarded as too "soft" (unscientific), and was seen as a tool to manipulate workers.

34. An example is provided by Kerr and Fisher (1957:282): "This group of sociologists has grown steadily in size and influence during the past few years, bringing with it certain charges against the intellectual apparatus with which the economists have worked. For those with a sense of history of ideas, there is a haunting familiarity to the charges. For they are the charges levelled by the church and aristocracy against the abstract, individualistic conception of the *philosophes*; they are the charges levelled by Burke against the French Revolution in the name of the prior rights of society and the group as against those of the artificial conception of reasoning man, by the German romantics of the 19th century in the name of the greater reality of the folk, by the Nazis against 'liberalism,' and by the Communists against cosmopolitanism. . . . This is the most modern episode in the attack on reason in the name of harmony, cohesion, and a traditional culture."

35. The selection of William Foote Whyte as IRRA president in 1963 would appear to contradict this claim, given Whyte's status as the leading exponent of the human relations school in industrial relations. By 1963, however, the battle between the ILE and PM wings over human relations was effectively over and the human relations group was well into the process of divorcing itself from industrial relations. My perception, therefore, is that by 1963 Whyte was a politically "safe" candidate because the human relations movement no longer posed an effective challenge to the ILE hegemony of the field, whereas a decade earlier Whyte's selection would have potentially opened the door to a true sharing of political power and intellectual perspectives. (This interpretation is supported by Whyte, who

said in a telephone conversation that he was surprised to learn that he had been selected as president, had largely ceased being actively involved in the organization by the early 1960s, and thought his selection was motivated by a desire on the part of the IRRA to honor his past work and accomplishments in the field and demonstrate a belated sense of ecumenicism.)

Other members of the PM school might have been selected as president in the 1950s–early 1960s had the IRRA been truly committed to the inclusion of a variety of viewpoints and disciplines. Examples include Douglas McGregor, former director of the Industrial Relations Section at MIT and author of the influential book *The Human Side of Enterprise* (1960); Chris Argyris, research director at the Yale Labor-Management Center and author of the much cited book *Personality and Organization* (1957); and Robert Dubin, a sociologist who had written numerous articles and books on industrial relations topics. The one person chosen during the 1950s to be IRRA president who did have close links to the human relations school was E. Wight Bakke. It is probably not coincidental that of all the people writing on human relations topics Bakke had the closest association with both the discipline of economics and the ILE wing of the IRRA (as evidenced, for example, by the book *Unions, Management, and the Public* [1948], co-edited by Bakke, Clark Kerr, and Charles Anrod).

36. The concept of a "web of rules" and the importance of these rules for structuring the system of industrial relations (the ILE portion) was first developed by Kerr and Siegel (1955).

37. It is ironic in this regard that Dunlop drew much of the inspiration for his systems model from the work of sociologist Talcott Parsons (see the appendix to chapter 1 of *Industrial Relations Systems*), who, in turn, was heavily influenced by Vilfredo Pareto, whose writings inspired Elton Mayo to conceptualize the factory as a self-contained social system.

38. Dunlop, in a telephone interview, expanded on his position. He perceived that in the 1950s, industrial relations (the ILE portion) was composed of a set of interrelated intellectual concepts that made it worthy of scientific inquiry, but that human relations was devoted largely to the development and application of managerial "tools" for practitioners and thus had little intellectual interest per se. He still maintains that the substantive aspects of the employment relationship are principally determined by conditions external to the organization (see Dunlop 1993). And he believes that the rules of the workplace (where rules are broadly defined to include both formal and informal conventions, standards, and policies) encompass the aspect of the employment relationship that is most amenable to scientific investigation. Thus, Dunlop did not accept Myers's compromise because the variation in the dependent variable Myers was trying to explain (the tenor of labor-management relations) is not, in Dunlop's opinion, one that any theory can ever say much about.

39. Further support of this interpretation comes from an earlier article by Dunlop (1954:92) in which he states, "This paper [a survey of research in

industrial relations] considers the locus of industrial relations to be union and management organizations and their interactions at all levels." The only precedent for this narrow labor-management definition of industrial relations I can find in the pre–World War II literature is an article by Leo Wolman in the 1932 edition (7:710–17) of the *Encyclopedia of the Social Sciences.* Wolman's discussion of the field of industrial relations is focused almost entirely on developments in the labor movement and union-management relations. One possible reason for this restricted view is that Wolman was research director for the Amalgamated Clothing Workers' Union until 1931.

Fiorito (1990) and Meltz (1991) strongly dispute the claim made here that the theoretical model contained in *Industrial Relations Systems* unduly neglects the role of management, the nonunion sector, and behavioral aspects of employment relations. I believe their arguments are unconvincing, however. Fiorito claims, for example, that the *real* (his emphasis) IR systems model factors in all the considerations cited above, yet his citation to this "real" model is not Dunlop's book but unpublished lecture notes from a class taught by Milton Derber. Dunlop's book must be judged on its own merits, however, and not someone else's classroom interpretation. Likewise, Meltz argues that it is difficult to understand charges that Dunlop neglected behavioral aspects of employment relations when he explicitly distinguishes between formal and informal rules. But nowhere in the book are these informal rules (or the informal work groups that often devise these rules) discussed in any substantive way.

40. Dunlop gives considerable emphasis to the interactions between unions and companies as organizations but pays very little attention to such topics as the reasons workers are motivated to join unions and the conditions that determine a union's policies and practices regarding bargaining demands, structure, and strategy. In this respect his perspective on industrial relations research is even narrower than that of the ILE school.

Dunlop's omission of the "internal" dimension is consistent, however, with the position he had taken in two earlier academic debates. The first was with Arthur Ross and centered on Dunlop's (1944) "economic" model of trade unions and on Ross's (1948) "political" model. Ross gave considerable emphasis in his book to the role of union leaders and social and psychological factors (e.g., "orbits of coercive comparison") in the determination of union wage policy. Dunlop claimed this position overemphasized the internal organizational dynamics of unions and neglected the impact of the external economic environment. The second debate was with William Foote Whyte (see Dunlop 1950; Whyte 1950) over the pros and cons of the human relations framework for IR research. This framework, as noted earlier, emphasizes that much collective behavior has social or psychological origins (e.g., desire for affiliation in a social group, development of group norms and sanctions to protect the collective welfare of the group) rather than economic origins, a position Dunlop heavily criticized. His stance on this matter made it difficult for him to include within his theoretical model in *Industrial Relations Systems* topics such as union-joining since much of the literature on this subject tended to emphasize the social and psychological motives discussed in the human relations literature (see, for example, Hoxie 1917, Tannenbaum 1921, and Leiserson 1959:16–31).

Since Dunlop had unsurpassed familiarity with the internal workings of both firms and unions, it is clear beyond a doubt that he was cognizant of the internal organizational dimension as a practical matter. That he omitted it from his theory has to be interpreted as reflecting his perception that internal organizational, psychological, and sociological factors play a relatively minor role in the operation of the industrial relations system (as stated in his 1950 article). This is an entirely acceptable position, but it would have been better if he had explicitly discussed this proposition in the book and provided empirical support for it, rather than adopt it as an unstated assumption. There is some evidence that Dunlop's position may have softened over the years, for in an article published in 1988 he discusses at length the important role played in wage determination by the informal social organization in the plant and cites a book by Elton Mayo as evidence.

6. THE HOLLOWING OUT OF INDUSTRIAL RELATIONS

1. The first editor of the journal was Arthur Ross. He briefly discussed the reasons for establishing it and its intended purpose in a note at the beginning of the first issue (Ross 1961). Three themes therein deserve mention. First, Ross framed the intellectual domain of industrial relations quite broadly to include all aspects of the employment relationship (see the statement to this effect on the inside cover of each issue). Second, the motivation for establishing the journal was clearly problem-solving, not science-building per se. Thus, Ross (p. 5) states: "The heart of the matter [the reasons for founding the journal] is that economic and political changes have undermined a great deal of what seemed reasonably well established in industrial relations in 1940 or 1950. A whole new set of issues have been created . . . [and] we desire to participate in the examination of these new issues and the search for solutions." Third, as evident in the quotation, Ross perceived that the problems most in need of examination in industrial relations had changed considerably relative to ten to twenty years earlier. He listed four specific issues as meriting attention: technological change, the effects of increased competition in product markets, the increased demand of workers and their families for economic security and the basic necessities and amenities of life, and the altered values and attitudes toward work among young people and white-collar workers.

    Clark Kerr, then president of the University of California system, played an instrumental part in getting the journal started. In a telephone conversation, he related that part of the purpose of the journal was to chart a new direction for industrial relations that would largely parallel the path taken by the book *Industrialism and Industrial Man* (Kerr et al. 1960). Thus, the intent was to move away from the preoccupation with unions and labor-management relations that had characterized IR research in the 1950s toward a dynamic, comparative analysis of the evolution of industrial society, its major institutions, and the manner in which work is organized and performed. He thought that, although the journal has been quite successful in its own right, it has largely failed in guiding IR research along this new path. As will become clear, the principal reason for this failure is that the trend toward pure science-building research in academia was incompatible with the research agenda mapped out by Kerr and his colleagues.

2. The narrowing of the subject domain of IR after 1960 complicates use of the term *industrial relations* in this and subsequent chapters since it is no longer clear whether the term applies to IR broadly conceived (all aspects of the employment relationship) or to IR narrowly conceived (labor-management relations). From 1960 onward, most academics and practitioners used *industrial relations* in its narrow sense, a convention that I follow from here on (unless the broad interpretation is clearly implied or is specifically stated).

3. Representative of this point of view is the statement by Wilensky in his *Syllabus of Industrial Relations* (1954:6) that "few students identified with the field confine it to union-management or employee relations."

4. A small number of articles did not fit into any of these topical areas and were thus excluded from the calculations.

5. I mentioned earlier (note 1) that the founders of *Industrial Relations* intended it to include research on all aspects of the employment relationship. The data cited here suggest that the journal had modest success in the 1960s in this regard (and certainly more so than the *ILR Review*) but that during the 1970s it lost a considerable degree of its disciplinary and topical eclecticism.

6. It is my perception that behavioral research on even narrowly defined IR topics (e.g., subjects pertaining to unions and labor-management relations) declined during the 1960s and 1970s. The increasing percentage of papers published in the IR journals by economists (as documented earlier) certainly supports this position. Since the late 1970s, however, a modest rebirth of interest in behavioral research has occurred in industrial relations. That IR is still conceived narrowly in this research is suggested by yet another symposium on the subject, this one published in the winter 1988 issue of *Industrial Relations*. Five of the seven papers focused on a collective bargaining subject.

7. This statement was affirmed by William Form in a telephone interview. When the first edition of the book was written, industrial sociology did not exist as a distinct field of study. Hence, he and Delbert Miller sought to take various strands of largely unconnected research on labor (e.g., social stratification, sociometry, organization theory, human relations) and

provide an intellectual structure for them. These strands of research were all part of industrial relations, they believed, and thus figure 3–1 was developed to illustrate these interrelationships. By the early 1960s, Form said, figure 3–1 no longer accurately described industrial relations, and the relationship of industrial sociology to it, and was thus dropped.

8. Historically, the institutionalists had given great attention to the role of protective labor legislation and social insurance programs as methods to resolve labor problems, a fact reflected in the presence of courses and even majors in IR curricula on topics such as Social Security, unemployment compensation, and workers' compensation, as well as the numerous sessions devoted to them at early IRRA meetings. After 1960, however, interest in these subjects among IR academics waned considerably, leaving the field even more narrowly constituted than its ILE version of the 1950s. Partially offsetting this trend, however, was the increased attention given at IRRA meetings, if not in IR curricula, to the labor market problems of disadvantaged groups such as minorities and the poverty-stricken. The early institutionalists had largely neglected these topics.

9. According to Hilde Behrend (1963) and John Berridge and John Goodman (1988), a debate over the broad versus the narrow definition of industrial relations also took place among British academics. One view that received support from several prominent scholars (e.g., Hugh Clegg, Allan Flanders, George Bain) was that industrial relations was the "study of job regulation," a definition that included union and nonunion work situations in principle but in effect narrowed the field to the study of union situations only.

10. William Form, in a telephone interview, cited several reasons sociologists largely ceased active participation in industrial relations. The most important reason, he believed, was the growing preoccupation of sociologists with issues of theory and methodology (i.e., science-building), a trend that caused research to become more inward-looking. Another factor was that the structuralists, who had dominated sociology, were gradually supplanted by social psychologists. The structuralists placed great emphasis on collective action and institutions, while the psychologists emphasized determinants of individual behavior. Finally, many sociologists took a Marxist or radical perspective on labor issues, which was incompatible with the more conservative, pluralistic ideology in industrial relations. Although sociology and industrial relations largely went separate ways in the 1960s and 1970s, according to Form, in the 1980s a modest rekindling of interest in IR topics occurred among sociologists.

11. An extensive bibliography of behavioral science research on unions and collective bargaining is contained in Lewin and Feuille 1983 and in individual chapters of Strauss, Gallagher, and Fiorito 1991. The latter is a good example of the revival of behavioral research in industrial relations (narrowly defined).

12. The absorption of human relations into organizational behavior was facilitated by the disrepute that the former had fallen into by the late 1950s,

due in part to theoretical deficiencies and in part to disillusionment in response to the excessive claims of its adherents to the effectiveness of such applied human relations techniques as T-groups and supervisor training. As Strauss (1970:145) said: "For many managers human relations was stereotyped, not as a field of study, but as a namby-pamby, be-good approach to management. Those who looked upon their fields as research-oriented science, rather than a set of preachy values, began to search for a new name and approach."

13. *Personnel Psychology* was established in 1948 to promote research on the application of pscyhological principles to personnel management. Although it was arguably the most research-oriented of the personnel journals, only one-fourth of the members of its editorial board were academics and the articles were relatively narrow in focus and practitioner-oriented. Typical of these articles were several in the first issue, including "Vision Tests for Precision Workers at RCA," "Interest Tests Reduce Factory Turnover," "Testing Programs Draw Better Applicants," and "An Attitude Survey in a Typical Manufacturing Plant."

14. Several "humanistic" theories of motivation (e.g., Maslow's hierarchy of needs, McGregor's theory X and theory Y) played an important role in the movement from the human relations to the human resources view of management. Whereas human relations had stressed improved social conditions as the principal mechanism to improve employee morale and productivity, Maslow and McGregor emphasized "self-actualization" (development and use of one's human potential) on the job. The implication for managerial practice was that, instead of improving conditions external to the job (e.g., communication skills), it was better to improve the job itself and to increase the opportunities given workers for participation and decision-making through such means as self-managed work teams and other forms of empowerment. This new perspective proved quite compatible with the "investment in people" idea and quickly became a central part of human resources theory.

15. The difference in approach between the old and the new generation of labor economists is clearly revealed in the texts of Lester (1941; 2d. ed., rev., 1964), Cartter and Marshall (1967), and Fleisher (1970). Lester's book is one of the last examples of the institutional or labor problems approach to the subject, while Fleisher's is one of the first examples of the market-oriented or neoclassical approach. Cartter and Marshall attempted to bridge the two approaches by devoting half their book to a demand-supply analysis of labor markets and the other half to a more descriptive analysis of unions and collective bargaining. A decade later this approach was obsolete because of the ongoing shift in labor economics toward competitive theory and formalized model-building. For another illustration of the cleavage that existed between the neoinstitutional and neoclassical approaches to the study of labor economics, compare Ross (1964) and Becker (1976).

16. Although the 1950s-era labor economists associated with the ILE school largely ceased active research in labor economics per se, several continued to publish in the field of industrial relations. The two most notable examples were Dunlop and Kerr, who authored articles and books on IR subjects throughout the 1970s and 1980s (Dunlop more so than Kerr). This publication record, augmented by their highly visible public service careers and work as top-level arbitrators and mediators in labor disputes, made them the two most influential "father figures" of the field in the 1980s.

17. Interdisciplinary research also waned in other fields of study. William Sewell (1989) notes, for example, that a great wave of enthusiasm for interdisciplinary research emerged in social psychology immediately after World War II and led to the founding of several significant interdisciplinary research centers but that by the 1970s interdisciplinary research had almost vanished. He attributes the decline to the threat posed by interdisciplinary research to the traditional departmental structure of American universities, the lack of adequate funding for such research, the lack of a breakthrough in integrative theory, and the concentration on research methods.

18. George Shultz (1964:25) said of this problem: "The field of industrial relations is thus confronted by a dilemma. On the one hand, the potential contribution of the several disciplines, *as disciplines,* is widely recognized; yet, on the other hand, the tradition of tackling a problem on its own terms tempts the industrial relations student to be a sort of jack-of-all disciplines. As master of none, however, he may well lose the essential analytical power of each and, in the process, lose the really professional content so essential to careful and precise analysis. This interdisciplinary trap is especially dangerous where degree programs in industrial relations as such are offered. . . . The effort to cover all aspects of the field almost inevitably leads to the professional content of each individual discipline being seriously diluted" (emphasis in original).

19. Jack Barbash supports this supposition (1989a:3): "If we are not bound by one theory it is just possible that common values inform our work."

20. Paul Webbink (1954:103) alludes to this in his reference to the "apparent resistance on the part of some economists toward the participation in industrial relations research of collaborators or competitors from other disciplines."

21. Clark Kerr (1978:132) observed that "before World War II . . . the field [industrial relations] had no core; it was fractionated among: the neoclassicists . . . the institutionalists . . . the Marxists . . . the antimonopolists . . . and the 'Human Relations' school." He then discusses the events of the 1950s (p. 134): "The field now had a core to it. The core might be identified as 'neo-institutionalism,' drawing on theory and practice, on the operation of competitive markets and organized power, and the various mixtures of them; concerned with the impact of institutions on markets and of markets on institutions."

22. My view is that the split between the PM and the ILE schools was caused by three types of "forces" that could be labeled as "push," "pull," and "dissolving." The push came from the antagonistic attitude of the ILE school toward the human relations movement and the policy implications it represented; the pull from the attractiveness of establishing a separate field of study devoted to the study of organizations and management from a behavioral science perspective; and the dissolving from the pressures of science-building, which weakened the incentives for cross-disciplinary collaboration. Although the "push" force from the ILE school was a contributing factor and no doubt hastened the divorce between it and the PM school, I suspect that the impact of the "pull" and "dissolving" forces were equally if not more important and that the effective demise of the "marriage" between the two groups was a matter of when not if.

23. That industrial relations became more "liberal" and "pro-union" after 1960 is supported by the research of Goddard (1992b). Based on statistical analysis of data from an attitudinal survey of Canadian faculty members teaching employment-related courses, he concluded that faculty in IR centers were more "left-wing" than faculty from either management or economics departments. Since the latter two groups were the ones that tended to drop out of the field of industrial relations after 1960, the net effect was that the field swung toward the more liberal end of the ideological spectrum.

7. INDUSTRIAL RELATIONS IN DECLINE

1. Union membership in Canada increased from 3.2 million to 4.0 million in the 1980s, while it declined in the United States from 22 million to 16 million. The divergent growth rates in the two countries were reflected in the equally divergent fortunes of academic industrial relations. Canadian IR experienced a modest boom as new academic programs were created and faculty hired, while academic IR in the United States experienced a marked decline. The labor movement in Great Britain also experienced a decline in membership and power during the 1980s (not unexpectedly since the social and economic policies of Margaret Thatcher closely paralleled those of Reagan), but academic IR weathered the decade in better shape than its American cousin.

2. Two early examples of the negative view of labor unions held by the Chicago economists are provided by Henry Simons (1948) and Milton Friedman (1951). Also see Harry Johnson and Peter Mieszkowski (1969). A relatively balanced view of unions by a Chicago-trained economist is provided by Albert Rees (1989).

3. Regarding the origins and meaning of the term *human resources*, John Storey (1989:4) says: "The term is in fact not new: one can find examples of its use nearly forty years ago. . . . But for many years the term carried no special significance and it tended to be used more or less interchangeably with a whole host of alternative formulations to signal what most would under-

stand as personnel management. In the 1980s it has, however, come to denote a radically different philosophy and approach to the management of people at work. . . . In its reworked usage it often purports to signal the interweaving of a number of elements which, in sum, demarcate it sharply from personnel management as commonly understood."

4. A survey by William G. Caples in the late 1950s (Caples 1958) found that there were twelve graduate-level (master's and/or Ph.D. degree) IR programs. Paradoxically, Herman's data (1984:A–5) show a significant decline between 1974 and 1984 in the number of M.A. and M.B.A. programs with a concentration in IR and HR. I believe this result is spurious, however, because the 1974 data include a more heterodox group of subfields (e.g., labor economics, education, political science) than does the 1984 data.

5. Estimates of the number of IR and HR programs in the United States vary widely, as the data cited indicate. Fifty-seven IR and HR units belong to the University Council of Industrial and Human Resource Programs, although six are outside the United States and an undetermined number are research units that have no degree program. Hoyt Wheeler (1988b) puts the number of autonomous IR and HR graduate programs at about twenty-five to thirty. He estimates that about two-thirds are IR and one-third are HR in orientation.

6. The position of the IR academic programs toward management education has traditionally been ambivalent. On the one hand, the great majority of IR graduates, both in the 1950s and in recent years, have taken jobs in management (Caples 1958; Fossum 1987). On the other hand, the majority of the administrators and faculty of the programs have a philosophical commitment to pluralism and collective bargaining. The curriculum and value system imparted to the students have thus been generally more union-oriented than most firms desire but is justified on the grounds that it provides students with a balanced perspective. This position is clearly reflected in the remarks of Arnold Tolles (1958:253): "The fact that the majority of graduates were to be employed by management did not imply that the curriculum must be management-oriented. . . . The teaching should be less concerned with providing tools than with broadening the perspective of the student." Tolles's position was a viable one in the 1950s when few business schools provided much in the way of personnel coursework or programs, but it is increasingly untenable today (for job market reasons, if not intellectual ones), when business schools offer comprehensive programs in OB and HRM that are expressly tailored to meet the needs of management.

7. The term *industrial relations* has become a handicap even for programs that have maintained an ILE focus. Cleveland State University, for example, recently renamed the Industrial Relations Center the Labor-Management Center. According to the center's director, the major reason for doing so was that the city's public sector unions had become its largest constituency

and they objected to the word *industrial* because it inaccurately suggested that the center primarily served blue-collar manufacturing workers.

8. In the 1950s, for example, the University of Iowa established an interdisciplinary department of labor and management in the business school. Its primary focus was labor-management relations, and most of the faculty had a background in institutional economics or law. In the early 1970s, the department was reorganized to include more of a human resource and behavioral science orientation, and the name was changed to the Department of Industrial Relations and Human resources. The department was reorganized again in 1989 to bring in the organizational behavior program and faculty, and the name was changed again, this time to the Department of Management and Organization. The net effect of these changes has been to shift the program steadily from IR to HR to OB. The only vestige of industrial relations remaining is several traditional IR courses and a master's of arts degree in IR. The former chairperson of the program, Tony Sinicropi, stated in a telephone conversation that IR is "the lowest rung on the departmental ladder" and will probably be phased out.

    Another example is the IR program at Georgia State. It was created in 1973 and housed in the business school. Until the late 1980s, the emphasis of the program was on labor-management relations and all of the active faculty were ILE-oriented. In 1987, the personnel program in the management department was moved to the institute and the program was renamed personnel and employment relations. Currently, only one out of the ten required or elective courses pertains to collective bargaining per se. Both the PM and the ILE schools are represented in the faculty, but the proportion of labor economists active in the program has fallen significantly.

9. The last IR-labeled, free-standing, multidisciplinary, degree-granting IR institute to be established that I know of was the Center for Labor and Industrial Relations at the New York Institute of Technology, created in 1978. Two IR-related research units were established in the 1980s, however: the Labor Research Center at the University of Rhode Island and the Industrial Relations Center in the Graduate School of Business at Columbia University. The Columbia unit was subsequently disbanded late in the decade.

10. One sign of the renewed interest in IR theory was the creation in the mid-1980s of a special study group devoted to industrial relations as a field and industrial relations theory within the International Industrial Relations Association.

11. In contrast to the United States, a number of articles on IR theory were published in Great Britain during the 1970s. Examples include Blain and Gennard 1970, Ward et al. 1975, Singh 1976, and Walker 1977. Also see Hameed 1982. The discussion in these articles tends to be rather desultory, however.

12. A review and assessment of Kochan's book by six leading IR scholars is provided in the winter 1982 issue of *Industrial Relations*. See, in particular, the review by Derber.

13. For a series of reviews of the book, see the April 1988 issue of *Industrial and Labor Relations Review*. Additional in-depth reviews are in Chelius and Dworkin 1990.

14. Freeman and Medoff can also be criticized for several sins of omission. Although they do not acknowledge it, the idea that unions lead to various forms of economic efficiencies (e.g., reduced turnover, higher productivity) has a long intellectual history. See Millis and Montgomery (1945:370–73), for example. They also ignore the ILE school's fundamental economic justification for collective bargaining—that it eliminates labor's inequality of bargaining power—and thus cede to their critics that union wage gains are a monopolistic form of price distortion.

15. See the January 1985 issue of *Industrial and Labor Relations Review* for a series of reviews of the book.

16. The renewed interest in IR theory in the 1980s led to introspection similar to that in the 1960s regarding the disciplinary status of the field, the deficient state of IR theory, the pros and cons of interdisciplinary research, and research methodology. See Cappelli 1985; R. Adams 1988, Hebert, Jain, and Meltz 1988; Chelius and Dworkin 1990; and Goddard 1992a.

17. The "notice to potential contributors" in the October 1989 issue supports the view that the journal's mix of articles had become lopsided in favor of labor economics and collective bargaining topics. It says (p. 3): "Members of the Editorial Board are concerned that many scholars believe the journal welcomes only papers on labor economics and collective bargaining... We should like to assure potential contributors that we welcome papers from *all* the specialties of our field, including organizational behavior, labor law, labor history, human resources, personnel management, income security, union administration, and international and comparative labor relations" (emphasis in original).

18. A decade earlier (1976) a review committee under the direction of Richard Lester had performed many of the same functions as the Kerr-Dunlop committee. The conclusions and recommendations of that committee are in its final report (IRRA 1977).

19. The report of the Lester committee (IRRA 1977) noted that a frequently heard complaint from members was that the intellectual substance of the publications of the IRRA needed to be upgraded. Although progress has been made on this front in recent years, I believe this complaint still has merit. In an attempt to provide hard evidence of this deficiency, I examined volumes 42 and 43 (October 1988–July 1990) of the *Industrial and Labor Relations Review* and added up the number of citations to articles in the three publications of the IRRA: the proceedings of the winter and spring meetings and the annual research volume. (The articles in the proceedings of the spring meeting are also published in the August issue of *Labor Law*

Journal, which I therefore included.) For comparison purposes, I also added up the number of citations to *Industrial Relations* and the *Journal of Labor Research.* My presumption is that the "quality" of a publication will be reflected in the number of citations that are made to articles contained in it. The results were as follows: winter IRRA proceedings, 24; spring IRRA proceedings, including *Labor Law Journal,* 3; IRRA research volume, 10; *Industrial Relations,* 49; and the *Journal of Labor Research,* 38. These data indicate, I believe, that the proceedings of the spring meeting have a near-zero impact on IR research, that the annual research volume is of marginal importance (more than half the citations to the volume were to several articles in the 1987 volume edited by Kleiner et al.), and that the proceedings of the winter meeting have a perceptible but nevertheless modest impact. Taken as a whole, the publications of the IRRA therefore seem relatively peripheral to academic research in the area of employer-employee relations.

20. The report of the Lester committee (IRRA 1977:10) states in this regard: "A frequently expressed criticism by young members, but also by some over 50 years of age, is that the meetings and other Association activities are too dominated by the more senior members." This problem was acknowledged again in the work of the Kerr-Dunlop committee (IRRA 1988b:1): "We need to increase the participation of younger members in the IRRA. In many cases, new scholars feel at a disadvantage in opportunities to be on the program." Several positive steps have recently been taken to address this problem, including having a poster session and dissertation roundtable, improving communications to the membership concerning submission deadlines and procedures, and using an open-submission process to select session topics for the winter meeting instead of a "by-invitation" method. The principal source of the complaint has not been entirely remedied, however, which is the limited number of competitive paper sessions at the winter meeting. On the recommendations of the Lester committee, the IRRA began to include three to four contributed paper sessions in each program of the winter meeting (out of a total of eighteen to twenty). The Kerr-Dunlop committee did not recommend any further increase in the number of such sessions, an unfortunate decision in that it perpetuates the long-standing feeling among a significant proportion of the membership that it is who you know, not what you know, that at least in part determines who is included on the program.

21. Everett Kassalow (1985:13) said in his IRRA presidential address that "the United States continues to need a strong and growing labor movement." It is difficult to measure an organization's ideological climate, but a person who said the opposite almost certainly would be neither welcome nor nominated for high office in the organization.

22. Academics who have served as IRRA president since 1975 include Gerald Somers, Irving Bernstein, Ray Marshall, Charles Killingsworth, Jack Barbash, Milton Derber, Jack Stieber, Everett Kassalow, Lloyd Ulman, Phyllis

Wallace, Robert McKersie, and James Stern. All but two are economists (Bernstein and McKersie), all the economists are in what I consider the ILE school (certainly none is a neoclassical economist of the Chicago school), and none has taken a stance in their published writings that could be construed as being even mildly critical of the basic principles and purposes of trade unionism and several (e.g., Marshall, Derber, Barbash, Kassalow) are clearly supportive of trade unionism. It is also instructive to examine who has *not* been elected president of the organization: prominent labor economists affiliated with the University of Chicago (e.g., Albert Rees, Melvin Reder, H. Gregg Lewis), academics who have been critical of unions and collective bargaining (e.g., Herbert Northrup), and persons whose primary interest is in the management side of employer-employee relations (e.g., Edward Lawler, Peter Drucker, Paul Lawrence).

23. It is difficult to quantify feelings of disenfranchisement and estrangement, but one circumstantial piece of evidence exists. The Kerr-Dunlop committee commissioned a survey of the IRRA membership in which a wide range of questions were asked concerning the activities and programs of the association. Only an 18 percent response rate was obtained. In a letter to the committee, David Lewin (1988b:9) said: "One wonders (dishearteningly) whether the bulk of the IRRA membership has given up. The 18 percent response rate to the recent survey suggests a 'yes' answer to this question, as do many of the comments reproduced in the report of the survey. At the 1987 annual meeting in Chicago, numerous IRRA members speculated about the lack of even one 'younger' scholar on the Review Committee. My purpose in mentioning these sensitive matters is not to apportion blame; instead it is to suggest that the Review Committee *may* have before it substantial evidence of the disillusionment of a large portion of the Association's membership—particularly its younger members" (emphasis in the original).

8. INDUSTRIAL RELATIONS IN THE 1990s AND BEYOND

1. According to Irving Bernstein (1985), "reform cycles" occur about every thirty years in the United States. The peaks of three such cycles occurred during the progressive era, the New Deal Era, and the period of New Frontier and Great Society. He speculates, therefore, that the mid–1990s will see the birth of another reform movement, largely in reaction to the excesses of the Reagan and Bush years. Although certain events make this scenario plausible (e.g., the loss of employment security by all ranks of American workers and the stagnation of real family income), it remains highly problematic. Were such a reform movement to appear, however, it would clearly be a favorable development for industrial relations.

2. The HR side of the field has produced many highly acclaimed, more popular-oriented books in recent years that examine the management of people and the conduct of employer-employee relations. These include *In Search of Excellence* (Peters and Waterman 1982) and *When Giants Learn to Dance*

(Kanter 1989). The challenge for IR is to produce a stream of equivalent works. Probably the most noteworthy in recent years is *And the Wolf Finally Came* (Hoerr 1988), although its message does not inspire enthusiasm for the study and practice of industrial relations.

3. The continued commitment of IR scholars to the New Deal system is evident in the report published in the winter 1983 issue of *Industrial Relations* (pp. 125–31) that summarized the conclusions of a two-day conference entitled "The Future of Industrial Relations," attended by twenty-nine of the field's leading researchers. The report states (p. 129, 131): "The conferees identified strongly with free collective bargaining. . . . To the extent that the conference had a theme, it was that of continuing faith in the efficacy of collective bargaining as the cornerstone of the American industrial relations system. . . . The conference closed with what came close to a consensus: our economic and social problems can best be resolved through tripartite union-management-government discussion and collaboration."

4. One of the first persons to question the relevance of the term *industrial relations* to a service, white-collar economy was Thomas Spates (1944). IR scholars have advanced two arguments in an attempt to rebut this criticism. Barbash (1989b:114), for example, claims that *industrial* must be interpreted broadly to include any large-scale, efficiency-directed enterprise, while Marshall (1987:67) claims that *industrial* should be interpreted in a generic sense to mean a particular line of business activity, such as the service industry or banking industry. I suspect these arguments will not be successful, given the widespread tendency of people in both academe and business to equate *industrial* with *manufacturing*.

5. The atrophy of the IRRA is reflected in the increase in the average age of its members. In 1977, the membership's average age was forty-six, which the Lester report (IRRA 1977:3) characterized as "fairly mature." The IRRA ceased asking members for their birth year in the late 1970s, but other evidence strongly suggests that the average age of the membership has almost certainly increased. For example, based on a sample of the academic members listed in the 1972 and 1990 IRRA membership directories who had Ph.D., D.B., or J.D. degrees and whose family names began with the letters A-D, I found that the average years in which they received their doctoral degrees were 1959 and 1972, respectively. Thus, in 1972, the average academic member had been out of school for thirteen years, while in 1990 the average member had been out of school for eighteen years (a 38 percent increase).

Another indicator of organizational decline is that the association is having an increasingly difficult time finding presidential nominees who meet the requirements of distinguished contributions to the field and a record of active participation in the organization, including past service on the executive board. Most of the people who meet the first requirement (e.g., Richard Freeman, Edward Lawler, William Usery) are not active members, while an ever-diminishing number of active members have a prominent national reputation.

6. The founders of the IRRA wanted to promote an active interchange between academics and practitioners and for that reason opened its ranks to persons from both groups. Efforts were made, in turn, to obtain a balanced representation among practitioners by including members from the three parties to the employment relationship—business, labor, and government—in the organization. The mixing of academics and practitioners was intended to foster a cross-fertilization between academic research and real-world practice, a goal I strongly support and one the IRRA has made important contributions toward achieving.

   But this organizational structure has also resulted in the representatives of organized labor having a disproportionate influence on the association's programs and policies. In theory, the inclusion of business people should have provided a political counterweight to organized labor, particularly since the former represent a greater share of the IRRA's national membership than the latter. In practice, however, it has not worked this way. First, organized labor has a larger stake than business firms in keeping the association in the ILE camp and thus takes a more activist role in it. Second, the business people nominated for office in the IRRA come from unionized companies and for reasons of both philosophy and self-interest have strong incentives to avoid staking out a position that union members might construe as antilabor. And, third, the academic leaders of the IRRA have traditionally been extra-sensitive to the opinions of organized labor on policy and program issues, both because of their ILE philosophical bent and their desire to avoid internal political battles. For these reasons, organized labor, in coalition with other allies (e.g., arbitrators and mediators) who have a vested interest in preserving the traditional collective bargaining system, exercise greater political power in the IRRA than is suggested by their membership numbers, giving them, in my estimation, effective veto power over substantive matters of policy. This opinion is supported by the comment of a long-time member of the IRRA in written correspondence to me: "Management doesn't give a damn, but labor has an almost ironclad veto on everything the IRRA does."

7. A similar exercise in strategic planning is provided in Cutcher-Gershenfeld 1991. A number of his proposals parallel those made here.

8. The term *employment relations* appeared at the same time as *industrial relations* but never achieved the popularity of the latter term. Several doctoral dissertations written in the 1920s used the term *employment relations* in their titles, for example, but the term then largely faded from the literature (but see Yoder et al. 1958). Recently, however, *employment relations* has made something of a comeback, as indicated by its adoption in the titles of academic degree programs at Georgia State University, the University of South Carolina, and the University of Cincinnati. The case for replacing the term *industrial relations* with *employment relations* is made by Wheeler

(1988a), whose major argument is that *employment relations* better indicates the central subject matter of the field—the employment relationship. Wheeler's usage of the term *employment relations* (and, I think, its intended usage in the program titles mentioned above) is different from what is proposed in the text. As advocated here, employment relations would be used as the new name for the field of industrial relations narrowly defined, while Wheeler would use it as the name for the field of industrial relations broadly defined (both current-day IR and HR). Although I have made use of the latter interpretation in other places (Kaufman 1991b), on reflection I think the term is not general enough to serve as an umbrella label for IR and HR combined. The reason is that employment relations gives emphasis to the word *relations,* which is central to IR, but omits any term suggestive of HR, such as *human resources* or *management.* Further, practitioners often associate employment relations with the subfield of employee relations in personnel management, rather than with the employment relationship as an intellectual concept.

9. The distinction between external and internal perspectives in research on the employment relationship is made by Somers (1969, 1972) and is implicit in the debate between John Dunlop (1950) and William Foote Whyte (1950) over the merits of the human relations model.

10. The dividing line between internal and external is not a hard and fast one but rather a useful generalization for distinguishing between two approaches to the study of employment-related outcomes in (and between) organizations. The reality of this distinction is best seen by examining research in the areas that represent the "pure cases": micro-organizational behavior and neoclassical labor economics. Micro OB seeks explanations for employment outcomes in variables that reside internal to the organization (often internal to the individual), while the environment or "context" external to the organization is generally treated as a given (Cappelli 1990). Neoclassical labor economics, by contrast, looks at market forces external to the organization as the cause of these same phenomena and generally treats factors internal to the organization as a given (or "black box") (Lewin and Feuille 1983).

   Two other fields provide the intellectual bridge between these two polar cases. They are, respectively, industrial relations and organization theory (macro OB). Industrial relations studies the transmission process between the multidisciplinary array of external environmental forces and the structures, practices, and behaviors internal to the firm. Organization theory does much the same, but the perspective is from inside the firm looking out. Since there is clearly conceptual overlap, the internal versus the external distinction tends to get fuzzy in practice in research projects that are close to the interface of the two fields (see Begin 1990). The external versus the internal distinction nevertheless has considerable explanatory power as a general way of typing the theoretical and empirical approach to research in the fields of HR and IR.

11. The reorientation I advocate, and the reasons it is necessary, is amply illustrated by the textbooks currently used in traditional IR and HR courses. The typical IR course uses a text devoted to the subject of collective bargaining and labor-management relations, while the typical HR course uses a book that focuses on the practice of human resource management. While there is some overlap in material (the HR book will have a chapter or two on labor relations, the IR book a chapter or two on the structure and functions of management), the student comes away with the impression that IR and HR are largely separate subjects whose major intellectual dividing line is that one deals with unions and the other with management. Not only does this dichotomy fundamentally misrepresent the true nature of the differences that have historically distinguished the PM and ILE perspectives on the employment relationship, but given the small and dwindling size of the union sector in the economy, it obviously places the continued survival of IR courses and curricula in jeopardy.

    Both on intellectual and pedagogical grounds, the preferable approach is to combine the IR and HR courses into one introductory course; make the mission of the course the study of the institutions, practices, and outcomes of the employment relationship and the public policies that structure and regulate this relationship; and present IR and HR as different approaches to the analysis of these subjects. In turn the distinction between IR and HR should be made on the basis of the differences in their underlying assumptions about the employment relationship (e.g., conflict of interests versus congruence of interests), their theoretical approach to the study of the subject (e.g., emphasis on internal versus external environments), and recommendations concerning policy and practice. This approach, essentially the one taken by the labor problems texts of the 1930s, needs to be rediscovered and used as the basis for an introductory employment relations course in every college curriculum. (I think the intellectual value-added from such a course in M.B.A. programs, for example, would be significantly greater than that obtained from the standard core course in organizational behavior.) *Human Resources Management and Industrial Relations*, by Thomas Kochan and Thomas Barocci (1985), provides one example of the approach I am advocating.

12. A corollary is that some union-related topics traditionally considered within the corpus of industrial relations would become part of HR, such as the determinants of membership commitment to the union as an organization and studies of militancy among union members.

13. Dunlop's model of industrial relations systems focuses on the employment relationship, integrates various external environmental variables (e.g., technology, law, product and labor market forces, ideology), has a cross-disciplinary perspective, and is avowedly science-building in purpose. While certain aspects of the model are questionable (e.g., the focus on rules as the dependent variable in IR research), it nevertheless illustrates the feasibility and fecundity of the approach advocated here. This generally

favorable reference to Dunlop's model contrasts sharply with the critical review it received in chapter 5. My major objection there was that it purported to be a general model of industrial relations when, in fact, it omitted consideration of the internal perspective of the PM school, which was still very much a part of industrial relations in the 1950s. This criticism, while of continuing relevance from a historical perspective, is moot for present-day industrial relations to the extent that the field is defined more narrowly, as advocated here. Nonetheless, I continue to feel that the excessively imperialistic stance the book takes vis-à-vis the PM school works against constructive dialogue.

14. Strike studies are a good example. Both HR and IR scholars publish research on strikes, but the studies have far more in common within HR and IR categories than across categories (see Gallagher and Gramm 1991). Thus, the strike studies by externally oriented researchers, such as economists and sociologists, typically use the number of strikes from a time-series or cross-section data set as the dependent variable and attempt to explain the variation with various independent variables that measure characteristics of the external environment (unemployment rate, size of union membership, and so on). HR researchers, in contrast, tend to look at either attitudinal constructs related to strike intentions or the psychological consequences of strike action as the dependent variable and attempt to explain the variation with independent variables that measure personal demographic and psychological characteristics (gender, feelings of inequity).

15. A particular challenge to the ILE model in this regard is Fox's (1974) contention that a system of workplace governance based on a pluralist ideology will inevitably experience a secular decline in performance because of the mutual low-trust, high-conflict relationships that exist between workers and employers.

16. See Strauss (1990) and Cappelli (1990) for alternative suggestions of how IR should be reconceptualized. Both argue that IR should take a relatively macro perspective on organizational and employment issues. Strauss further argues that two of the major topical areas of IR should be "employment systems" and "justice systems." Although both are insightful concepts, they do not represent a division of knowledge that clearly separates IR from HR, a division that I contend is not only inherent to the study of the employment relationship, but one that also facilitates science-building.

17. The title *industrial and labor relations* adopted by the IR program at Cornell University in the 1940s originally had the requisite level of generality but no longer does. As I interpret it, the name was meant to convey that the program covered all aspects of the employment relationship (the original meaning of the term *industrial relations*) but that particular emphasis was placed on unionized employment situations (the meaning of the term *and labor relations*). Since most people today regard the terms *industrial relations* and *labor relations* as equivalent, this label has a significantly narrower meaning; in effect that the program addresses *only* unionized employment

situations. Because this meaning is neither correct nor viable in the long run from a marketing perspective, I predict that eventually the name of the Cornell program will be changed (or some other strategem found to accomplish the same purpose). Doing so will mark the end of an era.

18. The term *research* should also be dropped from the title since it has little relevance to the practitioner members of the association, who outnumber the academic members by a wide margin. My suggestion for a new title is the American Employment Relations Association or the Association for the Advancement of Employment Relations.

19. Planning and organizing an independent meeting would, however, entail a significantly greater expense for the IRRA, an expense it may not be able to bear given its extremely tight budget. One option is to eliminate the spring meeting and use those funds to support an independently held winter meeting.

References

Adams, Leonard P. 1967. "Research Note: Cornell University, New York State School of Industrial and Labor Relations." *Industrial and Labor Relations Review* 20 (July): 730–33.

Adams, Roy. 1983. "Competing Paradigms in Industrial Relations." *Relations Industrielles* 38 (3): 508–29.

———. 1988. "Desperately Seeking Industrial Relations Theory." *International Journal of Comparative Labour Law and Industrial Relations* 4 (1): 1–10.

———. 1992. "All Aspects of People at Work: Unity and Division in the Study of Labour and Labour Management." In *Industrial Relations Theory: Its Nature, Scope and Pedagogy*, ed. Roy Adams and Noah Meltz. Melbourne: Longman Cheshire. Forthcoming.

Adams, Thomas S., and Helen L. Sumner. 1905. *Labor Problems*. New York: Macmillan.

Appelbaum, Eileen. 1979. "Post-Keynesian Theory: The Labor Market." *Challenge* 21 (Jan.-Feb.): 39–48.

Arensberg, Conrad D. 1951. "Behavior and Organization: Industrial Studies." In *Social Psychology at the Crossroads*, ed. John H. Rohrer and Muzafer Sherif, 324–52. New York: Harper.

Arensberg, Conrad D., et al. 1957. *Research in Industrial Human Relations: A Critical Appraisal*. New York: Harper and Row.

Arensberg, Conrad D., and Geoffrey Tootell. 1957. "Plant Sociology: Real Discoveries and New Problems." In *Common Frontiers of the Social Sciences*, ed. Mirra Komarovsky, 310–37. Glencoe, Ill.: Free Press.

Argyris, Chris. 1954. "The Present State of Research in Human Relations in Industry: A Working Paper." New Haven: Labor and Management Center, Yale University.

———. 1957. *Personality and Organization: The Conflict between System and the Individual*. New York: Harper and Row.

References

Armstrong, Michael. 1988. *A Handbook of Human Resource Management*. New York: Nichols.

Aronson, Robert L. 1961. "Research and Writing in Industrial Relations—Are They Intellectually Respectable?" In *Essays on Industrial Relations Research—Problems and Prospects*, 19–44. Ann Arbor: Institute of Labor and Industrial Relations, University of Michigan and Wayne State University.

Ashenfelter, Orley, and George Johnson. 1969. "Bargaining Theory, Trade Unions, and Industrial Strike Activity." *American Economic Review* 50 (March): 35–49.

Aspley, John C., and Eugene Whitmore. 1943. *The Handbook of Industrial Relations*. Chicago: Dartnell.

Atherton, Wallace. 1973. *Theory of Union Bargaining Goals*. Princeton: Princeton University Press.

Baker, Helen. 1939. *The Determination and Administration of Industrial Relations Policies*. Princeton: Industrial Relations Section, Princeton University.

Bakke, E. Wight. 1946. *Mutual Survival: The Goal of Unions and Management*. New Haven: Labor and Management Center, Yale University.

———. 1950. *Bonds of Organization: An Appraisal of Corporate Human Relations*. New York: Harper and Row.

———. 1953. *The Fusion Process*. New Haven: Labor and Management Center, Yale University.

Bakke, E. Wight, Clark Kerr, and Charles Anrod. 1948. *Unions, Management, and the Public*. New York: Harcourt Brace.

Balderston, C. Canby. 1935. *Executive Guidance of Industrial Relations*. Philadelphia: University of Pennsylvania Press.

Barbash, Jack. 1979. "The American Ideology of Industrial Relations." In *Proceedings of the 1979 Spring Meeting, Industrial Relations Research Association*, 453–57. Madison: IRRA.

———. 1984. *The Elements of Industrial Relations*. Madison: University of Wisconsin Press.

———. 1986. "The New Industrial Relations." In *Proceedings of the 1986 Spring Meeting, Industrial Relations Research Association*, 528–33. Madison: IRRA.

———. 1989a. "Introduction." In *Theories and Concepts in Comparative Industrial Relations*, ed. Jack Barbash and Kate Barbash, 3–6. Columbia: University of South Carolina Press.

———. 1989b. "Equity as Function: Its Rise and Attrition." In *Theories and Concepts in Comparative Industrial Relations*, ed. Jack Barbash and Kate Barbash, 114–22. Columbia: University of South Carolina Press.

———. 1991a. "Industrial Relations Concepts in the U.S.A." *Relations Industrielles* 46 (1): 91–118.

———. 1991b. "John R. Commons and the Western Industrial Relations Tradition." In *Comparative Industrial Relations: Contemporary Research and Theory*, ed. Roy Adams, 21–36. London: HarperCollins.

Barkin, Solomon. 1950. "A Trade Unionist Appraises Management Personnel Philosophy." *Harvard Business Review* 28 (Sept.): 59–64.

References

———. 1957. "Human Relations in the Trade Unions." In *Research in Industrial Human Relations,* ed. Conrad Arensberg et al., 192–213. Madison: IRRA.

Barnard, Chester. 1938. *The Functions of the Executive.* Cambridge: Harvard University Press.

Barnes, William E., ed. 1886. *The Labor Problem: Plain Questions and Practical Answers.* New York: Harper and Bros.

Beaumont, Philip. 1990. *Change in Industrial Relations.* London: Routledge.

Beaumont, Richard A. 1962. "A Broadening View of Industrial Relations." In *Behavioral Science Research in Industrial Relations,* ed. Industrial Relations Counselors, 3–11. New York: IRC.

Becker, Gary, 1957. *The Economics of Discrimination.* Chicago: University of Chicago Press.

———. 1976. *The Economic Approach to Human Behavior.* Chicago: University of Chicago Press.

Beer, Michael, and Bert A. Spector. 1984. "Human Resources Management: The Integration of Industrial Relations and Organizational Development." In *Research in Personnel and Human Resources Management,* vol. 2, ed. Kendrith Rowland and Gerald Ferris, 261–97. Greenwich, Conn.: JAI Press.

Begin, James P. 1987. "What's Actually Happening? The IR Academic Survey." In *Proceedings of the Fortieth Annual Meeting, Industrial Relations Research Association,* 467–73. Madison: IRRA.

———. 1990. "An Organizational Systems Perspective on the Transformation of Industrial Relations." In *Reflections on the Transformation of Industrial Relations,* ed. James Chelius and James Dworkin, 53–72. New Brunswick, N.J.: IMLR Press.

Behrend, Hilde. 1963. "The Field of Industrial Relations." *British Journal of Industrial Relations* 1 (Oct.): 383–94.

Bell, Daniel. 1947. "Adjusting Men to Machines." *Commentary* 3 (Jan.): 79–88.

Bendix, Reinhard. 1956. *Work and Authority in Industry.* New York: Wiley.

Bendix, Reinhard, and Lloyd Fisher. 1949. "The Perspectives of Elton Mayo." *Review of Economics and Statistics* 31 (Nov.): 312–21.

Berg, R. M. 1931. *Bibliography of Management Literature.* New York: American Society of Mechanical Engineers.

Bernstein, Irving. 1960. *The Lean Years: A History of the American Worker, 1920–1933.* Boston: Houghton Mifflin.

———. 1970. *The Turbulent Years: A History of the American Worker, 1933–1941.* Boston: Houghton Mifflin.

———. 1985. "The Emergence of the American Welfare State: The New Deal and the New Frontier–Great Society." In *Proceedings of the Thirty-eighth Annual Meeting, Industrial Relations Research Association,* 237–42. Madison: IRRA.

Berridge, John, and John Goodman. 1988. "The British Universities Industrial Relations Association: The First Thirty-five Years." *British Journal of Industrial Relations* 26 (July): 155–77.

255

References

Blain, A. N. J., and J. Gennard. 1970. "Industrial Relations Theory: A Critical Review." *British Journal of Industrial Relations* 8 (Nov.): 387–407.

Bloomfield, Daniel. 1919. *Selected Articles on Employment Management.* New York: Wilson.

———. 1920. *Modern Industrial Movements.* New York. Wilson.

———. 1931. "Preventive Management: The Next Step in Industrial Relations." In *Preventive Management: Mental Hygiene in Industry,* ed. Henry B. Elkind, 3–22. New York: B. C. Forbes.

Bloomfield, Meyer. 1923. "Man Management: A New Profession in the Making." In *Problems in Personnel Management,* ed. Daniel Bloomfield, 3–15. New York: Wilson.

Blum, Solomon. 1925. *Labor Economics.* New York: Henry Holt.

Blumer, Herbert. 1948. "Sociological Theory in Industrial Relations." *American Sociological Review* 12 (Oct.): 271–78.

Boivin, Jean. 1989. "Industrial Relations: A Field and a Discipline." In *Theories and Concepts in Comparative Industrial Relations,* ed. Jack Barbash and Kate Barbash, 91–108. Columbia: University of South Carolina Press.

———. 1991. "The Teaching of Industrial Relations in Canadian Universities." Laval University, Sainte Foy, Quebec. Unpublished.

Bossard, James, and J. Frederic Dewhurst. 1931. *University Education for Business.* Philadelphia: University of Pennsylvania Press.

Bradley, Phillips. 1945. "Survey of Selected Labor and Management Educational Projects." In *Report of the Board of Temporary Trustees of the New York State School of Industrial and Labor Relations,* 63–113. State of New York Legislative Document, no. 20. Albany: Williams Press.

Brissenden, Paul. 1926. "Labor Economics." *American Economic Review* 16 (Sept.): 443–49.

Britt David, and Omer Galle. 1974. "Industrial Conflict and Unionization." *American Sociological Review* 37 (Feb.): 46–57.

Brody, David. 1980. *Workers in Industrial America: Essays on the Twentieth Century Struggle.* New York: Oxford University Press.

———. 1989. "Labor History, Industrial Relations, and the Crisis of American Labor." *Industrial and Labor Relations Review* 43 (Oct.): 7–18.

Brown, H. F. 1935. "IR Activities Survive Crucial Test." *Personnel Journal* 13 (5): 258–62.

Brown, J. Douglas. 1952. "University Research in Industrial Relations." In *Proceedings of the Fifth Annual Meeting, Industrial Relations Research Association,* 2–7. Madison: IRRA.

———. 1976. *The Industrial Relations Section of Princeton University in World War II: A Personal Account.* Princeton: Industrial Relations Section, Princeton University.

Cain, Glen. 1976. "The Challenge of Segmented Labor Market Theories to Orthodox Theory: A Survey." *Journal of Economic Literature* 14 (Dec.): 1215–57.

Calder, John. 1924. *Modern Industrial Relations.* London: Longman, Green.

Caples, William G. 1958. "A Survey of the Graduate Curriculum in Industrial Relations." In *Proceedings of the Eleventh Annual Winter Meeting, Industrial Relations Research Association*, 224–36. Madison: IRRA.

Cappelli, Peter. 1985. "Theory Construction in Industrial Relations and Some Implications for Research." *Industrial Relations* 24 (Winter): 90–112.

———. 1990. *Economics and Organizational Behavior: Finding a Middle Path for Industrial Relations.* Department of Management Working Paper no. 001. Philadelphia: Wharton School, University of Pennsylvania.

Cappelli, Peter, and John Chalykoff. 1985. "The Effects of Management Industrial Relations Strategy: Results of a Survey." In *Proceedings of the Thirty-Eighth Annual Meeting, Industrial Relations Research Association*, 171–78. Madison: IRRA.

Carpenter, O. F. 1926. "Instituting Employee Representation." In *Industrial Government*, ed. John R. Commons, 340–64. New York: Macmillan.

Cartter, Allan M., and F. Ray Marshall. 1967. *Labor Economics: Wages, Employment, and Trade Unionism.* Homewood, Ill.: R. D. Irwin.

Catchings, Waddill. 1923. "Our Common Enterprise." In *Problems in Personnel Management*, ed. Daniel Bloomfield, 481–502. New York: H. W. Wilson.

Chamberlain, Neil. 1948. *The Union Challenge to Management Control.* New York: Harper.

———. 1960. "Issues for the Future." In *Proceedings of the Thirteenth Annual Meeting, Industrial Relations Research Association*, 101–9. Madison: IRRA.

———. 1963. "The Institutional Economics of John R. Commons." In *Institutional Economics: Veblen, Commons, and Mitchell Reconsidered*, 63–94. Berkeley: University of California Press.

Chapple, Eliot D. 1949. "The Interaction Chronograph: Its Evolution and Present Application." *Personnel* 25 (4): 295–307.

———. "Applied Anthropology in Industry." 1952. In *Anthropology Today*, ed. A. L. Kroeber, 819–31. Chicago: University of Chicago Press.

Chelius, James, and James Dworkin. 1990. "An Overview of the Transformation of Industrial Relations." In *Reflections on the Transformation of Industrial Relations*, ed. James Chelius and James Dworkin, 1–18. New Brunswick, N.J.: IMLR Press.

Chester, C. M. 1939. *Management's Responsibilities in Industrial Relations.* Personnel Series no. 36. New York: American Management Association.

Chinoy, Ely. 1952. "The Tradition of Opportunity and the Aspirations of Automobile Workers." *American Journal of Sociology* 57 (March): 453–59.

Clark, Kim B. 1984. "Organization and Firm Performance: The Impact on Profits, Growth and Productivity." *American Economic Review* 74 (Dec.): 883–919.

Coats, A. W. 1983. "John R. Commons as a Historian of Economics: The Quest for the Antecedents of Collective Action." In *Research in the History of Economic Thought and Methodology*, vol. 1, ed. Warren J. Samuels, 147–61.

References

Cochrane, James L. 1979. *Industrialism and Industrial Man in Retrospect.* Ann Arbor: University Microfilms International.

Commons, John R. 1909. "American Shoemakers, 1648–1895: A Sketch of Industrial Evolution." *Quarterly Journal of Economics* 24 (Nov.): 39–98.

———. 1911. "Organized Labor's Attitude toward Industrial Efficiency." *American Economic Review* 1 (Sept.): 463–72.

———. 1919. *Industrial Goodwill.* New York: McGraw-Hill.

———. 1920. "Management and Unionism." In *Proceedings of the Industrial Relations Association of America,* 125–30. Chicago: IRRA.

———. 1921. "Industrial Relations." In *Trade Unionism and Labor Problems,* ed John R. Commons, 1–16. 2d ser. New York: Augustus Kelley.

———. 1924. *Legal Foundations of Capitalism.* New York: Macmillan.

———. 1926. "The Opportunity of Management." In *Industrial Government,* ed John R. Commons, 263–72. New York: Macmillan.

———. 1934a. *Myself.* Madison: University of Wisconsin Press.

———. 1934b. *Institutional Economics.* New York: Macmillan.

———. 1950. *Economics of Collective Action.* New York: Macmillan.

Commons, John R., and John Andrews. 1916. *Principles of Labor Legislation.* New York: Harper.

Commons, John R., Sam Lewisohn, Ernest Draper, and Don Lescohier. 1925. *Can Business Prevent Unemployment?* New York: Alfred Knopf.

Cooke, William N. 1985. "Toward a General Theory of Industrial Relations." In *Advances in Industrial and Labor Relations,* vol. 2, ed. David Lewin, 223–52. Greenwich, Conn.: JAI Press.

Craig, David R., and W. W. Charters. 1925. *Personal Leadership in Industry.* New York: McGraw-Hill.

Cross, John. 1969. *The Economics of Bargaining.* New York: Basic Books.

Cutcher-Gershenfeld, Joel. 1991. "The Future of Industrial Relations as an Academic Field: A Strategic Planning Approach." In *The Future of Industrial Relations,* ed. Harry C. Katz, 145–60. Ithaca: ILR Press.

Dalton, Dan, and William Todor. 1981. "Win, Lose, Draw: The Grievance Process in Practice." *Personnel Administrator* 26 (May–June): 25–29.

Dalton, Melville. 1950. "Unofficial Union-Management Relations." *American Sociological Review* 15 (Oct.): 611–19.

Daugherty, Carroll. 1936. *Labor Problems in American Industry.* 4th ed. Boston: Houghton Mifflin.

Davis, Keith. 1957. *Human Relations in Industry.* New York: McGraw-Hill.

Denison, Edward F. 1985. *Trends in American Economic Growth, 1929–1982.* Washington, D.C.: Brookings Institution.

Derber, Milton. 1964. "Divergent Tendencies in Industrial Relations Research." *Industrial and Labor Relations Review* 17 (July): 598–611.

———. 1967. *Research in Labor Problems in the United States.* New York: Random House.

———. 1968. "The Changing Patterns of Research." In *The Role of Industrial*

References

Relations Centers, Proceedings of a Regional Meeting of the International Industrial Relations Research Association, 43–48. Madison: Industrial Relations Research Institute, University of Wisconsin.

———. 1982. "Comments." *Industrial Relations* 21 (Winter): 84–92.

———. 1987. *A Brief History of the Institute of Labor and Industrial Relations*. Champaign: Institute of Labor and Industrial Relations, University of Illinois.

Derber, Milton, et al. 1950. "An Inter-disciplinary Approach to the Study of Labor-Management Relations." In *Proceedings of the Third Annual Meeting, Industrial Relations Research Association*, 250–96. Madison: IRRA.

———. 1953. *Labor-Management Relations in Illini City*. Champaign: Institute of Labor and Industrial Relations, University of Illinois.

Dickman, Howard. 1987. *Industrial Democracy in America: Ideological Origins of National Labor Relations Policy*. LaSalle, Ill.: Open Court.

Doherty, Robert F. 1987. "Discussion." *Proceedings of the Annual Meeting, Industrial Relations Research Association*, 494–95. Madison: IRRA.

Dorfman, Joseph. 1959. *The Economic Mind in American Civilization*. Vols. 4 and 5, *1918–33*. New York: Viking.

———. 1963. "The Background of Institutional Economics." In *Institutional Economics: Veblen, Commons, and Mitchell Reconsidered*, 1–44. Berkeley: University of California Press.

Douglas, Paul H. 1919. "Plant Administration of Labor." *Journal of Political Economy* 27 (July): 544–60.

———. 1921. "Shop Committees: Substitutes for, or Complements to, Trade Unions." *Journal of Political Economy* 29 (Feb.): 89–107.

———. 1922. "Personnel Problems and the Business Cycle." *Administration* 4 (July): 15–28.

Douglas, Paul H., Curtis N. Hitchcock, and Willard E. Atkins. 1925. *The Worker in Modern Economic Society*. Chicago: University of Chicago Press.

Drucker, Peter. 1954. *The Practice of Management*. New York: Harper and Bros.

Dubin, Robert. 1949. "Union-Management Co-operation and Productivity." *Industrial and Labor Relations Review* 2 (Jan.): 195–209.

———. 1960. "A Theory of Conflict and Power in Union-Management Relations." *Industrial and Labor Relations Review* 13 (July): 501–18.

Dubofsky, Melvin. 1985. "Industrial Relations: Comparing the 1980s with the 1920s." In *Proceedings of the Thirty-Eighth Annual Meeting, Industrial Relations Research Association* 227–36. Madison: IRRA.

Dunlop, John T. 1944. *Wage Determination under Trade Unions*. New York: Macmillan.

———. 1950. "Framework for the Analysis of Industrial Relations: Two Views." *Industrial and Labor Relations Review* 3 (April): 383–93.

———. 1954. "Research in Industrial Relations: Past and Future." In *Proceedings of the Seventh Annual Meeting, Industrial Relations Research Association*, 92–101. Madison: IRRA.

259

———. 1958. *Industrial Relations Systems.* New York: Holt.

———. 1977. "Policy Decisions and Research in Economics and Industrial Relations." *Industrial and Labor Relations Review* 30 (April): 275–82.

———. 1984a. "Industrial Relations and Economics: The Common Frontier of Wage Determination." In *Proceedings of the Thirty-Seventh Annual Meeting, Industrial Relations Research Association,* 9–23. Madison: IRRA.

———. 1984b. *Dispute Resolution: Negotiation and Consensus Building.* Dover, Mass.: Auburn House.

———. 1988. "Labor Markets and Wage Determination: Then and Now." In *How Labor Markets Work,* ed. Bruce E. Kaufman, 47–87. Lexington, Mass.: Lexington Books.

———. 1993. "Organizations and Human Resources, Internal and External Markets." In *Labor Economics and Industrial Relations: Markets and Institutions,* ed. Clark Kerr and Paul Staudohar. Stanford: Stanford University Press. Forthcoming.

Dunlop, John T., Frederick H. Harbison, Clark Kerr, and Charles A. Myers. 1975. *Industrialism and Industrial Man Reconsidered.* Princeton: Inter-University Study of Human Resources in National Development.

Dunnette, Marvin D., and Bernard M. Bass. 1963. "Behavioral Scientists and Personnel Management." *Industrial Relations* 3 (May): 115–30.

Dworkin, James. 1988. "IR Graduate Study in Business Schools: The Case of Purdue University." In *Proceedings of the Forty-first Annual Winter Meeting, Industrial Relations Research Association,* 459–67. Madison: IRRA.

Ehrenberg, Ronald. 1990. "Do Compensation Policies Matter?" *Industrial and Labor Relations Review* (special issue) 43 (Feb.): 3S-10S.

Eilbirt, Henry. 1959. "The Development of Personnel Management in the United States." *Business History Review* 33 (Autumn): 345–64.

Eisner, J. Michael. 1967. *William Morris Leiserson: A Biography.* Madison: University of Wisconsin Press.

Ely, Richard T. 1886. *The Labor Movement in America.* New York: Thomas Y. Crowell.

———. 1938. *Ground under Our Feet: An Autobiography.* New York: Macmillan.

Estey, J. A. 1928. *The Labor Problem.* New York: McGraw-Hill.

Estey, Martin. 1960. "Unity and Diversity in Industrial Relations Education: The Report of the IRRA Survey." In *Proceedings of the Thirteenth Annual Meeting, Industrial Relations Research Association,* 92–100. Madison: IRRA.

Farber, Hank S., and Harry C. Katz. 1979. "Interest Arbitration, Outcomes, and the Incentive to Bargain." *Industrial and Labor Relations Review* (Oct.): 55–63.

Faunce, William A. 1967. "Research Note: Michigan State University, School of Labor and Industrial Relations." *Industrial and Labor Relations Review* 20 (July): 737–38.

Feis, Herbert. 1923. "The Kansas Court of Industrial Relations: Its Spokesmen, Its Record." *Quarterly Journal of Economics* 37 (Aug.): 705–33.

Ferguson, Robert H. 1965. Review of *Economics of Labor*, 2d ed., by Richard Lester. *Industrial and Labor Relations Review* 18 (Jan.): 271–74.

Filene, A. Lincoln. 1919. "The Key to Successful Industrial Management." *Annals of American Academy* 85 (Sept.): 9–11.

Filley, Alan. 1968. "The Industrial Relations Graduate Programs." In *The Role of Industrial Relations Centers, Proceedings of a Regional Meeting of the International Industrial Relations Research Association*, 71–77. Madison: Industrial Relations Research Institute, University of Wisconsin.

Fiorito, Jack. 1987. "Political Instrumentality Perceptions and Desires for Union Representation." *Journal of Labor Research* 8 (Summer): 271–89.

———. 1990. "Comments: The Wider Bounds of IR Systems." In *Reflections on the Transformation of Industrial Relations*, ed. James Chelius and James Dworkin, 96–106. New Brunswick, N.J.: IMLR Press.

Fisher, Lloyd. 1953. *The Harvest Labor Market in California*. Cambridge: Harvard University Press.

Fleisher, Belton. 1970. *Labor Economics*. Englewood Cliffs, N.J.: Prentice-Hall.

Follett, Mary Parker. [1925] 1942. "Business as an Integrative Unity." In *Dynamic Administration: The Collected Papers of Mary Parker Follett*, ed. Henry Metcalf and L. Urwick, 71–94. New York: Harper and Bros.

———. [1926] 1942. "Constructive Conflict." In *Dynamic Administration: The Collected Papers of Mary Parker Follett*, ed. Henry Metcalf and L. Urwick, 30–49. New York: Harper and Bros.

Form, William. 1979. "Comparative Industrial Sociology and the Convergence Hypothesis." *Annual Review of Sociology* 5: 1–25.

Fortune. 1946. "The Fruitful Errors of Elton Mayo." November, 181–83; 238–48.

Fossum, John A. 1987. "The Evolving Market for IR Professionals: Meeting the Needs." In *Proceedings of the Fortieth Annual Meeting, Industrial Relations Research Association*, 482–89. Madison: IRRA.

Foulkes, Fred. 1980. *Personnel Policies in Large Nonunion Companies*. Englewood Cliffs, N.J.: Prentice-Hall.

Fox, Alan. 1974. *Beyond Contract: Work, Power, and Trust Relations*. London: Faber and Faber.

Franke, Richard H., and James D. Kaul. 1978. "The Hawthorne Experiments: First Statistical Interpretation." *American Sociological Review* 43 (Oct.): 623–42.

Franke, Walter. 1987. "Accommodating to Change: Can IR Learn from Itself?" In *Proceedings of the Fortieth Annual Meeting, Industrial Relations Research Association*, 474–81. Madison: IRRA.

Freeman, Richard B. 1988. "Contraction and Expansion: The Divergence of Private and Public Sector Unionism in the United States." *Journal of Economic Perspectives* 2 (Spring): 63–88.

Freeman, Richard B., and James Medoff. 1984. *What Do Unions Do?* New York: Basic Books.

Fried, Amy E. 1987. *Industrial Relations Research Institute: A Brief History, 1947–1987*. Madison: Industrial Relations Research Institute, University of Wisconsin.

Friedman, Milton. 1951. "Some Comments on the Significance of Labor Unions for Economic Policy." In *The Impact of the Union*, ed. David McCord Wright, 204–34. New York: Harcourt Brace.

———. 1953. *Essays in Positive Economics*. Chicago: University of Chicago Press.

Friedman, Milton, and Anna Schwartz. 1963. *A Monetary History of the United States: 1867–1960*. Princeton: Princeton University Press.

Furniss, Edgar S. 1925. *Labor Problems*. Boston: Houghton Mifflin.

Gallagher, Daniel G., and Cynthia Gramm. 1991. "Integrating Behavioral and Economic Perspectives of Strike Activity: Promise or Illusion?" James Madison University, Harrisonburg, Va. Unpublished.

Gallagher, Daniel G., and George Strauss. 1991. "Union Membership Attitudes and Participation." In *The State of the Unions*, ed. Daniel Gallagher et al., 139–74. Madison: IRRA.

Gardner, Burleigh B. 1946. "The Factory as a Social System." In *Industry and Society*, ed. William Foote Whyte, 4–20. New York: McGraw-Hill.

Getman, Julius, Stephen Goldberg, and Jeanne Herman. 1976. *Union Representation Elections: Law and Reality*. New York: Russell Sage Foundation.

Ginsburg, Woodrow, E. Robert Livernash, Herbert Parnes, and George Strauss. 1970. *A Review of Industrial Relations Research*, vol. 1. Madison: IRRA.

Goddard, John. 1992a. "Beyond Empiricism: Towards a Reconstruction of IR Theory and Research." In *Advances in Industrial and Labor Relations*, ed. David Lewin, David Lipsky, and Donna Sockell. Forthcoming.

———. 1992b. "Contemporary Industrial Relations Ideologies: A Study of the Values and Beliefs of Canadian Academics." *Relations Industrielles*. Forthcoming.

Golden, Clinton S., and Virginia D. Parker. 1955. *Causes of Industrial Peace*. New York: Harper and Bros.

Golden, Clinton S., and Harold J. Ruttenberg. 1942. *The Dynamics of Industrial Democracy*. New York: Harper and Bros.

Goldthorpe, John. 1984. *Order and Conflict in Contemporary Capitalism*. Oxford: Clarendon Press.

Gordon, Robert A., and James E. Howell. 1959. *Higher Education for Business*. New York: Columbia University Press.

Gouldner, Alvin W. 1954. *Patterns of Industrial Bureaucracy*. Glencoe, Ill.: Free Press.

Graham, Rev. Robert C. 1948. "The Industrial Relations Curriculum in Colleges and University." Master's thesis, Catholic University.

Gray, Wayne B. 1987. "The Cost of Regulation: OSHA, EPA and the Productivity Slowdown." *American Economic Review* 77 (Dec.): 998–1006.

Greenwood, Ronald G., and Charles D. Wrege. 1986. "The Hawthorne Studies." In *Papers Dedicated to the Development of Modern Management*, ed. Daniel Wren, 24–35. Norman Okla.: Academy of Management.

Gulick, Charles A. 1932. "Industrial Relations in Southern Textile Mills." *Quarterly Journal of Economics* 46 (Aug.): 720–42.

Haber, Samuel. 1964. *Efficiency and Uplift: Scientific Management in the Progressive Era, 1890–1920.* Chicago: University of Chicago Press.

Haber, William. 1930. *Industrial Relations in the Building Industry.* Cambridge: Harvard University Press.

Haire, Mason. 1955. "Role Perceptions in Labor-Management Relations." *Industrial and Labor Relations Review* 8 (Jan.): 204–16.

Hameed, Syed. 1982. "A Critique of Industrial Relations Theory." *Relations Industrielles* 37 (1): 15–31.

Hansen, Alvin H. 1922. "The Economics of Unionism." *Journal of Political Economy* 30 (Aug.): 518–30.

Harbison, Frederick H. 1946. "The Basis of Industrial Conflict." In *Industry and Society*, ed. William Foote Whyte, 168–82. New York: McGraw-Hill.

Harbison, Frederick H., and Robert Dubin. 1947. *Patterns of Union-Management Relations.* Chicago: Science Research Associates.

Hart, C. W. M. 1948. "Industrial Relations Research and Social Theory." *Canadian Journal of Economics and Political Science* 15 (Feb.): 53–73.

Harter, LaFayette G., Jr. 1962. *John R. Commons: His Assault on Laissez Faire.* Corvallis: Oregon State University Press.

Hausman, Leonard, Orley Ashenfelter, Bayard Rustin, Richard Schubert, and Donald Slaiman. 1977. *Equal Rights and Industrial Relations.* Madison: IRRA.

Hebert, Gerard, Hem C. Jain, and Noah M. Meltz. 1988. *The State of the Art in Industrial Relations.* Kingston and Toronto: Industrial Relations Centre, Queen's University, and Centre for Industrial Relations, University of Toronto.

Heckscher, Charles. 1988. *The New Unionism.* New York: Basic Books.

Heldman, Dan, James Bennett, and Manuel Johnson. 1981. *Deregulating Labor Relations.* Dallas: Fisher Institute.

Heneman, Herbert, Jr. 1968. "Contributions of Current Research." In *The Role of Industrial Relations Centers, Proceedings of a Regional Meeting of the International Industrial Research Relations Association*, 49–58. Madison: IRRA.

———. 1969. "Toward a General Conceptual System of Industrial Relations: How Do We Get There?" In *Essays in Industrial Relations Theory*, ed. Gerald G. Somers, 3–24. Ames: Iowa State University Press.

Heneman, Herbert, Jr., and John G. Turnbull. 1952. *Personnel Administration and Labor Relations.* New York: Prentice-Hall.

Heneman, Herbert, Jr., et al. 1960. *Employment Relations Research.* Madison: IRRA.

Herman, Georgianna. 1984. *Personnel and Industrial Relations Colleges: An ASPA Directory.* 2d ed. Berea, Ohio: American Society for Personnel Administration.

References

Herzberg, Frederick, Bernard Mausner, and Barbara Snyderman. 1959. *The Motivation to Work*. New York: Wiley.

Hicks, Clarence J. 1941. *My Life in Industrial Relations*. New York: Harper and Bros.

Hicks, John R. 1932. *The Theory of Wages*. New York: Macmillan.

Hills, Steven. 1975. "Organizational Behavior and Theoretical Models of Industrial Relations." In *Proceedings of the Twenty-eighth Annual Winter Meeting, Industrial Relations Research Association*, 47–55. Madison: IRRA.

———. 1992. "Integrating Industrial Relations with the Social Sciences." In *Industrial Relations Theory: Its Nature, Scope and Pedagogy*, ed. Roy Adams and Noah Meltz. Melbourne: Longman Cheshire. Forthcoming.

Hirsch, Barry. 1991. *Labor Unions and the Economic Performance of Firms*. Kalamazoo, Mich.: W. E. Upjohn Institute.

Hoerr, John P. 1988. *And the Wolf Finally Came*. Pittsburgh: University of Pittsburgh Press.

Hoffstadter, Richard. 1963. *The Progressive Era: 1900–1915*. Englewood Cliffs, N. J.: Prentice Hall.

Holliday, W. T. 1934. "Employee Representation." *Personnel* 10 (May): 99–104.

Homans, George C. 1950. *The Human Group*. New York: Harcourt Brace.

———. 1954. "Industrial Harmony as a Goal," In *Industrial Conflict*, ed. Arthur Kornhauser, Robert Dubin, and Arthur Ross, 48–58. New York: McGraw-Hill.

Homans, George C., and Jerome Scott. 1947. "Reflections on Wildcat Strikes." *American Sociological Review* 12 (June): 278–87.

Houser, J. David. 1927. *What the Employer Thinks*. Cambridge: Harvard University Press.

Hoxie, Robert. 1915. *Scientific Management and Labor*. New York: Appleton.

———. 1917. *Trade Unionism in the United States*. New York: Appleton.

Hyman, Richard. 1975. *Industrial Relations: A Marxist Introduction*. London: Macmillan.

Industrial Relations Counselors. 1949. *Industrial Relations Work at Certain Universities*, pts 1–3. New York: IRC.

———. 1962. *Behavioral Science Research in Industrial Relations*. New York: IRC.

Industrial Relations Research Association. 1977. *Report of the Comprehensive Review Committee of the Industrial Relations Research Association*. Madison: IRRA.

———. 1988a. *Report of the IRRA Comprehensive Review Committee*. Madison: IRRA.

———. 1988b. *Recommendations from the IRRA Working Group on Winter and Spring Meetings*. Madison: IRRA.

———. 1990. *Membership Directory*. Madison: IRRA.

Industrial Relations Section, California Institute of Technology. 1939. *The Industrial Relations Section: An Initial Report of Progress*. Pasadena: California Institute of Technology.

References

Industrial Relations Section, Princeton University. 1930. *Selected Book List for the Office of an Industrial Relations Executive*. Princeton: Princeton University.

———. 1939. *Problems and Policies in Industrial Relations in a War Economy: A Selected, Annotated Bibliography*. Princeton: Princeton University.

———. 1986. *The Industrial Relations Section of Princeton University, 1922–1985*. Princeton: Princeton University.

Jacoby, Sanford. 1985. *Employing Bureaucracy: Managers, Unions, and the Transformation of Work in American Industry, 1900–1945*. New York: Columbia University Press.

———. 1990. "The New Institutionalism: What It Can Learn from the Old." *Industrial Relations* 29 (Spring): 316–40.

Johnson, George. 1984. "Changes over Time in the Union-Nonunion Wage Differential." In *The Economics of Trade Unions*, ed. Jean-Jacques Rosa, 3–19. Boston: Kluwer Nijhoff.

Johnson, Harry, and Peter Mieszkowski. 1969. "The Effects of Unionization on the Distribution of Income: A General Equilibrium Approach." *Quarterly Journal of Economics* 84 (Nov.): 539–61.

Johnson, Robert W. 1949. "Human Relations in Modern Business." *Harvard Business Review* 27 (Sept.): 29–55.

Jucius, Michael J. 1948. *Personnel Management*. Chicago: Irwin.

Justin, Brother F. S. C. 1949. "The Study of Industrial and Labor Relations in Catholic Colleges." *Industrial and Labor Relations Review* 3 (Oct.): 70–75.

Kanter, Rosabeth Moss. 1989. *When Giants Learn to Dance*. New York: Simon and Schuster.

Kassalow, Everett. 1985. "Trade Unionism: Once More into the Future." *Proceedings of the Thirty-eighth Annual Meeting, Industrial Relations Research Association*, 1–13. Madison: IRRA.

Katz, Harry C. 1991. *The Future of Industrial Relations*. Ithaca: ILR Press.

Kaufman, Bruce E. 1988. "The Postwar View of Labor Markets and Wage Determination." In *How Labor Markets Work*, ed. Bruce E. Kaufman, 145–203. Lexington, Mass.: Lexington Books.

———. 1989a. "Labor's Inequality of Bargaining Power: Changes over Time and Implications for Public Policy." *Journal of Labor Research* 10 (Summer): 285–98.

———. 1989b. "Models of Man in Industrial Relations Research." *Industrial and Labor Relations Review* 43 (Oct.): 72–88.

———. 1991a. "Labor's Inequality of Bargaining Power: Myth or Reality?" *Journal of Labor Research* 12 (Spring): 151–66.

———. 1991b. "Research Expectations in IR/HR Units: The View from the Beebe Institute." In *Proceedings of the Forty-fourth Annual Winter Meeting, Industrial Relations Research Association*, 502–9. Madison: IRRA.

———. 1993. "The Evolution of Thought on the Competitive Nature of Labor Markets." In *Labor Economics and Industrial Relations: Markets and Institutions*, ed. Clark Kerr and Paul Staudohar. Stanford: Stanford University Press. Forthcoming.

References

Kaufman, Bruce E., and Paula E. Stephan. 1987. "The Determinants of Inter-industry Wage Growth in the 1970s." *Industrial Relations* 26 (Spring): 186–94.

Kelly, Laurence. 1987. "Industrial Relations at Queen's: The First Fifty Years." *Relations Industrielles* 42 (3): 475–99.

Kennedy, Dudley R. 1920. "The Future of Industrial Relations." *Industrial Management*, March, 227–31.

Kerr, Clark. 1950. "Labor Markets: Their Character and Consequences." *American Economic Review* 40 (May): 278–91.

———. 1954a. "The Balkanization of Labor Markets." In *Labor Mobility and Economic Opportunity*, ed. E. Wight Bakke, 92–110. New York: Wiley.

———. 1954b. "Industrial Relations and the Liberal Pluralist." In *Proceedings of the Seventh Annual Meeting, Industrial Relations Research Association*, 2–16. Madison: IRRA.

———. 1978. "Industrial Relations Research: A Personal Retrospective." *Industrial Relations* 17 (May): 131–42.

———. 1983. "A Perspective on Industrial Relations Research—Thirty-six Years Later." In *Proceedings of the Thirty-sixth Annual Winter Meeting, Industrial Relations Research Association*, 14–21. Madison: IRRA.

———. 1988. "The Neoclassical Revisionists in Labor Economics (1940–1960)—RIP." In *How Labor Markets Work*, ed. Bruce E. Kaufman, 1–46. Lexington, Mass.: Lexington Books.

Kerr, Clark, John Dunlop, Frederick Harbison, and Charles Myers. 1960. *Industrialism and Industrial Man*. Cambridge: Harvard University Press.

Kerr, Clark, and Lloyd H. Fisher. 1950. "Effects of Environment and Administration on Job Evaluation." *Harvard Business Review* 28 (May): 77–96.

———. 1957. "Plant Sociology: The Elite and the Aborigines." In *Common Frontiers of the Social Sciences*, ed. Mirra Komarovski, 281–309. Glencoe, Ill.: Free Press.

Kerr, Clark, and Abraham Siegel. 1954. "The Interindustry Propensity to Strike: An International Comparison." In *Industrial Conflict*, ed. Arthur Kornhauser, Robert Dubin, and Arthur Ross, 189–212. New York: McGraw-Hill.

———. 1955. "The Structuring of the Labor Force in Industrial Society: New Dimensions and New Questions." *Industrial and Labor Relations Review* 8 (Jan.): 151–68.

Keynes, John Maynard. 1936. *The General Theory of Employment, Interest, and Money*. New York: Harcourt Brace.

Keyserling, Leon. 1945. "Why the Wagner Act?" In *The Wagner Act: Ten Years Later*, ed. Louis Silverberg, 5–33. Washington, D.C.: Bureau of National Affairs.

Kleiner, Morris M., et al. 1987. *Human Resources and the Performance of the Firm*. Madison: IRRA.

Knox, John B. 1955. *The Sociology of Industrial Relations*. New York: Random House.

Kochan, Thomas. 1980. *Collective Bargaining and Industrial Relations*. Homewood, Ill.: R. D. Irwin.

————. 1992. "Teaching and Building Middle-Range Industrial Relations Theory." In *Industrial Relations Theory: Its Nature, Scope, and Pedagogy,* ed. Roy Adams and Noah Meltz. Melbourne: Longman Cheshire. Forthcoming.

Kochan, Thomas, and Thomas Barocci. 1985. *Human Resources Management and Industrial Relations.* Boston: Little Brown.

Kochan, Thomas, Harry Katz, and Robert McKersie. 1986. *The Transformation of American Industrial Relations.* New York: Basic Books.

Kochan, Thomas, Robert B. McKersie, and Peter Cappelli. 1984. "Strategic Choice and Industrial Relations Theory." *Industrial Relations* 23 (Winter): 16–39.

Kochan, Thomas, et al. 1979. *Dispute Resolution under Factfinding and Arbitration.* New York: American Arbitration Association.

Kornhauser, Arthur. 1948. "The Contribution of Psychology to Industrial Relations Research." In *Proceedings of the First Annual Meeting, Industrial Relations Research Association,* 172–88. Champaign: IRRA.

————. 1954. "Human Motivations Underlying Industrial Conflict." In *Industrial Conflict,* ed. Arthur Kornhauser, Robert Dubin, and Arthur Ross, 62–85. New York: McGraw-Hill.

Kornhauser, Arthur, Robert Dubin, and Arthur Ross. 1954. *Industrial Conflict.* New York: McGraw-Hill.

Krislov, Joseph, and John Mead. 1987. "Changes in IR Programs since the Mid-Sixties." *Industrial Relations* 26 (Spring): 208–12.

Landsberger, Henry A. 1958. *Hawthorne Revisited.* Ithaca: Cornell Sudies in Industrial and Labor Relations, vol. ix.

————. 1967. "The Behavioral Sciences in Industry." *Industrial Relations* 7 (Oct.): 1–19.

Lange, W. H. 1928. *The American Management Association and Its Predecessors.* Special Paper no. 17. New York: American Management Association.

Lawler, Edward, III. 1986. *High Involvement Management.* San Francisco: Jossey-Bass.

Lawshe, C. H., et al. 1953. *The Psychology of Industrial Relations.* New York: McGraw-Hill.

Leiserson, William M. 1923. "Employee Management, Employee Representation, and Industrial Democracy." In *Problems in Personnel Management,* ed. Daniel Bloomfield and Meyer Bloomfield, 503–16. New York: H. W. Wilson.

————. 1929. "Contributions of Personnel Management to Improved Labor Relations." In *Wertheim Lectures on Industrial Relations,* 125–64. Cambridge: Harvard University Press.

————. 1935. "Collective Bargaining." In *Collective Bargaining,* 21–28. Personnel Series no. 19. New York: American Management Association.

————. 1959. *American Trade Union Democracy.* New York: Columbia University Press.

Lens, Sidney. 1974. *The Labor Wars.* New York: Anchor.

Lescohier, Don D. 1935. "Working Conditions." In *History of Labor in the*

United States, 1896–1932, vol. 3. ed. John R. Commons et al., 51–396. New York: Macmillan.

Lester, Richard A. 1941; 2d. ed., rev., 1964. *Economics of Labor.* New York: Macmillan.

———. 1946a. "Shortcomings of Marginal Analysis for Wage-Employment Problems." *American Economic Review* 36 (March): 63–82.

———. 1946b. "Wage Diversity and Its Theoretical Implications." *Review of Economics and Statistics* 28 (Aug.): 152–59.

———. 1947a. "Marginalism, Minimum Wages, and the Labor Market." *American Economic Review* 37 (March): 135–48.

———. 1947b. "Reflections on the Labor Monopoly Issue." *Journal of Political Economy* 55 (Dec.): 13–36.

———. 1951. *Labor and Industrial Relations: A General Analysis.* New York: Macmillan.

———. 1952. "A Range Theory of Wage Differentials." *Industrial and Labor Relations Review* 5 (July): 433–50.

———. 1954. *Hiring Practices and Labor Competition.* Princeton: Industrial Relations Section, Princeton University.

———. 1973. "Manipulation of the Labor Market." In *The Next Twenty-five Years of Industrial Relations,* ed. Gerald G. Somers, 47–55. Madison: IRRA.

Levitan, Sar, Wilbur Cohen, and Robert Lampman. 1968. *Towards Freedom from Want.* Madison: IRRA.

Lewin, David. 1987. "Industrial Relations as a Strategic Variable." In *Human Resources and the Performance of the Firm,* ed. Morris Kleiner et al., 1–41. Madison: IRRA.

———. 1988a. "The Industrial Relations (IR) Content of MBA Degree Programs in the U.S." In *Proceedings of the Forty-first Annual Winter Meeting, Industrial Relations Research Association,* 474–78. Madison: IRRA.

———. 1988b. Letter to IRRA Comprehensive Review Committee on the survey of the membership of the Industrial Relations Research Association.

———. 1991. "The Contemporary Human Resource Management Challenge to Industrial Relations." In *The Future of Industrial Relations,* ed. Harry C. Katz, 82–99. Ithaca: ILR Press.

Lewin, David, and Peter Feuille. 1983. "Behavioral Research in Industrial Relations." *Industrial and Labor Relations Review* 36 (April): 341–60.

Lewin, Kurt, R. Lippitt, and R. White. 1939. "Patterns of Aggressive Behavior in Experimentally Created Social Climates." *Journal of Social Psychology* 10 (May): 271–99.

Lewis, H. Gregg. 1951. "The Labor-Monopoly Problem: A Positive Program." *Journal of Political Economy* 69 (Aug.): 277–87.

———. 1956. "Hours of Work and Hours of Leisure." In *Proceedings of the Ninth Annual Meeting, Industrial Relations Research Association,* 192–206. Madison: IRRA.

———. 1963. *Unions and Relative Wages in the United States.* Chicago: University of Chicago Press.

References

Lewisohn, Sam A. 1926. *The New Leadership in Industry*. New York: E. P. Dutton.

Likert, Rensis. 1961. *New Patterns of Management*. New York: McGraw-Hill.

———. 1967. *The Human Organization: Its Management and Value*. New York: McGraw-Hill.

Lindblom, Charles. 1949. *Unions and Capitalism*. New Haven: Yale University Press.

Ling, Cyril C. 1965. *The Management of Personnel Relations: History and Origins*. Homewood, Ill.: R. D. Irwin.

McCone, John. 1920. "Organized Labor in Industry." In *Proceedings of the Industrial Relations Association of America*, 92–97. Chicago: IRAA.

McConnell, Campbell R. 1955. "Institutional Economics and Trade Unions." *Industrial and Labor Relations Review* 8 (April): 347–60.

McGregor, Douglas. 1960. *The Human Side of Enterprise*. New York: McGraw-Hill.

McGregor, Douglas, and Irving Knickerbocker. 1941. "Industrial Relations and National Defense: A Challenge to Management." *Personnel* 18 (July): 49–63.

Machlup, Fritz. 1946. "Marginal Analysis and Empirical Research." *American Economic Review* 36 (Sept.): 519–55.

———. 1951. *The Political Economy of Monopoly*. Baltimore: Johns Hopkins University Press.

McKersie, Robert B. 1990. "End of an Era: Industrial Relations Section Turns Fiftysomething." Massachusetts Institute of Technology. Unpublished.

McNulty, Paul. 1968. "Labor Problems and Labor Economics: The Roots of an Academic Discipline." *Labor History* 9 (Spring): 239–61.

———. 1980. *The Origin and Development of Labor Economics*. Cambridge: MIT Press.

Marshall, Alfred. 1920. *Principles of Economics*. 8th ed. London: Macmillan.

Marshall, Ray. 1987. "The Future of Private Sector Collective Bargaining." In *The Future of Industrial Relations*, ed. Daniel J. B. Mitchell, 63–87. Los Angeles: Institute of Industrial Relations, University of California.

Maslow, Abraham H. 1954. *Motivation and Personality*. New York: Harper and Row.

Mathewson, Stanley. 1931. *Restriction of Output among Unorganized Workers*. New York: Viking.

Mayo, Elton. 1925. "The Great Stupidity." *Harper's* 151 (July): 225–33.

———. 1929. "Maladjustment of the Industrial Worker." In *Wertheim Lectures on Industrial Relations*, 165–96. Cambridge: Harvard University Press.

———. 1930. *A New Approach to Industrial Relations*. Cambridge: Harvard Business School.

———. 1933. *The Human Problems of an Industrial Civilization*. New York: Macmillan.

———. 1945. *The Social Problems of an Industrial Civilization*. Cambridge: Harvard School of Business.

Meltz, Noah M. 1988. "Why Are There Few Academic Industrial Relations

269

Departments?" Centre for Industrial Relations, University of Toronto. Unpublished.

———. 1989. "Industrial Relations: Balancing Efficiency and Equity." In *Theories and Concepts in Comparative Industrial Relations,* ed. Jack Barbash and Kate Barbash, 109–13. Columbia: University of South Carolina Press.

———. 1991. "Dunlop's *Industrial Relations Systems* after Three Decades." In *Comparative Industrial Relations: Contemporary Research and Theory,* ed. Roy Adams, 10–20. Melbourne: Longman Cheshire.

Miles, Raymond. 1965. "Human Relations or Human Resources?" *Harvard Business Review* 43 (July–Aug.): 148–63.

Miller, A. Van Court. 1937. *Social Security and Industrial Relations.* Personnel Series no. 28. New York: American Management Association.

Miller, Delbert C., and William H. Form. 1951, 1964, 1980. *Industrial Sociology. An Introduction to the Sociology of Work Relations.* 1st ed., 2d ed., 3d ed. New York: Harper.

Millis, Harry A., and Royal E. Montgomery. 1938. *Economics of Labor,* vols. 1–2. New York: McGraw-Hill.

———. 1945. *Economics of Labor,* vol. 3. New York: McGraw-Hill.

Mills, C. Wright. 1948. "The Contribution of Sociology to Studies of Industrial Relations." In *Proceedings of the First Annual Meeting, Industrial Relations Research Association,* 199–222. Champaign: IRRA.

Mills, D. Quinn. 1981. "Management Performance." In *U.S. Industrial Relations, 1950–1980: A Critical Assessment,* ed. Jack Stieber et al., 99–128. Madison: IRRA.

Milton, Charles R. 1960. *"The Development of Philosophies of Personnel Administration."* Ph.D. diss., University of North Carolina.

Moore, Wilbert. 1951. *Industrial Relations and the Social Order.* Rev. ed. New York: Macmillan.

Morris, Richard. 1987. "The Early Uses of the Industrial Relations Concept." *Journal of Industrial Relations* 29 (Dec.): 532–38.

Myers, Charles A. 1955. "Conclusions and Implications." In *Causes of Industrial Peace under Collective Bargaining,* ed. Clinton Golden and Virginia Parker, 46–54. New York: Harper and Bros.

Myers, Charles A., and George P. Shultz. 1951. *The Dynamics of a Labor Market.* New York: Prentice Hall.

National Industrial Conference Board. 1929. *Industrial Relations Programs in Small Plants.* New York: National Industrial Conference Board.

———. 1931. *Industrial Relations: Administration of Policies and Programs.* New York: National Industrial Conference Board.

———. 1933. *Collective Bargaining through Employee Representation.* New York: National Industrial Conference Board.

Nelson, Daniel. 1975. *Managers and Workers: Origins of the New Factory System in the United States, 1880–1920.* Madison: University of Wisconsin Press.

———. 1982. "The Company Union Movement, 1900–1937: A Reexamination." *Business History Review* 54 (Autumn): 335–57.

Nyman, R. Carter. 1949. *Foundations for Constructive Industrial Relations*. New York: Funk and Wagnall's.

Olson, Olivia. 1894. *Solution of the Labor Problem*. Chicago: Hornstein Bros.

Osterman, Paul. 1987. "Choice of Employment Systems in Internal Labor Markets." *Industrial Relations* 26 (Winter): 46–67.

Pennock, George, A. 1930. "Industrial Research at Hawthorne." *Personnel Journal* 8 (5): 296–313.

Perlman, Mark. 1958. *Labor Union Theories in America*. Evanston, Ill.: Row, Peterson.

Perlman, Selig. 1922. *History of Trade Unionism in the United States*. New York: Macmillan.

———. 1928. *A Theory of the Labor Movement*. New York: Macmillan.

Persons, Charles E. 1927. "Labor Problems as Treated by American Economists." *Quarterly Journal of Economics* 41 (May): 487–519.

Peters, Thomas J., and Robert M. Waterman. 1982. *In Search of Excellence*. New York: Harper and Row.

Peterson, Joyce Shaw. 1987. *American Automobile Workers, 1900–1933*. Albany: State University of New York Press.

Pfiffner, John M. 1949. "A Human Relations Reading List." *Personnel* 26 (July): 133–45.

Phelps, Orme. 1955. *Introduction to Labor Economics*. 2d ed. New York: McGraw-Hill.

Rayback, Joseph G. 1966. *A History of American Labor*. New York: Free Press.

Reder, Melvin. 1982. "Chicago Economics: Permanence and Change," *Journal of Economic Literature* 20 (March): 1–38.

Rees, Albert. 1976. "H. Gregg Lewis and the Development of Analytical Labor Economics." *Journal of Political Economy* 84, pt. 2 (August): 53–57.

———. 1989. *The Economics of Trade Unions*. 3d ed. Chicago: University of Chicago Press.

Rehmus, Charles. 1985. "The Changing Role of Universities in Industrial Relations Training." In *Proceedings of the 1985 Spring Meeting, Industrial Relations Research Association*, 591–94. Madison: IRRA.

Reynolds, Lloyd. 1948. "Economics of Labor." In *Survey of Contemporary Economics*, ed. H. S. Ellis, 255–87. New York: Blakiston.

———. 1951. *The Structure of Labor Markets*. New York: Harper and Bros.

———. 1953. Review of *The Impact of the Union* by David McCord Wright. *American Economic Review* 43 (June): 474–77.

———. 1955. "Research and Practice in Industrial Relations." In *Proceedings of the Eighth Annual Meeting, Industrial Relations Research Association*, 2–13. Madison: IRRA.

———. 1957. "The Impact of Collective Bargaining on the Wage Structure." In *The Theory of Wage Determination*, ed. John Dunlop, 173–93. London: Macmillan.

———. 1988. "Labor Economics Then and Now." In *How Labor Markets Work*, ed. Bruce E. Kaufman, 117–43. Lexington, Mass.: Lexington Books.

Reynolds, Morgan O. 1984. *Power and Privilege: Labor Unions in America.* New York: Universe Books.

Rezler, Julius. 1968a. "The Place of the Industrial Relations Program in the Organizational Structure of the University." *Industrial and Labor Relations Review* 21 (Jan.): 251–58.

———. 1968b. "Administrative Arrangements in Industrial Relations Centers." In *The Role of Industrial Relations Centers, Proceedings of a Regional Meeting of the International Industrial Relations Association,* 1–11. Madison: Industrial Relations Research Institute, University of Wisconsin.

Roberts, Benjamin C. 1972. "Affluence and Disruption." In *Man and the Social Sciences,* ed. William A. Robson, 245–72. London: London School of Economics and Political Science.

Robinson, Joan. 1933. *The Economics of Imperfect Competition.* London: Macmillan.

Rockefeller, John D., Jr. 1923. "Representation in Industry." In *Problems in Personnel Management,* ed. Daniel Bloomfield and Meyer Bloomfield, 517–28. New York: H. W. Wilson.

Roethlisberger, Fritz J. 1977. *The Elusive Phenomena.* Cambridge: Harvard University Press.

Roethlisberger, Fritz J., and William J. Dickson. 1939. *Management and the Worker.* Cambridge: Harvard University Press.

Ross, Arthur M. 1948. *Trade Union Wage Policy.* Berkeley: University of California Press.

———. 1961. "Introduction to a New Journal." *Industrial Relations* 1 (1): 5–7.

———. 1964. "Labor Courses: The Need for Radical Reconstruction." *Industrial Relations* 4 (Oct.): 1–17.

Ross, Dorothy. 1991. *The Origins of American Social Science.* Cambridge: Cambridge University Press.

Rothbaum, Melvin. 1967. "Research Note: University of Illinois Institute of Labor and Industrial Relations." *Industrial and Labor Relations Review* 20 (July): 733–35.

Russell Sage Foundation. 1919. "Industrial Relations: A Selected Bibliography." *Bulletin of the Russell Sage Foundation Library* 35.

Ruttenberg, Stanley H. 1958. "Appraisal of Education in Industrial and Human Relations." In *Proceedings of the Eleventh Annual Meeting, Industrial Relations Research Association,* 243–47. Madison: IRRA.

Ryan, Frederick L. 1936. *Industrial Relations in the San Francisco Building Trades.* Norman: University of Oklahoma Press.

Sayles, Leonard, and George Strauss. 1953. *The Local Union: Its Place in the Industrial Plant.* New York: Harper.

Schatz, Ronald W. 1993. "From Commons to Dunlop: Rethinking the Field and Theory of Industrial Relations." In *Defining Industrial Democracy: Work Relations in Twentieth Century America,* ed. Howell Harris and Nelson Lichtenstein. Cambridge: Cambridge University Press. Forthcoming.

Schlabach, Theron F. 1969. *Edwin E. Witte: Cautious Reformer*. Madison: State Historical Society of Wisconsin.

Schlaifer, Robert. 1980. "The Relay Assembly Test Room: An Alternative Statistical Interpretation." *American Sociological Review* 45 (Dec.): 995–1005.

Schnelle, Kenneth, and Harland Fox. 1951. "University Courses in Industrial Relations." *Personnel Journal* 20 (Sept.): 128–33.

Schriesheim, Chester. 1978. "Job Satisfaction, Attitudes toward Unions, and Voting in a Union Representation Election." *Journal of Applied Psychology* 63 (Oct.): 548–52.

Schultz, Richard S., and Mathias B. Lynaugh. 1939. "Cooperation of Men, Management, and Psychologists in Industrial Relations." *Journal of Applied Psychology* 23 (Dec.): 733–43.

Scott, Walter Dill, and Robert C. Clothier. 1923. *Personnel Management*. New York: A. W. Shaw.

Selekman, Benjamin M. 1947. *Labor Relations and Human Relations*. New York: McGraw-Hill.

Selekman, Benjamin M., and Sylvia Selekman. 1950. "Productivity—and Collective Bargaining." *Harvard Business Review* 28 (March): 127–44.

Sewell, William. 1989. "Some Reflections on the Golden Age of Interdisciplinary Social Psychology." *Annual Review of Sociology* 15: 1–16.

Sherer, Peter D. 1991. "The Future of Industrial Relations as an Academic Field: New Directions for Research in Industrial Relations." In *The Future of Industrial Relations*, ed. Harry C. Katz, 164–69. Ithaca: ILR Press.

Shultz, George P. 1964. "Labor Courses Are Not Obsolete." *Industrial Relations* 4 (Oct.): 23–28.

———. 1968. "Priorities in Policy and Research for Industrial Relations." In *Proceedings of the Twenty-first Annual Winter Meeting, Industrial Relations Research Association*, 1–13. Madison: IRRA.

Simon, Herbert. 1947. *Administrative Behavior*. New York: Macmillan.

Simons, Henry. 1948. "Reflections on Syndicalism." In *Economic Policy in a Free Society*, 121–59. Chicago: University of Chicago Press.

Singh, R. 1976. "Systems Theory in the Study of Industrial Relations: Time for a Re-appraisal." *Industrial Relations Journal* 7 (Autumn): 59–71.

Slichter, Sumner, 1919a. *The Turnover of Factory Labor*. New York: Appleton.

———. 1919b. "The Management of Labor." *Journal of Political Economy* 27 (Dec.): 813–39.

———. 1920. "Industrial Morale." *Quarterly Journal of Economics* 35 (Nov.): 36–60.

———. 1928. "What Is the Labor Problem?" In *American Labor Dynamics in the Light of Post-War Developments*, ed. J. B. S. Hardman, 287–91. New York: Harcourt Brace.

———. 1931. *Modern Economic Society*. New York: Henry Holt.

———. 1939. "The Changing Character of American Industrial Relations." *American Economic Review* 29, pt. 2 (March): 121–37 (Suppl.).

Slichter, Sumner, James Healy, and E. Robert Livernash. 1960. *The Impact of*

Collective Bargaining on Management. Washington, D.C.: Brookings Institution.

Smith, Adam. 1776. *The Wealth of Nations.* Edited by Edwin Cannan; with a preface by George J. Stigler. Chicago: University of Chicago Press, 1976.

Snyder, David. 1977. "Early North American Strikes: A Reinterpretation." *Industrial and Labor Relations Review* 30 (April): 325–41.

Social Science Research Council. 1928. *Survey of Research in the Field of Industrial Relations.* New York: Social Science Research Council.

Sokolsky, George E. 1936. *Management's Industrial Relations Problems.* Personnel Series no. 22. New York: American Management Association.

Somers, Gerald G. 1961. "The Labor Market and Industrial Relations Research." In *Essays on Industrial Relations Research—Problems and Prospects,* 45–72. Ann Arbor: Institute of Labor and Industrial Relations, University of Michigan and Wayne State University.

———. 1967. "Research Note: The University of Wisconsin, Industrial Relations Research Institute." *Industrial and Labor Relations Review* 20 (July): 739–41.

———. 1969. "Bargaining Power and Industrial Relations Theory." In *Essays in Industrial Relations Theory,* ed. Gerald G. Somers, 39–53. Ames: Iowa State University Press.

———. 1972. "The Integration of In-Plant and Environmental Theories of Industrial Relations." In *International Conference on Trends in Industrial and Labor Relations,* 385–88. Jerusalem: Jerusalem Academic Press.

———. 1975. "Collective Bargaining and the Social-Economic Contract." In *Proceedings of the Twenty-eighth Annual Winter Meeting, Industrial Relations Research Association,* 1–7. Madison: IRRA.

Somers, Gerald G., Edward Cushman, and Nat Weinberg. 1963. *Adjusting to Technological Change.* Madison: IRRA.

Spates, Thomas. 1937. *Industrial Relations Trends.* Personnel Series no. 25. New York: American Management Association.

———. 1938. *The Status of Industrial Relations.* Personnel Series no. 32. New York: American Management Association.

———. 1944. *An Objective Scrutiny of Personnel Administration.* Personnel Series no. 75. New York: American Management Association.

———. 1960. *Human Values Where People Work.* New York: Harper.

Stagner, Ross. 1948. "Psychological Aspects of Industrial Conflict, I: Perception." *Personnel Psychology* 1 (Jan.): 131–44.

Stein, Herbert. 1990. *The Fiscal Revolution in America.* Washington, D.C.: American Enterprise Press.

Stephenson, Geoffrey, and Christopher Brotherton, eds. 1979. *Industrial Relations: A Social Psychological Approach.* New York: Wiley.

Stern, James. 1992. "Whither or Wither IRRA." In *Proceedings of the Forty-fifth Annual Winter Meeting, Industrial Relations Research Association.* Madison: IRRA. Forthcoming.

References

Stewart, Bryce. 1951. "Development of Industrial Relations in the United States." Industrial Relations Counselors. Unpublished.

Stigler, George. 1942. *The Theory of Competitive Price.* New York: Macmillan.

———. 1947. "Professor Lester and the Marginalists." *American Economic Review* 37 (March): 154–57.

———. 1949. *Five Lectures on Economic Problems.* London: Longmans, Green.

Stigler, George, and Gary Becker. 1977. "De Gustibus Non Est Disputandum." *American Economic Review* 67 (March): 76–90.

Stockton, Frank T. 1932. "Personnel Management in the Collegiate School of Business." *Personnel Journal* 12 (Dec.): 220–27.

Stoll, Clarence G., et al. 1937. *Practical Industrial Relations.* Personnel Series no. 26. New York: American Management Association.

Stone, R. W. 1932. *Personnel Management: An Appraisal.* Personnel Series no. 14. New York: American Management Association.

Storey, John, ed. 1989. *New Perspectives on Human Resource Management.* London: Routledge.

Strauss, George. 1968. "Human Relations—1968 Style." *Industrial Relations* 7 (May): 262–76.

———. 1970. "Organizational Behavior and Personnel Relations." In *A Review of Industrial Relations Research,* vol. 1. ed. Woodrow Ginsberg et al., 145–206. Madison: IRRA.

———. 1978. "Directions in Industrial Relations Research." In *Proceedings of the 1978 Annual Spring Meeting, Industrial Relations Research Association,* 531–36. Madison: IRRA.

———. 1979. "Can Social Psychology Contribute to Industrial Relations?" In *Industrial Relations: A Social Psychological Approach,* ed. Geoffrey Stephenson and Christopher Brotherton, 365–97. New York: Wiley.

———. 1984. "Industrial Relations: Times of Change." *Industrial Relations* 23 (Winter): 1–15.

———. 1989. "Industrial Relations as an Academic Field: What's Wrong with It?" In *Theories and Concepts in Comparative Industrial Relations,* ed. Jack Barbash and Kate Barbash, 241–60. Columbia: University of South Carolina Press.

———. 1990. "Toward the Study of Human Resources Policy." In *Reflections on the Transformation of Industrial Relations,* ed. James Chelius and James Dworkin, 73–95. New Brunswick, N.J.: IMLR Press.

———. 1992. "Present at the Beginning: Some Personal Notes on OB's Early Days and Later." In *Management Laureates: A Collection of Autobiographical Essays,* ed. Arthur Bedeian. Greenwich, Conn.: JAI Press. Forthcoming.

Strauss, George, and Peter Feuille. 1981. "Industrial Relations Research in the United States." In *Industrial Relations in International Perspective,* ed. Peter B. Doeringer, 76–144. New York: Holmes and Meier.

Strauss, George, Raymond Miles, Charles Snow, and Arnold Tannenbaum. 1974. *Organizational Behavior: Research and Issues.* Madison: IRRA.

References

Strauss, George, Daniel Gallagher, and Jack Florito. 1991. *The State of the Unions.* Madison: IRRA.

Tannenbaum, Frank. 1921. *The Labor Movement: Its Conservative Functions and Social Consequences.* New York: Putnam.

Tannenbaum, Robert, and Warren Schmidt. 1958. "How to Choose a Leadership Pattern." *Harvard Business Review* 36 (March–April): 95–101.

Taylor, Frederick. 1895. "A Piece Rate System, Being a Step toward Partial Solution of the Labor Problem." *Transactions* 16: 856–83.

Tead, Ordway. 1921. "The Problem of Graduate Training in Personnel Administration." *Journal of Political Economy* 29 (May): 353–67.

———. 1929. *Human Nature and Management.* New York: McGraw-Hill.

———. 1931. "Human Nature and Management." In *Preventive Management: Mental Hygiene in Industry*, ed. Henry B. Elkind, 23–52. New York: B. C. Forbes.

———. 1938. "Industrial Relations 1939 Model." *Personnel Journal* 17 (5): 160–67.

Tead, Ordway, and Henry C. Metcalf. 1920. *Personnel Administration: Its Principles and Practice.* New York: McGraw-Hill.

———. 1933. *Labor Relations under the Recovery Act.* New York: McGraw-Hill.

Teplow, Leo. 1976. "Industrial Relations Counselors at Fifty Years." In *People, Progress, and Employee Relations*, ed. Richard Beaumont, 3–8. Charlottesville: University of Virginia Press.

Thorndike, Edward L. 1922. "The Psychology of Labor." *Harper's*, June, 790–806.

Thurow, Lester. 1988. "Producer Economics." In *Proceedings of the Forty-first Annual Meeting, Industrial Relations Research Association*, 9–20. Madison: IRRA.

Time Magazine. 1952. "Human Relations: A New Art Brings Revolution to Industry." April 14, 96–97.

Tolles, Arnold. 1958. "Discussion." In *Proceedings of the Eleventh Annual Meeting, Industrial Relations Research Association*, 253–57. Madison: IRRA.

Trahair, R. C. S. 1984. *The Humanist Temper: The Life and Work of Elton Mayo.* New Brunswick: Transaction Books.

Tripp, L. Reed. 1964. "The Industrial Relations Discipline in American Universities." *Industrial and Labor Relations Review* 17 (July): 612–18.

U.S. Congress. 1916. *Industrial Relations: Final Report and Testimony.* Vol. 1. Washington, D.C.: Government Printing Office.

U.S. Department of Labor. Bureau of Labor Statistics. 1921. *Personnel Research Agencies.* Bulletin no. 299. Washington, D.C.: Government Printing Office.

———. 1930. *Personnel Research Agencies.* Bulletin no. 518. Washington, D.C.: Government Printing Office.

Van Metre, Thurman W. 1954. *A History of the Graduate School of Business, Columbia University.* New York: Columbia University Press.

Verma, Anil. 1985. "Relative Flow of Capital to Union and Nonunion Plants within a Firm." *Industrial Relations* 24 (Fall): 395–405.

References

Voos, Paula, and Lawrence Mishel. 1986. "The Union Impact on Profits: Evidence from Industry Price-Cost Data." *Journal of Labor Economics* 4 (Jan.): 105–33.

————. 1991. *Unions and Economic Competitiveness.* Armonk, N.Y.: M. E. Sharpe.

Walker, Kenneth, 1977. "Towards Useful Theorising about Industrial Relations." *British Journal of Industrial Relations* 15 (Nov.): 307–16.

Walter, Jack E. 1934. *Effect of the Depression on Industrial Relations Programs.* New York: National Industrial Conference Board.

Walton, Richard. 1985. "Toward a Strategy of Eliciting Employee Commitment through Policies of Mutuality." In *HRM: Trends and Challenges,* ed. Richard Walton and Paul Lawrence, 35–65. Cambridge: Harvard Business School Press.

Walton, Richard, and Paul Lawrence, eds. 1985. *HRM: Trends and Challenges.* Cambridge: Harvard Business School Press.

Walton, Richard, and Robert McKersie. 1965. *A Behavioral Theory of Labor Negotiations.* New York: McGraw-Hill.

Ward S., A Wagner, E. Armstrong, J. Goodman, and J. Davis. 1975. "Rules in Industrial Relations Theory." *Industrial Relations Journal* 6 (1): 14–30.

Ware, Caroline F. 1946. *Labor Education in Universities.* New York: American Labor Education Service.

Warner, W. Lloyd, and Joseph Low. 1947. *The Social System of the Modern Factory.* Vol. 4, *The Strike: A Social Analysis.* New Haven: Yale University Press.

Watkins, Gordon S. 1922. *An Introduction to the Study of Labor Problems.* New York: Thomas Crowell.

————. 1928. *Labor Management.* New York: McGraw-Hill.

Watkins, Gordon S., and Paul A. Dodd. 1940. *Labor Problems.* 3d ed. New York: Thomas Crowell.

Webb, Sidney, and Beatrice Webb. 1894. *A History of Trade Unionism.* London: Longmans, Green.

————. 1897. *Industrial Democracy.* London: Longmans, Green.

Webbink, Paul. 1954. "Methods and Objectives of Industrial Relations Research." In *Proceedings of the Seventh Annual Meeting, Industrial Relations Research Association,* 102–6. Madison: IRRA.

Weber, Arnold R. 1987a. "Understanding Change in Industrial Relations: A Second Look." In *Proceedings of the Fortieth Annual Meeting, Industrial Relations Research Association,* 10–23. Madison: IRRA.

————. 1987b. "Industrial Relations and Higher Education." In *The Future of Industrial Relations,* ed. Daniel J. B. Mitchell, 8–28. Los Angeles: Institute of Industrial Relations, University of California.

Weber, Arnold R., Frank H. Cassell, and Woodrow L. Ginsburg. 1969. *Public-Private Manpower Policies.* Madison: IRRA.

Weiler, Paul C. 1990. *Governing the Workplace.* Cambridge: Harvard University Press.

Weiss, Leonard W. 1966. "Concentration and Labor Earnings." *American Economic Review* 56 (March): 98–117.

Whalen, Charles. 1991. "Saving Capitalism by Making It Good: The Monetary Economics of John R. Commons." Hobart and William Smith Colleges, Geneva, N.Y. Unpublished.

Wharton School Industrial Research Unit and Labor Relations Council. 1989. *Report on Progress.* Philadelphia: Industrial Research Unit, Wharton School, University of Pennsylvania.

Wheeler, Hoyt. 1985. *Industrial Conflict: An Integrative Theory.* Columbia: University of South Carolina Press.

———. 1988a. "A Proposal for Renaming Our Field of Study 'Employment Relations,' " *UC Forum,* Newsletter of the University Council of Industrial Relations and Human Resource Programs. 1 (Spring–Summer): 5.

———. 1988b. "Is There a Pattern? A Report on a Survey of Graduate IR Curricula." In *Proceedings of the Forty-first Annual Meeting, Industrial Relations Research Association,* 445–51. Madison: IRRA.

Whyte, William Foote. 1944. "Pity the Personnel Man." *Advanced Management* 19 (4): 154–58.

———. 1948. *Human Relations in the Restaurant Industry.* New York: McGraw-Hill.

———. 1950. "Framework for the Analysis of Industrial Relations: Two Views." *Industrial and Labor Relations Review* 3 (April): 393–401.

———. 1951a. "Social Science and Industrial Relations." *Personnel* 27 (Jan.): 258–66.

———. 1951b. *Patterns for Industrial Peace.* New York: Harper.

———. 1955. *Money and Motivation: An Analysis of Incentives in Industry.* New York: Harper.

———. 1959. *Man and Organization: Three Problems in Human Relations in Industry.* Homewood, Ill.: R. D. Irwin.

———. 1965. "A Field in Search of a Focus." *Industrial and Labor Relations Review* 18 (April): 305–22.

———. 1987. "From Human Relations to Organizational Behavior: Reflections on the Changing Scene." *Industrial and Labor Relations Review* 40 (4): 487–500.

Wilensky, Harold L. 1954. *Syllabus of Industrial Relations: A Guide to Reading and Research.* Chicago: University of Chicago Press.

Williams, Whiting. 1918. *Human Relations in Industry.* Washington, D.C.: U.S. Department of Labor.

———. 1920. *What's on the Worker's Mind.* New York: Scribner and Sons.

Williamson, Jeffrey G., and Peter H. Lindert. 1980. *American Inequality: A Macroeconomic History.* New York: Academic Press.

Willits, Joseph H. 1931. *What's Ahead in Light of Ten Years' Progress?* Personnel Series no. 13. New York: American Management Association.

Witte, Edwin. 1947. "The University and Labor Education." *Industrial and Labor Relations Review* 1 (Oct.): 3–17.

———. 1954. "Institutional Economics as Seen by an Institutional Economist." *Southern Economic Journal* 21 (Oct.): 131–40.

Wolman, Leo. 1932. "Industrial Relations." In *Encyclopedia of the Social Sciences*. 7: 710–17. New York: Macmillan.

Woods, Donald. 1968. "Discussion." In *The Role of Industrial Relations Centers, Proceedings of a Regional Meeting of the International Industrial Relations Association*, 87–90. Madison: Industrial Relations Research Institute, University of Wisconsin.

Wren, Daniel A. 1985. "Industrial Sociology: A Revised View of Its Antecedents." *Journal of the History of the Behavioral Sciences* 21 (Oct.): 310–20.

———. 1987. *The Evolution of Management Thought*. 3d ed. New York: Wiley.

Wright, David McCord. 1951. *The Impact of the Union*. New York: Harcourt Brace.

Yoder, Dale. 1931. "Introductory Courses in Industrial Relations." *Personnel* 7 (Feb.): 123–27.

———. 1933. *Labor Economics and Labor Problems*. New York: McGraw-Hill.

———. 1938. *Personnel and Labor Relations*. Englewood Cliffs, N.J.: Prentice-Hall.

———. 1952. "What's in a Name?" *Personnel Journal* 30 (March): 367–69.

———. 1958. "Research Needs for the Second Decade." In *Proceedings of the Tenth Annual Meeting, Industrial Relations Research Association*, 2–10. Madison: IRRA.

Yoder, Dale, Herbert Heneman, John Turnbull, and C. Harold Stone. 1958. *Handbook of Personnel and Labor Relations*. New York: McGraw-Hill.

INDEX

ABOUT THE AUTHOR

Bruce E. Kaufman is director of the W.T. Beebe Institute of Personnel and Employment Relations and is a professor of economics at Georgia State University, where he has served on the faculty since 1977. He received his Ph.D. in economics from the University of Wisconsin and has published widely in the field of industrial relations.